THE RECONSTRUCTION OF RELIGION

D1153614

THE RECONSTRUCTION
OF RELIGION

Lessing, Kierkegaard, and Nietzsche

JAN-OLAV HENRIKSEN

William B. Eerdmans Publishing Company
Grand Rapids, Michigan / Cambridge, U.K.

© 2001 Wm. B. Eerdmans Publishing Co.
All rights reserved

Wm. B. Eerdmans Publishing Co.
255 Jefferson Ave. S.E., Grand Rapids, Michigan 49503 /
P.O. Box 163, Cambridge CB3 9PU U.K.

www.eerdmans.com

Printed in the United States of America

06 05 04 03 02 01   7 6 5 4 3 2 1

Library of Congress Cataloging-in-Publication Data

Henriksen, Jan-Olav.
The reconstruction of religion: Lessing, Kierkegaard,
and Nietzsche / Jan-Olav Henriksen.
p.   cm.
Includes bibliographical references.
ISBN 0-8028-4927-X (pbk. : alk. paper)
1. Religion — Philosophy — History.
2. Lessing, Gotthold Ephraim, 1729-1781 — Religion.
3. Kierkegaard, Søren, 1813-1855 — Religion.
4. Nietzsche, Friedrich Wilhelm, 1844-1900 — Religion.
I. Title.

BL51.H463 2001
210'.92'2 — dc21
2001040384

The publication of this book was made possible
through a generous grant from the
Research Council of Norway.

Contents

Acknowledgments

I want to thank the following for making this book possible:

My American friends LeRon Shults and Wentzel van Huyssteen, who encouraged me to finally try to publish something in English. I doubt that I would have embarked on this project without their support.

The Research Council of Norway, which gave a grant for publication that was of great importance to the book's finalization, and David Cameron, Ph.D., who corrected my English and was of great help. Language errors and peculiarities that still remain I take responsibility for.

My children Christine and Andreas, as well as my doctoral student Maud Stenseng, helped with reading the proofs in a hectic closing session. I am deeply grateful.

Finally, I want to thank the staff at Eerdmans Publishing Company for receiving the book so well, and for all their work to make this presentable in English better than mine. I am deeply impressed by their openness to, and the effort they put into, a book by an overseas scholar not familiar with the American scene.

This book has been written over the last four years in and between many other tasks at the Norwegian Lutheran School of Theology. As the reader will perceive, it expresses some of the author's own commitments when dealing with philosophy of religion and theology. In this connection, I want to express my gratitude to my employer, who sees the need for pursuing many different roads to the understanding of what Christian faith, and, more generally, religion, means in the present. That is also what this book is about.

Ås, south of Oslo, June 2001   J.-O.H.

Chapter One

INTRODUCTION

Three Writers Facing the Modern Challenges to Religion

The period between 1750 and 1890 proved to be most disturbing for adherents of Christianity. Established orthodox truth was challenged from the "outside" by historical criticism offered by authors who were rather hostile to traditional Christian faith (e.g., H. Reimarus, D. F. Strauss). The Enlightenment strand of the modern mentality proved to be full of criticism, of hostility to and polemics against religion. At the same time, from "inside" the Christian communities, new ways of formulating traditional beliefs were offered by representatives of the emerging, so-called liberal theology. We find the most outstanding attempt of this type in the work of F. Schleiermacher. Moreover, religion became an object for new and conflicting concerns, arising from the development of the natural sciences, as well as from increasingly secular modes of thought. Consequently, we encounter in this period a plurality of interpretations of the importance and meaning of religion and religious faith.[1]

1. For the historical background of the Enlightenment movement and its criticism of religion, see P. Gay, *The Enlightenment: An Interpretation*, vol. 1: *The Rise of Modern Paganism*. However, Gay seems to agree with Cassirer, *Philosophie der Aufklärung*, p. 180, in that this movement is falsely interpreted if it is only seen as irreligious and hostile to Christian faith. Cassirer writes, and I quote this in order to present the background of my own study: "The strongest impulses of thought in the Enlightenment and its real

1

One could perhaps say that this period put the Christian faith itself to a test. Faith needed to be able to formulate and express itself in new terms, to reconstruct itself on the basis of other conditions than those present in the prevailing traditions. Remarkably, this actually happened: Despite deep and thoroughgoing criticism, even hostility, theological reflection found new ways of responding to the challenges of the times, thereby also integrating the valid concerns of the modern world. We could say that what happened was a critical reappropriation of what was given in the Christian tradition. This resulted in different reconstructions of what religion is, some favorable and some unfavorable to this tradition and its content.

For anyone interested in the presuppositions of religious belief in a modern and postmodern world, these transformations in theological and religious expressions are of great interest. They are of interest not only of themselves, but in order to understand and clarify some of the important conditions for religious life today as well. Perhaps one of the most striking features that come to mind in this period is the emphasis on the importance of *religious subjectivity*. This insistence on founding religious concerns on personal subjectivity rather than on the doctrinal corpus of truths given in tradition can be seen in the Enlightenment understanding of natural religion over against "the supranatural," as well as in Schleiermacher's notion of the feeling of absolute dependence ("das schlechthinnige Abhängigkeitsgefühl") and Kierkegaard's insistence on subjectivity as truth. The principle of subjectivity finally finds its most critical expression in Nietzsche's interpretation of religion as framed and shaped by the will to power.

The writings of Lessing, Kierkegaard, and Nietzsche give access to three very different approaches to the relationship between religion and modernity. Lessing is a "free mind" and a typical representative of the Enlightenment period, not so much concerned with Christianity as with religion and its practical side. Kierkegaard is a deeply religious person, and develops his reconstruction of Christianity in strong opposition to the main theological and philosophical currents of his time. Nietzsche, famous for his announcement of the death of God, is partly hostile to the religious life and thoughts of his times. At the same time, his writings re-

---

spiritual power are not based on its deviation from faith, but on the new ideal of faith that it establishes, and on the new forms of religion that it embodies."

2

veal a deep ambiguity toward Christ himself. If we classify the authors as belonging to specific periods, Lessing can be seen as the representative of the Enlightenment way of dealing with religion before Schleiermacher and Hegel, while Kierkegaard is critical of the way religion expresses itself in the modernized clothes of Hegelianism and the established Danish church. Nietzsche is easily identified (but in a way that requires far more elaboration than can be given here) as the author who anticipates some of the postmodern approaches to human subjectivity and religion. Hence he also is open to interpretations that would have seemed alien, even disturbing, to Lessing and Kierkegaard, had they known them. However, he seems to be ignorant of the highly reflective level on which they dealt with religion.

Hence, by turning to these authors and their work, we have the possibility of understanding religion from several different angles. I have found it fruitful to compare and reflect on the resemblance and the similarities among the three. I do not think that there are many direct connections in terms of influence among them (but in some cases there are, e.g., between some of Lessing's work and Kierkegaard's). My interest in not historical, but more theoretical and philosophical, since I think these authors can provide means for reflecting about under what conditions religion can be understood, and hence how it can be reconstructed theoretically in the framework of modernity. The outcomes of their reflective processes, however, differ considerably.

It should be clear that I do not investigate the totality of the views they present, but offer an interpretation of elements that still prove to be interesting in the light of today's questions. I want to reread and interpret the historical material their works offer in order to understand the present situation better.[2] The positive contribution of this book will thus probably be not so much the new insights it offers on the individual authors as the attempt to frame them and compare them in relation to the challenges posed by the modern conditions for religion. I think such a comparison can expose striking features and connections in terms of how they deal with the questions posed.

Despite all their differences, the three also have a common trait: they are writers in the true sense of the word, that is, they write literature

---

2. In this I follow the lines of the hermeneutical philosophy of H. G. Gadamer in *Wahrheit und Methode*.

of high quality.[3] Each is recognized as an important contributor to the culture of his own language. No doubt, this is partly due to the fact that they, as writers, can give a sensitive and careful interpretation of the subjects they are treating. By perceiving the challenges of their contemporary situation in a way that is fully conscious of what is at stake, they can offer an approach that is concerned with what is new and important. In addition, all three "wear masks" when they write, that is, they occasionally hide their own identity or position when they publish their works (even Nietzsche insists on "wearing a mask," although he always publishes in his own name).[4]

None of the three writers is part of "the religious or academic establishment," despite the fact that their links with it are not totally lacking. Still, they are all eagerly interested in the meaning of religion, and interpret it from the borderlines between culture, religion/theology, and philosophy. They address important aspects of the challenges posed by the modern mind to traditional religion, and present their own options for the future of religion.[5] In discussing attitudes, phenomena, and insights that arose and were established in the modern period, they, at the same time, give us who live on the threshold to a postmodern period a chance of gaining insight into the problems of maintaining a Christian faith today.

Another striking similarity among the three is that none of them is able to identify with the contemporary, "official" form of religion. This goes without saying for Nietzsche, but this issue is also important for understanding the framework in which Lessing's and Kierkegaard's thinking takes place. Consequently, in Lessing and Kierkegaard the problem of *appropriation* of tradition is strongly present, because they see that in order to preserve a responsible believing subject, one can neither subscribe uncritically to any element in tradition nor exhibit any attitude of servility toward it. They hold a specific understanding of (religious) subjectiv-

---

3. In the literature, the common traits of Kierkegaard and Nietzsche are often recognized, but that this also is the case with Lessing is observed less often. For an interesting comparison between Kierkegaard and Nietzsche, see Kellenberger, *Kierkegaard and Nietzsche: Faith and Eternal Acceptance*, 2ff.

4. The problem of identity and subjectivity will be treated more extensively in the following chapters.

5. Cf. Kellenberger's statement that Kierkegaard and Nietzsche "both probed beneath the surface of religion" (*Kierkegaard and Nietzsche*, 3). But the ways in which they did this, and hence *reconstructed* religion theoretically, were very different.

ity necessary in order to maintain a responsible, and what seems for them an adequate, religious belief.

By contrast, Nietzsche makes the supposition of subjectivity itself appear as an element of the production of religion and metaphysics, and hence makes its constructive and changing appearance transparent. At the same time, just like the others, he offers a criticism of what knowledge of history can provide as a resource for the development of the human subject.

A final feature that the writers have in common, one that is distinctively modern, is the eclectic character of their work. This is perhaps the other side of their lack of a systematic and coherent system of thought. Such eclecticism is, according to Peter Gay, quite common among Enlightenment thinkers, but it seems to apply for all our authors as well.[6] When they constantly seem to change position, see things from different angles, they are then not only providing different relevant perspectives on the same case. They also anticipate the postmodern insight that no stance is final, that it is always possible to make some other reflection. Hence they exhibit a mode of thought that we still find in today's postmodern culture.

Modernity: Religion as Construction

For any modern believer, religion is not something to be taken for granted, a situation or personal condition that exists without giving rise to questions and challenges about the forms of faith handed down through history. Modernity means a critical reaction against any traditionally given content. Hence it demands a mode of reflection that makes religion and religious beliefs transparent and viable in their present forms. Since the Enlightenment, many thinkers have attempted to establish such transparency by reconstructing religion theoretically on the basis of the new conditions offered by modernity. Thereby they have contributed to modern reconstructions of religion developed in order to cope with the question about what religion means in the present.

In this study, I look at how three specific authors developed different theoretical reconstructions of religion during a period of a little more

---

6. For eclecticism in the Enlightenment period, see Gay, *Enlightenment*, 160-61.

than a hundred years. I try to unravel some of the main strands in their individual webs of reconstruction, in order to disclose how they integrate these strands into the webs that shape their thinking. I try to see how strands from traditional religion and theology were interwoven with important modern ideals into a more or less coherent web. This totally new web not only exhibits what the thinkers hold that religion is (and has been) actually about (the "essence" of religion). It also contains their opinion about on what terms religion still can have meaning today.

The three strands from traditional religion and theology that I look for are:

- The understanding of the *historical content* that forms the basis of Christian religion, and how this can be appropriated in a meaningful way as being relevant for the present.
- The understanding of the *truth* of this religion. Linked to this is of course also the question of the uniqueness of Christianity. As anyone who knows something about Christianity in modernity is aware of, these are persistent questions accompanying this religion through the times from the Enlightenment to the present day.
- How Christians can be sure of their convictions, in a situation where *pluralism, subjectivism, and historical critique* offer strong challenges to any religious commitment.

Important traits of modernity that are relevant for the present study have been outlined in the often-cited, still interesting book by Peter Berger, *The Heretical Imperative.* I present some insights from this book, as Berger's position is very close to what I see as a possible and fruitful framework for the interpretations that I offer in the following analysis. As a sociologist, Berger reaffirms his previously expressed insight into the dependence of religious convictions on socially given plausibility structures. In modernity, however, such structures are pluralized, just as institutions are.[7] As pluralism grows, the individual who needs social confirmation of his or her own beliefs seems to have less and less chance of gaining just this. The weakening of the institutions that used to supply this kind of support is not making this predicament easier to resolve.[8]

7. P. L. Berger, *The Heretical Imperative,* 17.
8. As we shall see, none of the three authors in question seems to put any empha-

Berger insists, I think rightly, that this applies for all kinds of convictions and beliefs. As the individual moves between different cultural and institutional spheres, she cannot be sure that what she finds valid in one of them also is valid in another.

> In the modern situation, certainty is hard to come by. It cannot be stressed enough that this fact is rooted in pretheoretical experience — that is, in ordinary, everyday social life. This experience is common to the proverbial man in the street and to the intellectual who spins out elaborate theories about the universe. The built-in uncertainty is common to both as well.[9]

Here Berger points out the social conditions for what I would call *the erosion of commitment*. This social erosion of the reasons for commitment need not be total, but arises from the fact that the individual constantly finds herself in situations where she cannot relate to her own ideas or beliefs without also making reflections on their provisional character, the possible weakness and error contained in them, and their contextual conditioning.[10] All such elements imply that *reflexivity* turns religion into an option that is no longer presented in a finished form by fate and tradition. Religion now becomes an option demanding the exercise of choice and active, personal construction. This construction includes the religious form as well as its content. I refer to this active reflection of the historically given religious content as *the subjective appropriation made necessary by modernity* (cf. above). That this appropriation is actually subjective also in the individual sense is clear in that no one can be expected to develop a worldview or a religious position that is identical to what is given in a religious tradition. The religious tradition no longer has one coherent and stable recipient of its form and content. The plurality of worldviews and personal conditions, as well as differences in back-

---

sis on the institutional side of religion. This confirms Berger's position, and also seems to indicate that there really is a possibility for using his insights as a framework for an analysis of the three.

9. Berger, *Heretical Imperative*, 19.

10. Berger points to three different problems that arise from the heretical imperative and are deeply connected to it: the problem of false religious experience, the status of one's preferred historical religion in relation to others, and the problem of religious certainty (ibid., 145ff.). As we shall see, Nietzsche addresses most clearly the first, Lessing the second, and Kierkegaard the third of these.

ground and experience, together with the lack of stable structures and patterns of plausibility, make identical transmission and reception of religion impossible. Again quoting Berger:

> The more choices, the more reflection. The individual who reflects inevitably becomes more conscious of himself. That is, he turns his attention from the objectively given outside world to his own subjectivity. As he does this, two things happen simultaneously: The outside world becomes more questionable, and his inner world becomes more complex. Both of these things are unmistakable features of modern man.[11]

This description suits very well the three authors I analyze here. As we shall see, for all of them religion is no longer an objectively presented option, but something to be regarded in terms of *how it functions for the subject and her personal development*. Hence their reconstruction of religion and their own understanding of what constitutes the "inner world" of subjectivity are closely related. In other words, they all seem to link their understanding of "the essence of religion" to important elements in the subject. But despite this background, they have different approaches to religion that mirror different constructive options. In this, they probably also mirror different cultural contexts and stages in the relationship between modern society and religion.

An element in the modern appropriation — or rejection — of religion is that it can no longer be taken for granted. This is the natural consequence of what has been said so far. Some describe this as *the problem of authority*. In modernity, there is no other authority than the subject and what the subject can make her own. To view this as a problem is to assess religion in modernity on the basis of religious elements important to the premodern period, and I do not make much out of this here. The situation in which modern religion finds itself — it can no longer be taken for granted — opens the possibility of simultaneously exposing it to criticism and relating to it with personal commitment. The deobjectivation of religion means its subjectivation,[12] and this turn to the subjective sphere as the basic one is the condition on which all of our authors must be understood.

11. Ibid., 22.
12. See ibid., 26.

Given this background, Berger's notion of *the heretical imperative* in modernity becomes understandable, even enlightening, when we read the works of Lessing, Kierkegaard, and Nietzsche. Heresy was traditionally understood as a position that deliberately (by choice) deviated from that which was secured by authority. Authority is what makes heresy possible.[13] Heretics denied authority apart from themselves. As long as there existed a stable and plausible structure of tradition, affirmed by authority, heresy in terms of choice of something different, based on personal preferences, was an option for the few. But as Berger puts it, the social condition of such "heresy" has changed with the coming of the uncertainties of modernity:

> By contrast, the modern situation is a world of religious uncertainty, occasionally staved off by more or less precarious constructions of religious affirmation. . . . For premodern man, heresy is a possibility — usually a rather remote one; for modern man, heresy typically becomes a necessity. Or again, modernity creates a new situation in which picking and choosing becomes an imperative.[14]

One consequence following from Berger's analysis is for the most part tacitly expressed in his work: he makes clear how religion as a consequence of the demand for personal choice needs an increasingly stronger basis in personal experience in order to maintain its plausibility for the individual.[15] As time goes by, however, experiences can be forgotten, they can fade and dim. Hence striving for new, refreshed, and stronger experiences can be seen as a correlate to the lack of common social plausibility, and the deobjectification of religion. It would probably be wrong to say that experience replaces the authority of tradition, but it nevertheless becomes that by which the individual is able to "warm up" and maintain her own religious affirmation and certainty.[16] This also mirrors the

---

13. Ibid., 27.

14. Ibid., 28 (without the original italics).

15. For how personal experience, and not historical demonstration, provided the means for being assured about the truth of a religious position, see Cassirer, *Philosophie*, 236.

16. This is a point that can be made very clear — negatively — in relation to Nietzsche. He seems never to have had any positive experience of religion, and lived so isolated that he could not gain insight into the positive possibilities of social life that religion offers in a way that could have opened his eyes to this. I do not state this to make an im-

9

change of authority that took place during the development of a modern construction of religion. It is no longer the formal authority of tradition that the subject recognizes, but a functional authority that can be recognized as long as religion contributes to the shaping of and interpretation of experiences that are important to the subject.

My personal reasons for writing this book are as follows. First, by and through analyses like the following, I want to provide a means for the critical self-reflection of a religious position. More specifically, I want to underscore and develop perspectives on Christianity in modernity that I think are important in order to understand how this belief is actually reformulated under contemporary conditions. Many Christians today have, I think, some vague idea that their faith is not in every respect or expression similar to that of the first Christians. But why this is so, and on what basis their belief is reconstructed today, are not always transparent to them. What I want to do, then, is simply to try to contribute to more transparency in this matter, without claiming that I have done all that is to be done about it. Consequently, I also think that we find tools and insights in Lessing, Kierkegaard, and Nietzsche that are important for understanding religious subjectivity in the contemporary, increasingly postmodern world.

Still, many will argue that Christianity is founded on more than subjective and personal experience, and is more than just a way of framing and articulating such experience. They are convinced that something happened in the history of Jesus Christ that can be understood as revelation, that is, as a disclosure of something new, something not accessible for humanity by means of only personal and common experience and our own reason. This does not rule out, however, that our understanding of this past history of necessity must be historically relative to our own context, our contextually based reason, and that the contextual appropriation of this marks out the constructive element in any religion, including Christianity. Hence I think we have to see Christianity as developing — in order to cope with and meet the challenges, forms of thought, and

---

portant point about Nietzsche, but to indicate that religion in modernity exhibits clearly that there are social and cultural conditions that determine the individual's resources for developing a personal appropriation of religion, as well as the actual shape religion becomes. The statement of Gibbon, quoted in Gay, *Enlightenment*, 210, seems to fit Nietzsche well: "The enemies of religion never know it, because they hate it, and often they hate it because they do not know it."

social conditions of its own contemporary culture. The three authors considered here help us to understand more of what this means.[17]

Anticipations of Postmodernism?

In the previous section, I have suggested that a constructive element is involved in the modern way of framing religion (as well as in every other form of religion). This element becomes fully conscious in the reflection of many postmodern writers, of whom Nietzsche is one of the first. As I stress the anticipatory element in the author's thought rather strongly in the following chapters, however, here I content myself with several comments in order to clarify the reasons for this anticipation.

Postmodernity is not, in my mind, first and foremost to be understood as a historical period, but more as a dimension of the understanding we develop of culture, intimately connected to many of the elements we find in the modern way of describing and understanding reality.[18] The postmodern approach to culture and religion implies an alternative construction and an alternative description of many of the same elements, problems, and phenomena that are identified as modern, or framed by theories of modernity. This means that although the thinkers I investigate can be described as being distinctly modern, they also exhibit elements that, from another point of view, can be seen as anticipations of theories and problems we find in recent, theoretical, and postmodern frameworks. This is especially clear from the following considerations.

Postmodern theory implies an increased emphasis on the reflexivity of reflexivity, thereby taking up the moment of reflexivity already contained in much modern theory and strengthening it. Hence it underscores reflection on thinking itself, and on what human thinking and culture are able to produce, communicate, and bring forth.

Therefore the postmodern elements anticipated in Lessing, Kierkegaard, and Nietzsche do not represent a break with the modern, but are consequences of it, in which modernity develops into its corollary

---

17. Here I find myself in agreement with N. H. Gregersen, *Teologi og Kultur: Protestantismen mellem assimilation og isolation (Theology and culture: Protestantism between assimilation and isolation)*.

18. For a more detailed argument regarding this see Henriksen, *På Grensen til Den andre (At the other's border)*, 22ff.

mode: postmodernity. This can be seen in how the following elements, found in one or more of the authors, are developed:

- the understanding of pluralism (especially in Lessing and Nietzsche), or the appreciation of a plurality of approaches to a problem or case (as we can see in all of them);
- the constructive element, which expresses itself in how all three understand subjectivity as something developing, fragile, contingent, not given, and formative for religion;[19]
- the tendency toward detachment, disengagement, and irony, in how they develop what I call double reflexivity;[20]
- the stress on the objective uncertainty of any religious truth.

As one can recognize, the elements that I depict here as elements of a postmodern attitude are also found in the description by Berger mentioned in the previous section. Hence there is a continuity that seems to indicate that the problems that Lessing, Kierkegaard, and Nietzsche handle could very much be our own, even if we live in a in a situation more marked by postmodern cultural traits than they did.

There is, however, one distinct difference between a postmodern and a modern approach to the theoretical reconstruction of religion. This is clearly disclosed in the change of framework for dealing with the elements just listed. The postmodern situation lacks a common narrative, within which these elements can be organized, and that can give a coherent and common way of relating religion, personal experience, and other forms of knowledge to each other.[21] The postmodern condition also implies that there is no recognizable center for the organization of our cultural constructions. This is a conviction that is not shared by Lessing and Kierkegaard. Nietzsche alone seems to anticipate this postmodern element in a way that also accepts the full consequences of it.

19. In this respect, e.g., Kierkegaard's opposition against Hegel's *System* can be read and understood as well. For a more detailed exposition of how he anticipates postmodernity in this, see Westphal, *Becoming a Self,* viii-ix, 3, 115, et passim.

20. What is meant by this expression will be clarified in chapter five below.

21. Cf. Lyotard, *The Postmodern Condition* — a book that probably exhibits this better than any other. Here we also see why both Lessing and Kierkegaard, although they can be read as anticipating some elements more commonly identified as postmodern, are still very much modern in their reconstructions of religion.

Technical Information and a Reflection on the Scope of This Study

The present study is not intended to cover all aspects of the thought of Lessing, Kierkegaard, and Nietzsche. I rather wish to highlight the strands in the web that were mentioned in the first section of this chapter. In an academic context, the scope of the present study aims at presenting results that have relevance for the study of religion in a modern and postmodern culture, as well as for the philosophy of religion. It will also probably have some relevance for the history of ideas. What is presented does not, however, place itself strictly within the limits of one or another of these fields of research.

As for secondary literature, I have used material that contributes to the understanding of the topics I discuss, without any attempt to make a study that relates itself to all the material available. Within the limits set for this study, I could consider only a selection of works. As the following is more of a systematic than a historical study, however, I have not emphasized a comprehensive interaction with the existing secondary literature. Also, in the case of Kierkegaard and Nietzsche the literature is so vast that it is not possible to cover it in a study like the present one. This may be a shortcoming of the book, but it is deliberate. I think, however, that the argument of the book profits from less discussion of other interpretations, since it offers the opportunity for more attention to the primary sources. All translations are mine.

Finally, I have to admit that I see a paradox in a project like this. In a way, this book is "backward looking." I write about authors who published their works more than a hundred years ago. But the aim of the study is to look to the past in order to understand the present and cope with the future. I think Lessing, Kierkegaard, and Nietzsche all teach us that religion can develop in different ways, and that this development could mean progress or decline, depending on what we see as the importance of its content for human life. They challenge us to reconsider to what extent religion has something important to say about and contribute to human life, and to our social and cultural conditions. Consequently, this book is written from interests shaped by the current situation. I think we always do this when we deal with the past, and I do not apologize for it. But anyone who reads this in order to get an exhaustive picture of how the thought worlds of Lessing, Kierkegaard, or Nietzsche frame religion should rather look elsewhere.

Chapter Two

LESSING

*Conceptual Differentiation,
Critique of Tradition, and
Acceptance of Plurality*

Introduction

As indicated in the introduction, this book is written on the assumption that there are elements in the Enlightenment critique of religion that still prove important as a framework for critical self-reflection in recent theology and philosophy of religion. The critique offered by Enlightenment thinkers discusses such features as dogmatism, intolerance, and the function of theological discourse in society (which does not necessarily need to be positive). By reflecting on their contributions, we can construct a more elaborate basis for the understanding of the conditions for formation of religious subjectivity in a modern setting.

Lessing is an interesting case because he is not quite typical in his contemporary setting. He would perhaps be more typical, at least for some important trends, in the present. He is well trained and educated, and knows a lot about theology without being a theologian. He is an active participant in the cultural debate. He does not feel at home in the church, but at the same time he does not detach himself totally from it. He is uncomfortable with the theology of his contemporaries, but is still unable to formulate and express a fully coherent alternative to this theology.[1] Hence he stands both "inside" and "outside" established religion.[2] In all this, he could be an archetype of a more recent attitude among people who to a large extent have drawn the consequences of experiences similar to his and privatized their relation toward religion and church,[3] without holding any kind of definite position themselves.[4]

However, Lessing holds some important notions that guide him in his work on religion. In the following, I investigate his understanding of true religion and the predicament of humanity — two ideas that are linked closely in his thought. In the course of the analysis, we shall also see how Lessing develops a network of conceptual distinctions that helps him to reconstruct religion in a way that also takes into consideration the specific challenges it faces in his times.[5]

---

1. In the following, I quote from Lessing's *Werke* by way of simple references in the text to volume and page, e.g., 8:234.

2. Lessing's relation to traditional and orthodox religion is, however, far more complex than these short sentences indicate. It is clear that Lessing rather early in his career broke completely away from orthodox Christianity (Allison, *Lessing and the Enlightenment,* 60). But he became more positive toward Christianity after 1770 (ibid., 81), despite his strong argument with the orthodox pastor Goeze. Since I am less interested in Lessing's personal affairs than in the position(s) he develops in his writings, I have chosen to ignore the aspect of his historical development in the following. For a more extensive treatment of this point, see Gay, *Enlightenment,* 60ff.; and Saine, *Problem of Being Modern,* 214-15.

3. See the introduction above on Berger's description of the modern subject.

4. The task of placing Lessing securely in one final position is not easy, as can also be seen in the literature on him, where he is made into anything from an anti-Christian *Aufklärer* to a reflective Christian. E.g., we see how Fittbogen, *Die Religion Lessings,* 101, makes Lessing into a writer who develops a Lutheran position only for tactical reasons in his criticism of Reimarus's documents. Fittbogen sees him as an antitheological *Aufklärer.* But in this he makes Lessing's position clearer and firmer than it actually was. He concludes that Lessing must be seen at as the founder of "Neo-Protestantism" (310). His position is countered by L. P. Wessel, *G. E. Lessing's Theology — A Reinterpretation: A Study in the Problematic Nature of the Enlightenment,* 15: "Therefore it is not logical consistency, but rather the generative and suggestive possibilities of an idea that interested Lessing. The purpose of an idea is to inspire further reflection. This, indeed, constitutes . . . Lessing's thinking." This is not only a more apt remark on Lessing's position, but also one in which we can see how he anticipates the explorative and experimenting mode of reflection we find in recent, postmodern thought.

5. See how the establishment of such distinctions are viewed as important also in the works of others: "A large part of his thinking is thus to be described as a task of analytical differentiation" (Thielicke, "Vernunft und Existenz bei Lessing — Das Unbedingte in der Geschichte," 101). See J. von Lüpke, *Wege der Weisheit,* 14.

Setting the Stage: Lessing's
Historical Position and Contribution

Natural religion was, without doubt, the most important concept used to reconstruct theology during the Enlightenment. A look into how this concept works in the reconstruction of religion also casts light on how religion undergoes important changes in its function during that period. These changes are simply not possible to understand without the concept of natural religion.

Natural religion is a concept that is intended to depict the religious dispositions given with the very existence of human beings. A human being is understood as a religious being. The concept should not be confused with that of natural *theology,* which is the rational and theoretical explication of this religion in a more or less coherent doctrinal summary.[6] I speak here deliberately of a *disposition* for religion: this disposition has to be cultivated and developed in order for religion to function properly.

Already from this two suppositions appear that seem important as elements for the construction of Lessing's thought. First, the human being is described as having a natural relation to religion — religion is something that belongs to being human. Second, this natural religion functions as a normative concept on the basis of which one can evaluate the content of any *positive* religion, and hence the individual development of a person's religious character. In order to appropriate the position of natural religion, one has to undergo a process of formation. This formation is — as we shall see below — particularly connected to the practice of reason. We shall see how this formation is an important element in Lessing's thought.

The traditional, orthodox dogmatics also made use of and affirmed the notion of natural religion. But the construction of the context for the notion differed from the one we find in Enlightenment thought. Affirmation of this notion was only possible as long as the naturally given religious disposition was seen as in need of correction. The natural dispositions had to be renewed through the insights given in special revelation, which was found in the Bible. Such correction was needed due to the sin-

---

6. For this and the following, see F. Wagner, *Was ist Religion? Studien zu ihrem Begriff und Thema in Geschichte und Gegenwart,* 35ff.

fulness of human beings. Sin darkened the rational faculties of human beings. Thus, from the orthodox point of view, "enlightenment" had to come from the content of revelation.

It is exactly this understanding of sin as a basic *conditio humana* in the construction of religion that alters in function during the time of Lessing.[7] The Enlightenment provides a more positive, less sin-oriented understanding of the human being and his or her religiosity. Once the natural conditions of the human being are no longer understood on the basis of humanity's innate sinfulness, the naturally given *ratio* proves itself capable of illuminating human existence without the help of a supernatural revelation. Now, instead of the Bible, reason provides the means for enlightenment. This elimination of the concept of sin as central to the construction of the features of true religion gives a new perspective on the whole concept of religion.

This has profound consequences for the development of religious subjectivity (a religious self-relation) as well. The subject is no longer mainly understood as wanting, as in need of restoration from the corruption of sin. Sin is not understood as a deficit inflicted from some distant historical past, and plays no central role in the self-understanding of the subject. Instead, the *wanting* elements that the subject can recognize as such in his own life stem from the lacking or not yet fulfilled development of his own humanity. This want is thus interpreted in a teleological framework that directs and interprets the subject from its own future realization of possibilities, more than from humanity's past "fall into sin." As we shall see, this reshaping of the interpretative framework not only plays a significant role in Lessing's work but also serves as the background for Kierkegaard's and Nietzsche's interpretation of the human quest for self-realization.[8]

Consequently, the configuration of the relationship between natural religion and reason found in orthodox dogmatics is radically altered. Now, by affirming the independence and sufficiency of a naturally given reason — no longer perceived as being distorted by sin — one can use this reason for directing a critique against traditional theology and religion.

7. For this see also the extensive presentation in Saine, *Problem of Being Modern,* 198ff.

8. On the changing conditions for this part of theological anthropology, see W. Pannenberg, *Gottesebenbildlichkeit als die Bestimmung des Menschen in der neueren Theologiegeschichte;* and *Anthropologie in theologischer Perspektive,* esp. 46ff.

This offers a basis for an increasingly critical public attitude toward the positively given Christian religion, and some of the content in the Bible as well.[9] Once the self-understanding of the religious believer is not determined by the consciousness of being a sinner, one also gets a new consciousness that is able to oppose the authority of the pastoral office and the theologians. This is part of the general context within which Lessing develops his understanding of religion and authority. In order to fulfill this critical task, however, one has to operate with a counternotion of religion that can function normatively. As indicated, it is *natural religion* that serves as the new normative concept. F. Wagner summarizes the development thus:

> Neither can religion withdraw from the inquiries of reason. Hence the concept of religion is subjected to a definite *change of function*. Religion as *natural religion* is stripped of its theological framework and conditions, and becomes an object of processes of critique and argument, which takes place on the basis of a reason self-conscious about its own autonomy.[10]

In order to clarify this further, we could use a comparison between natural law and natural religion as they were understood after the Enlightenment transformation. Natural law and natural religion are not based on historical facts, but on what reason can gain insight into by itself, independent of the changing historical circumstances. As such, they function as critical points of departure for the evaluation of every historically given compilation or codex of norms and law, or of any positive religion. The notion of natural law or natural religion also gives rise, however, to the paradox that it is itself divinely sanctioned, at the same time as it can be a critical tool over against any positively given religion that is also divinely sanctioned.[11] Natural right also expresses itself — as does natural religion — in a positive, historically given right, but not perfectly. Hence

---

9. On the social conditions for Lessing's critique and for the formation of his idea of the Enlightenment, see the introduction in Peter, *Stadien der Aufklärung.* Peter's book is especially useful as to how traditional morality goes into crisis in this period. A thorough interpretation of the main lines in Lessing's criticism of theology can be found in Saine, *Problem of Being Modern,* chaps. 7 and 8.

10. Wagner, *Was ist Religion,* 35.

11. See D. Harth, *Lessing,* 190.

one cannot ignore history when one tries to find out what is naturally given right or religion, and what is not.

At this point it is tempting to anticipate the chapter on Nietzsche and point out how he sees religion as something *not* connected to, but in plain opposition to, what is given in history. Nietzsche seems to have an idea of religion as something that is in accordance with a suprahistorical norm, which is the basis on which everything given in history can be criticized. Like Lessing, however, he does not affirm how this religious content also expresses itself in historically positive forms. Nietzsche perceives religion as the "divinely sanctioned" condemnation of the historically given and as a way of neglecting the altering circumstances of history. This new configuration has important consequences that we have to investigate in order to set the stage for a more broadly developed presentation of Lessing's work.

As already mentioned, by this we get another way of understanding truth in religion. Truth is no longer something that a privileged authority can define from the "inside" of religion or theology, or something linked to the historical facticity of a revelation in a specific time and place. Truth has to be understood as expressing itself in personal experience. It is also linked to what can be affirmed as rational in the light of the autonomous reason and accepted by reason, which is not already committed to some specific religious point of view.

This affirmation of the autonomy of reason has two functions. First, it contributes to the heretical imperative, which makes the individual responsible for the development of a viable religious position.[12] This cannot be left to any other authority. Second, this is also part of the development of a bias in the understanding of the "core content" of religion, toward understanding the truth of religion in terms of its contribution to morality. This understanding forms part of Lessing's background but is also developed further by him. We can therefore agree with Allison in saying that Lessing is "the founder of a whole new conception of religious truth."[13]

To realize what this new conception means, it is important to see the understanding of religion that it implies. Religion consists only of moral truths and accidental historical doctrine with no important con-

12. See the introduction, esp. 9-10.
13. Allison, *Lessing*, vii.

20

tent beyond the moral. This, however, leads to a specific method for interpreting religion. The historical dimension of religion is either ruled out totally or serves simply as an illustration for moral truths. Hence history becomes relatively unimportant for understanding both religion and morality.

Given the rise of historical criticism, it is easy to understand why history is written off as unimportant for religion. It is conceived as lacking the ability to demonstrate its own trustworthiness. As we shall see, Lessing discusses the consequences of this in some of his writings.

We see this most clearly in the deistic position. The outcome of deism is that Christianity is true to the same degree that it is superfluous. It has no positive content besides the practice of morality. Morality is all that deserves a place in the true worship of God. As Allison states, this means that the "total sum of traditional Christian doctrine, as well as its historical claims, are not only religiously irrelevant, but morally pernicious."[14]

This is not the case in Lessing. He tries to establish a position that goes beyond what occupied the Enlightenment, namely, the question of the facticity of the Christian revelation. Hence he can also evaluate Christianity as one of the most important manifestations of the human spirit, irrespective of the obscurities of its historical background.[15]

More specifically, Lessing's work contributes to a dialogue on the historically given form of Christianity. This is combined with an understanding of reason that only makes it accept that which can be true independent of historically given circumstances (what Kant would call synthetic a priori judgments). His main contribution in this dialogue is the development of some important conceptual distinctions. He does not try to mediate between the different dimensions, levels, and frameworks he works out. These distinctions serve to make clear that it is hard to spell out compromises in the relation between reason and faith.[16]

Sociologically, the establishment of these distinctions can be attributed to the fact that the life-world of believers was becoming increas-

---

14. Ibid., 16.
15. See ibid., 164.
16. See H. Thielicke, *Vernunft und Existenz bei Lessing*, 8.

ingly more complicated and was in strong need of a more complex and powerful conceptual apparatus.[17] The apparatus Lessing develops is not intended to split revelation, tradition, and reason, but to see how they can be critically linked to one another in a new and more transparent reconstruction of religion that neither violates the autonomy of the religious subject nor ignores the historical conditions of religion.[18]

The development of a reconstructed relationship between reason and faith is thus deeply connected to the clear distinction between reason and religion. To uphold a distinction here seems essential for Lessing in order to maintain both: it is essential in order to maintain an adequate expression of what religion is about. Without it one would, as a believer, become more and more out-of-date because of scientific developments. The distinction between reason and religion is also needed to establish a notion of reason that reminds us of its own limits. As Harth puts it: "In order to protect the guiding pragmatic ideas of religion in spite of this, it seems necessary to reorganize its basis, without ignoring the growing complexity and without giving up the liberating use of reason."[19]

That Lessing's main contribution lies in developing conceptual distinctions that are still of use could give the impression that he was merely an analytical thinker. However, this would be hard to argue. He also has a profound personal understanding of what it means to be a human being in history, and hence a deep insight into the importance of historical development for religious subjectivity and subjectivity in general.[20] This is what we inquire further into now.

17. See W. Oelmüller, *Die unbefriedigte Aufklärung*, v: "Where the life-world became more differentiated, the differentiations of the process of enlightenment also became necessary."

18. See H. Küng, "Religion im Prozeß der Aufklärung," 97: "In spite of all its historical difficulties, Lessing will not depart from Christianity as one does with an old hat. He will reinterpret it and thereby transpose it forwards from its very inside in a skilled manner."

19. Harth, *Lessing*, 172.

20. See Oelmüller, *Aufklärung*, xii: "The horizon within which Lessing, Kant and Hegel develop their processes of Enlightenment is . . . history."

Lessing's Aim

Lessing wrote everything, including plays for the theater and reviews. If we take a closer look as his writings in the field of philosophy of religion, however, we could say that they consist mainly of *Streitschriften* (polemics). There are two notable exceptions: the drama *Nathan the Wise,* and the treatise *On the Education of the Human Race (Die Erziehung des Menschengeschlechts),* of which the first parts were published in a *Streitschift.* In all these writings, he advances the critique and discussion of already established, contemporary theological works. Hence he does not so much present us with a finished doctrine based on its own suppositions as with marginalia on other writers. Thus his main aim is to contribute to a critical discussion of all the main positions present in his contemporary world: orthodoxy, deism, neology. He also reflects on how the growing insight in religious pluralism implies a new understanding of religion. All this makes it possible to understand why he publishes the work of Reimarus, which is a critical treatise on some of the important assumptions in German Lutheranism at the time.[21]

Although Lessing often "hides himself"[22] by mainly presenting and discussing the work of others (e.g., Reimarus), we get glimpses of the direction in which he is moving. He attempts to formulate a critical point of departure from which the conflict between orthodoxy and Reimarus's position could be overcome,[23] in which the Christian religion would stand forth neither as exclusive and intolerant nor as mere fraud.

The position he tries to develop is based on an appropriation of the given religion that takes two basic elements of Enlightenment thinking

21. These publications, together with Lessing's comments on it, can be found in *Werke,* vol. 7.

22. Many authors see this "hiding" as a kind of Socratic move, similar to that found in Kierkegaard. See B. Boethe, *Glauben und Erkennen, 7,* who quotes Hans Urs von Balthasar: "This is the new in Lessing, that he . . . beyond enlightened faces . . . carries a mask." For the question of mediate communication in Lessing in general, see von Lüpke, *Wege der Weisheit,* 100ff. Kierkegaard's description of the uncertainty of immediate communication suits Lessing as well. Kierkegaard states in 16:130 how one cannot be sure where one is, and is challenged to take a serious point of view oneself, not in relation to the messenger, but the message. Any immediate communication dissolves the possibility of personal appropriation (see 16:136).

23. See Allison, *Lessing,* 49.

into consideration in a proper way. These are, first, that the individual's religious belief should be the result of rational conviction and not of blind acceptance of the authority of tradition; second, that these beliefs should be morally efficacious.[24] These two elements show how he is here in accord with the general modern way of framing religion. At the same time, we notice how he, uniquely among our three authors, relies heavily on the understanding of morality as an important criterion for what is a tenable religious position. This gives an important contrasting background for Kierkegaard's dictum in *Fear and Trembling* that the religious position could imply a suspension of the common. It is also an important background for Nietzsche's critique of the destructive merging of Christianity and morality in his own times.[25]

Truth and Human Development — Anthropological Teleology

For Lessing, truth has far greater value in the personal and existential sense than in the sense of having "the right opinion" about things. To understand the implications of this, one has to realize that Lessing rejects the possibility that a human being is able to possess any absolute truth. This does not mean, however, that the struggle for truth is without value for the human being. On the contrary, this struggle for truth is of great importance for humanity. The quest for truth, not to "have" truth itself, by way of possessing it, is what makes humanity human. In claiming this, Lessing reflects the Enlightenment position that it is reason properly used that makes the human being develop toward maturity. In this struggle, the human being can experience the growth of his/her own powers and capacities. "The quest for the truth is the medium in which human excellence grows" (8:33).

This basic description of human life in its relation to truth requires comment. Here we see how there is a teleology in human life,[26] where humanity is not only a question of becoming what one already is (as Nietz-

---

24. See ibid., 51.

25. See below, chapter four, on Nietzsche.

26. See what was said above on the reshaping of the framework for theological anthropology into a teleological one.

sche would say). To become human is also to be involved with truth. This is a notion that first of all presupposes that we are, as humans, capable of gaining insights into what the truth is, by means of our reason. But it also means that to struggle for truth is a necessary condition for becoming human and rising above the level of innocent immediacy that we share with the animals. In other words, the relation between humanity and truth as being necessary for full maturity shapes the basis for a normative understanding of humanity. As we will see in the chapter on Nietzsche, he is concerned with how this creates for him an unsustainable tension between the facticity and the alleged normativity in human subjectivity.

Now, what does this notion of truth mean in the context of religion? First, we should note explicitly that Lessing does not think that we are capable of attaining absolute truth. No one can possess it, and therefore no religious position can make the claim that it is totally different in quality from any other such position. This makes Lessing's position anti-absolutist.

Allison, upon whose study I draw heavily in the following, emphasizes what I could call Lessing's ability to differentiate between the historical foundation of a position and its religious truth.[27] Lessing no longer relates the question of truth to a historical foundation, but to how this religious content functions in the development of human subjectivity. The outcome of this, however, is a relativist, evolutionary conception of religious truth.[28] "Relativist" must here not be taken in the sense that truth is a result of arbitrary choice. It is to be understood as a position where the statement or position x can only be seen to be true when it is related and relative to a specific context of historical circumstances and stages of development in humankind. What this means is clarified further in the analysis below.

The human relationship to truth is a link to that which contributes to the developing excellence of the human. We *are* not excellent, but the relation to truth makes it possible for us to *become* excellent. If we give up the struggle for truth, we give up the struggle for human excellence. Our

27. Allison, *Lessing*, viii.
28. Ibid. Allison offers a good understanding of how this position in Lessing is closely linked to positions in his historical context, and argues that many of his conceptions must be seen in the light of his work with Leibnizian philosophy of religion.

relation to truth is then that which makes it possible for us to develop into true human beings. Consequently, if we give up the quest for truth, we give up the quest to become our real selves.[29]

Correspondingly, the one who thinks that he already possesses the truth stops the process of human development. "Der Besitz macht ruhig, träge, stolz" ("The possession [of truth] makes one calm, slow, and proud," 8:33). Hence knowledge that one does not have the truth serves as a tool for challenging human beings to search in order to come closer to the truth; it puts humans on the track of an "unending quest." This quest is a *conditio humana* — it is necessary for the human being in order to develop and be what he is meant to be: a rational and moral being, that is, one who lives based on his own powers, and who does not have to rely on the powers of others.

In this respect, Lessing seems, as indicated, to have a teleological understanding of humanity: humanity is linked to a transcendent aim, one that is set before us. If this link to the aim is ignored or one thinks that it is already here, one runs the risk of stunting the capacities for further development. This also has serious consequences in terms of morality and religion: the fulfillment of this aim is closely linked to how we can develop and use our innate abilities for being moral and rational.

This position can be distilled into a criticism of all dogmatic positions that claim to have or possess the truth. Seen in the light of this understanding, dogmatism is an obstacle to the development of true human capacities. Since it holds that the truth is already there, contained in the Bible or in a system of teaching, one can resign from further struggle and attempts to improve oneself and one's insight into the truth.[30] Dogmatism also destroys the ability to view one's own position from a critical distance.

Insight into the nonpossession of truth thus becomes an insight into what it means to be truly human. Interestingly, Lessing contrasts the human being and God in this connection. For God — the one who is eternal and who does not develop[31] — "naturally" possesses the truth. This is

29. See what was said above on truth as making a normative concept of the human possible. Again, we note the difference from Nietzsche, who has only scorn for such a normative understanding.

30. "To remain standing on one specific stage of development means also remaining behind everything that progresses forward" (H. Schultze, *Lessings Toleranzbegriff,* 79).

31. Note here how Lessing takes over a traditional understanding of God and reshapes it to his context.

not so for human beings. Hence the relationship to truth and the capacity to grow in maturity mark an important difference between God and human beings. One of the parables Lessing wrote, perhaps the most provocative to his contemporaries, expresses this:

> If God held all truth in his closed right hand, and in his left hand only the ever-active drive to seek truth, even under the condition that I would ever and always go astray in the search, and he said to me: "Choose!" I would humbly fall before his left hand and say: "Father, give! The pure truth is reserved for you alone" (8:33).

Truth in human life is truth in development and truth for development. Because we do not permanently possess the truth, we are not in a position to exclude others, or to say that we are closer to the truth than they are. Dogmatism in an exclusive sense is thus ruled out. Therefore this notion of truth serves both as a basis for relativizing different doctrinal positions in religion and as a humanely based argument for practicing tolerance among different opinions.

It is, however, not accurate to describe the relativizing of the notion of truth in Lessing as Hannah Arendt does: "Lessing's greatness does not merely consist in a theoretical insight that there cannot be one single truth within the human world but in his gladness that it does not exist, and that, therefore, the unending discourse among men will never cease so long as there are men at all."[32] Contrary to what Arendt seems to indicate, Lessing does believe in truth, and in the search for it.[33]

What is valid in Arendt's statement, however, is that Lessing's view has opened up another kind of discourse among human beings than that which occurs if one of the participants is theoretically justified in thinking that she possesses the truth. The insight that we share in a common struggle for or quest for truth creates another kind of human community. Or, to say it in a way more like Jürgen Habermas: no one has a privileged position in this quest, and this lack of privilege opens up a recognition of the other in her likeness to me.

Implicitly, this also rules out any dogmatically based way of estab-

---

32. H. Arendt, *Von der Menschlichkeit in Finsteren Zeiten,* 45-46.
33. See Oelmüller, *Aufklärung,* 66, who also underscores that tolerance for Lessing presupposes a notion of the quest for truth.

lishing religious subjectivity. Religious subjectivity has, on these terms, to be able to "stand back" from its own positive content, establish an ironic position, and recognize its own limits and limitations. Hence Lessing opens to the systemic incorporation of religious reflexivity in a way that also is aware of its restricting conditions. One can no longer be so sure of oneself that one withdraws from the scrutiny made possible by the awareness of the existence of positions different from one's own. (As we shall see, Kierkegaard tries to avoid this consequence by stressing the passionate element in religious subjectivity, but simultaneously his insistence on reflexivity in religious matters subverts these attempts.)

What has generated this critical attitude toward the possession of the truth? In order to understand this, we have to look a little into positions taken by Lessing's contemporaries, positions that can still be found among people who relate positively in some way to religion. Truth is understood in different ways by Lessing's contemporaries:

a. The orthodox position holds that religious truth is secured via the infallible (God-inspired) text of the Bible.
b. The position of neology, mediating between faith and reason, holds that religion is true because of its rational and moral content.
c. The rationalist position presents two options. Either religion is true because it is proved to be historically correct and we accept it only to the extent that is seems rationally or historically plausible. Or religion is based on deception and positions that can be maintained only by fraud. The latter position was adopted by Reimarus.[34]

Having in mind that Lessing establishes a position that moves beyond (a) and (c), thereby also relating critically to (b), we are now able to see what his conception of truth implies. On the one hand, he recognizes the honesty of orthodox theologians in admitting that they do not proceed rationally but base their convictions on a prior conviction that the Bible is the infallible Word of God. On the other hand, he is critical toward what we could call the neological reduction, that is, the attempt to establish a reconciliation between religion and reason. Such a position, taken to its log-

34. For this see Allison, *Lessing*, 80.

ical conclusion, empties Christianity of all doctrinal content that is not morally relevant.[35]

The two positions he confronts illustrate different attempts to deal with the problem of appropriation of the content present. In orthodoxy, appropriation of tradition leaves out any consideration of changing historical circumstances, and of the aim of human development. Hence we could say that orthodoxy lacks the contextual awareness that is necessary to understand religion's intimate links to the present. In the orthodox framework, it is simply not necessary to reflect on the aim for human development, since the whole truth lies outside the sphere of subjectivity. Paradoxically, this is also to some extent true of the position found in neology. Since religious truth is identified with moral and rational truth, which can be obtained by reason when exercised properly, one does not have to consider the stance of the subject in its historical context. According to Lessing, however, the main problem here is an unsound mix of reason and faith.[36]

The third position, rationalism, suffers from many of the same weaknesses as the others. Allison summarizes the challenge Lessing is confronted with in these positions:

> His problem . . . will be to find a standpoint in terms of which the positive significance of Christian thought may be appreciated without at the same time vitiating the truth in the deistic and Spinozistic critique of the traditional conception of revelation. *Within the context of eighteenth-century thought this implies the separation of the Christian religion from its historical or factual foundation, and it is precisely this separation which we shall see Lessing propose and defend.*[37]

This task can be fulfilled only in a complete repudiation of the approach of rationalist Enlightenment theology, which dealt with truth basically on historical terms. We see this especially when Lessing deals with Reimarus, where "for the first time in the eighteenth century the question of the facticity of the Christian revelation was held to be irrelevant for the truth of Christian religion."[38] We should add, however, that this

---

35. Ibid., 84-85.

36. For Lessing's critique of neology see the more extensive treatment by Gay, *Enlightenment,* 330ff.

37. Allison, *Lessing,* 83.

38. Ibid., 96.

does not rule out all Enlightenment ideals for the human subject. By developing his own critical position, Lessing offers resources that secure the autonomy of the religious subject. By asserting that religion has validity due to its inner or intrinsic truth, and not according to more objective, hence also more disputable, revelations, he now places the question and struggle for truth not so much in an "objective, historically true" revelation as in the fulfillment of the human destiny to become more rational, more moral: to grow toward the truth. This can still be taken to be basically an Enlightenment position.

On this basis it is possible to claim that Lessing has a consistent position in his work, and that against "neology, naturalism, and orthodoxy alike he endeavored to separate the question of the truth of the Christian religion, considered as a body of doctrine and ethic, from the question of the facticity of its alleged revelation." Inherent in this is, however, the fact that Lessing's position is "ultimately grounded in a rejection of the traditional concept of revelation."[39] If revelation means that the human being is given a kind of knowledge that cannot be obtained by human capacities, this is only consequent. But what is the content of revelation?

Lessing is clear that Christian truth cannot be "identified with the wholly rational natural religion of deism or neology." The reason for this is already presented in what has been said on truth and human development. But this also makes it possible to see the genesis of the appropriation of religion in the subject in a special light: Since "such truth is first grasped in history as revealed and as immediately grasped — felt — rather than rationally comprehended by the believer, it must be clothed in an obscure and authoritarian form."[40] This immediately leads to the question: What is the rational content, and what is the relation between this content and the positive, authoritarian form in which it confronts the believer?[41] As we shall see, the answer to this question cannot be given in a couple of sentences. Lessing spells it out in different contexts, and with quite different aims. It is, however, the totality of this picture that can tell us whether he presents a coherent conception of religious truth and revelation. Schematically, however, it develops along the following lines:

39. Ibid., 121.
40. Ibid., 124.
41. See ibid.

- In a discussion on the historical validity and relevance of the history behind the Christian faith *(Über die Beweis des Geistes und der Kraft),* he argues for a personal, subjectively based truth that actualizes the past in the present.
- In the discussion on the development of human maturity *(Erziehung des Menschengeschlechts)* he argues for the appropriation of this truth in and through historical development, taking changing cultural conditions into account.
- In the recognition of a common humanity, which thus establishes religious and doctrinal tolerance *(Nathan der Weise),* he argues for a common human stance in relation to truth, irrelevant of personal religious stance.
- While discussing the distinction between practical truth and doctrinal truth *(Testimonium Johannis, Nathan),* he develops a morally colored position on truth. Truth reveals itself in the practice of love.

Consequently, one can say that this approach, which uses a philosophy of religion that does not understand itself as being theological in general, serves as a "defense for a free faith," that is, a faith that is based on what can still be recognized and accepted on contemporary terms as being valid in a given religious tradition.[42]

Is There Religious Truth without Secure Historical Truth?
Toward a New Notion of Natural Religion

The core of Lessing's construction of the religious problematic can be identified as the struggle to answer the following question: How is it possible that the unconditional absolute truth is accessible to us? It cannot appear as such in history, because history is an accumulation of contingencies and irrationalities. His proposed solution to this is that the unconditional truth can appear only within the horizon of reason. Now, from a traditional Christian point of view, this is not a solution without

42. See Oelmüller, *Aufklärung,* xiii-xiv, also xv: "The Christian religion cannot any longer count on acceptance based on its traditional legitimation, as the religious subject now demands a personally convincing validity in issues of faith and salvation."

problems, as the core of Christianity consists of a historical revelation, where God reveals himself in events that must be considered as contingent. These events are understood as the revelation of the truth about human life and destiny. Moreover, what happens in this revelation history cannot be deduced as being necessary by reason alone.

Lessing holds that truth is connected more to reason than to contingent historical circumstances. But he has another reason for stating this. For him, religion is more a practice of the heart than a given opinion, "ein bloßes Meinen."[43] Historical contingencies are in themselves no way to this more practical truth. Hence there seems to be no unmediated way to the unconditional truth along the path that a historically based religion offers.[44]

This way of posing the cluster of problems and reconstructing Lessing's position is inspired by Thielicke. He develops this along the lines proposed by Kierkegaard. Though one-sided, this way of formulating the problem covers, to a great extent, one main element of the basic construction in Lessing's philosophy of religion. But there is more to be said.

Growing and critical awareness of the historical insecurity of the Bible, and consequently, the basis of Christian faith, makes it important for Lessing to discuss how we deal with the history the Bible records. Although he is critical toward basing religious truth on historical contingencies, he is aware that Christianity is a historically based religion. In our context, this is important because it can tell us something about the impact historical critique has on the formation of the religious subject — and how we are to approach and estimate such a critique. Much of the discussion of these problems is implicit in the controversy that followed Lessing's publication of Reimarus's fragments.

Lessing holds that historically based arguments in favor of Christianity are unconvincing because, even though they may be carried out correctly, they can later prove to rely on an incorrect interpretation of the circumstances. This makes him reluctant to give them much weight in securing the confidence of the believer.[45] It is in this light that one

43. For this see also the background in Cassirer, *Die Philosophie der Aufklärung*, 220-21 and 226, where this is developed with reference to the parable of the ring, to which we return below.

44. See Thielicke, *Vernunft und Existenz bei Lessing*, 8.

45. See ibid., 30.

should read his critical dictum that "contingent historical truths can never become proofs for the necessary truths of reason" ("Zufällige Geschichtswahrheiten können der Beweis von notwendigen Vernunfts-wahrheiten nie werden," 8:12).

This statement clearly presents the problem with which Lessing struggles. On the one hand, he differentiates between historical truth and truth achieved by reason. But he also seems to identify the truth of religion with the "necessary truths of reason." However, this should not be taken at face value. To claim that religion contains necessary truths of reason is very close to saying that religion can be proved rationally. That is not the case, and Lessing never claims such a thing. Moreover, such a position tends to ignore that at least in Christianity, doctrine is presented partly as an interpretation of history. This interpretation, which obviously must be taken in the light of what seems reasonable by critical reason, rests on principles that are not apparent in that history itself. The principles of interpretation must come from *reason*. If not, then the interpretation of history is offered solely on the basis of that historical interpretation itself, a position that leaves no room for autonomous, critical reason. And that is not Lessing's interest.[46]

On this basis, Lessing appears not to be a clear-cut rationalist. He does not claim that we can do away with historical experience, or that the history recorded in the Bible has no bearing whatsoever on understanding what Christianity is all about. But he uses the above-quoted dictum critically: The orthodox cannot use history to prove that it must be exactly and indisputably as they say. Historical arguments have no such power. Also, we cannot take for granted that the interpretation of history offered by a religious tradition is adequate. By this, we see how Lessing is open to the critical evaluation and appropriation of the content of religious traditions.[47] History, as it exists apart from such an appropriation, is a tacit danger to the subject, an instance that threatens it with heteronomy. The opposing force to this power of history is reason.[48]

46. For how this position can be read as a development of Leibniz's and Wolff's philosophies see Saine, *Problem of Being Modern*, 261-62.

47. "This is why history with the validities it carries to me is a heteronomous entity, that threatens the integrity of my own essence. Thus, I have to rework my own history . . . in order to become 'myself'" (Thielicke, *Vernunft und Existenz*, 2).

48. "The basic condition of a modern, enlightened autonomous reason consists in the postulate that I shall not start with anything other than myself. A reason that is

History can still *contain* some truth, and this can be accessed through reason. But there is no logical way from history to truth. This raises the question: Exactly how, then, is one to understand the relationship between history and reason?

In this context, Lessing does not seem concerned with the impact of historical criticism as such. This is because he does not see why the conviction that religion is true has to be based on historical events at all. Empirical elements have nothing to say about this conviction of the truth of religion. Religion is based on an internal conviction, a personal assurance that is independent of historical circumstances. By stating this, he limits the impact of historical criticism on traditional belief. He also states, however, that there is an internal relation between the human being's religious sentiment and the truth of religion, a truth which can be appropriated by going behind the different stories.

His supporting argument for this position is based on two important distinctions. First, he distinguishes between the Bible and religion. The Bible, its historical content, and its development can be submitted to critique. But this does not affect the religion in the heart of the human being (8:123). This is noteworthy, as this clearly establishes the basis of religion in the subject (see the introduction to this chapter on natural religion). The text of the Bible is a witness of human religiosity — and hence mediated reports of someone else's religious experience — not mine.[49]

Lessing accordingly makes a distinction between external historical truths and internal truths based on the conviction and feeling of confidence. He thinks that the human being is able to provide independent and autonomous support for the essential truths of religion, no matter what the Bible says (8:123). This is closely linked to his under-

---

disobedient to this postulate becomes subjected to the madness of authority, which hinders reason as an actual historical power from doing what it wants to, namely, to start with itself. However, this also implies that this reason has to make a total abstraction from history" (G. Rohrmoser, "Lessing und die religionsphilosophische Fragestellung der Aufklärung," 117).

49. A corresponding distinction to the one I present here, but one that I will not go further into, is between the arguments made for a case and the case itself. The case can have a good stance, even though the arguments for it are bad, Lessing insists. By making this distinction Lessing tries to soften the impact of his own critique of his contemporary theology, but also to show that the historical forms and arguments presented for Christianity need not be taken as the definitive criteria for judging its truth.

standing of an inner authority that is distinct from the "external" authority of tradition.

The distinction between Bible and religion plays an important role in Lessing's *Axiomata* against Hauptpastor Goeze (8:131). It serves as an instrument for separating spirit and letter in the Bible (136), where "spirit" corresponds to "the inner conviction" and "letter" to "historical facts." The basic tune of this argument is that there was a type of Christianity that preceded the Bible and gave rise to it (138ff.). Hence there could be Christianity without the Bible, although not without the essential content thereof (140).

What Lessing makes possible here by way of this argument is the existence of religion, and *in casu* Christian religion, without the existence of the Bible. Or, to put it differently: religion and spirit were existing and present before book and letter (140). Thus what Lessing promotes is a Christianity that does not stake everything on the Bible's formal authority. By saying that Scripture cannot be the sole source of Christian religion, Lessing, in his own words, tries to rescue it from insoluble problems (346). He argues for a truth independent of Scripture, and by doing so, he offers arguments that can make the Christian religion trustworthy without maintaining the Bible's formal authority or its absolute correctness in all historical matters.[50] The outcome is that not every attack on the Bible need be considered an attack on religion in general (344).

By advancing this position, Lessing marks a shift in the place of authority. Authority in questions of religion rests neither in the history of the Bible nor in pastoral authority but in the experience and feeling of the religious subject, and her interior convictions. However, this does not solve the main problem concerning the relation between religion and history. The "stories" told that gave rise to belief, feeling, and conviction still run the risk of being mere frauds. But Lessing does not seriously deal with this problem because for him it is less important than what he sees as the main source of religion.

To configure the basis of essential religious truth in this way, as I have said, opens one up to a notion of natural religion, that is, a religion that does not need a written source in order to establish itself. It also,

---

50. See what I said in the introduction about the shift from formal to functional authority.

however, opens one up to a fresh look at the authority of the apostles, that is, for those witnessing to the truth. Religion is not true because it is taught by teachers and apostles. Rather they preach and teach it because it is true (8:148-49). A fortiori, something is not true because God says it, but God says it because it is true (149). Stating this, Lessing expresses an opinion on the question of religious voluntarism that is in accordance with Enlightenment ideals. God is made subject to the independent criteria for truth. To put it another way, this position makes it possible to hold that the notion of God does not exclude the possibility of there being an autonomous religious believer with a critical attitude. It places the whole question of truth in relation to how the subject can experience the content of religion as "inner truth," not based on legitimacy from formal or personal authority.

Moreover, the authority of the Scriptures must be explained on the basis of their ability to create an internal experience of truth for the subject. If they do not have any such truth, then no other explanations can supply them with it (8:149-50). For example, the Scriptures are not more credible if someone argues that the Holy Spirit inspires them. Any support by external authority, any attempt to make the Scriptures stand out as true by adding some sort of theory or argument that is not in some way already contained in them, is in vain, according to Lessing. The experience of the truth of the Scriptures can only rest in their ability to convince us by themselves (50). This experience of truth is primarily given, and cannot be disturbed or affected by any historical circumstances.

In his famous treatise *Über den Beweis der Geistes und der Kraft (On the proofs and powers of the Spirit)*, Lessing makes a further distinction. He distinguishes between being contemporary to the events that the evangelists have recorded and being a secondhand listener to the reports of the same miraculous events. This distinction, he claims, is indisputable. We exist in different conditions from the disciples (but as one will remember, Kierkegaard disputes whether this gives the disciples an advantage over us).

The purpose of the distinction is partly to expose how the religious subject is configured on other suppositions in modern times than when Christianity originated. To be a contemporary, one has to have immediate access to a personal experience of the reality that gives rise to faith. As a contemporary, one has a better possibility to be attentive to and to be grasped by what is happening. To live in and to experience these events oneself is something completely different from having the same events presented to one in mediate reports (see 8:9-10).[51]

According to Lessing, being a believer is completely different in the time of Jesus than it is in our times. We do not have the same access to the events that gave rise to faith as Jesus' contemporaries had. Hence we do not have the same religious experience as them. What was once experienced as the immediate proofs and powers of the Spirit, in the present contains neither Spirit nor power. Instead, that experience has degenerated into a mere witness of the same. Lessing is clear that the report of an event is not the same as the event itself, just as a realized prophecy is not the same as a report of the same (8:10).

Speaking in terms of the anthropological foundations of religion, these distinctions serve as a way of pointing to the difference between mediate and immediate experience. They also show to what extent Enlightenment thinking is receptive to the understanding of how historically given content does — and does not — have an impact on the formation of the subject. Apparently, this distinction also serves as a qualitative marker. Mediate experience does not have the same quality as immediate experience, as it is mediated through a medium (8:10). The medium detaches the subject from an immediate relationship to history.

In summary, we obtain the following distinctions between the different material formations of religious subjectivity:

Engaged and committed subject	Detached subject
Immediate experience containing power and Spirit	Mediate experience, with neither power nor Spirit
Personal experience	Experience based on a medium: a testimony
Personal truth — inner based, rational	Critical distance and discussion of the historical truth of the reports
Contemporary participation	Past history

51. As we will see later, this position is criticized by Kierkegaard. He "brackets" the critical, detached, and insecure religious subject almost totally, and insists on passion instead of reason and reflection as a basis for a religious relationship. (This does not exclude reason and reflection totally, but it has no place in this basis.) For a further discussion on this, see chapter three below.

The critical distance made possible by the mediate way of relating to important religious events has its drawback in that these events now lack the power and Spirit that can cause the subject to believe in the same way as past authorities claimed.

Several elements should be noticed about Lessing's argument here:

- He does not question the historical validity of the reports in the Bible. The distinction is important even if they prove to be valid.
- Lessing seems to take for granted that one cannot have an immediate relation to something reported by others. In one way this seems to be true. However, much of what we hold and take as valid is based not on personal experience, but on transmission in culture. Such transmission also serves to build up our life-world, where we take things as being immediately given. Lessing's argument does not deny this. What he does deny is the possibility of having first-hand experiences like those of the first Christians when it comes to the basis for establishing religious faith. Religion must, in modern times, be related to another type of subjectivity. Also, his argument should not be taken as a denial of the position that one cannot have an immediate relation to religious truth. What he spells out are the limitations of a historical foundation of faith. As we shall see later, Kierkegaard develops just this point in important ways.

Believers in the past had every reason for their strong faith. They experienced something of great power that gave occasion to such a faith. How, asks Lessing, can we expect the same strong faith to rise in us, we that do not have the same occasions and causes for believing as they had? (8:11). Tacit in this question is the assumption that it is only possible to have a strong faith rooted in historical events if those events have been experienced in one's own life. Now, in our time, tales of miracles no longer have the power to "move" the subject (12).

This implies that arguments based on reports of what others have believed cannot have the same status as the original causes of their beliefs. It is at this stage that Lessing introduces the question of the historical validity of the reports of the Bible. He develops his argument carefully:

- The reports of the occasions causing religious faith are just as trustworthy as any other historical report (8:11).

- Since they are just as trustworthy as any other historical report — no more and no less — how can we then use them in a way that seems to make them more trustworthy? Is it legitimate to use them as the basis for a religious position that has its sources in something else than the same history? (The answer implied is: no.)
- Since no historical truth can be demonstrated, then no other truth can be demonstrated by this historical truth.
- Hence accidental truths of history can never become the proof of necessary truths of reason (8:12; see above).

Thus the circle is closed. In the development of this argument, I noted that Lessing used two distinctions: between a historical and a religious position, and between truths of history and truths of reason. Let us now take a closer look at the implications of these notions. These pairs of distinctions are interrelated and must not be juxtaposed. Truths of history are related to historical reports and are contingent. On the other hand, truths of religion are based on reason and are necessary. Hence truths of religion cannot be founded on contingent historical events that we determine to be true. That would also make the basis of a religious position utterly insecure (see 8:12).

Lessing insists that the only thing that can be built on historical events is historical knowledge. Hence there is no pathway from the historical to the metaphysical or to a doctrinal position: the historical can only give a basis for other historical elements. As the doctrinal and the historical are thus conceptually separated, it becomes impossible to infer from the historical to the doctrinal or metaphysical (8:14). Consequently, for Lessing, mere historical facts cannot move the subject to hold a truth that is independent of history. The faith of the subject thus becomes detached from the history from which faith takes its point of departure.

Paul Rilla has commented on the implications of this position. He says that by making such a sharp distinction between the content of faith and the content of historical knowledge, Lessing attempts to overcome the tendencies of the Enlightenment to bring forth a norm, which lets feudally determined elements of faith appear as acceptable for the bourgeois world.[52] This norm itself, however, seems to require a belief, and this is what

52. P. Rilla, *Lessing und sein Zeitalter*, 452.

Lessing illustrates with his critique. In other words, the attempt to affirm a unity of faith and reason, which Lessing does not consider to be desirable, presupposes a subjective disposition that Lessing succeeds in bringing to light. Rilla's comment is worth noticing because he demonstrates how closely linked Lessing's reconstruction of religion and religious subjectivity is to his political and social context. Although presumably enlightened, the positions he criticizes appear to be oblivious to their basic assumptions.

We can now see how the awareness or consciousness of the distance in time and space between the first believers and us is given a distinctively new meaning. This meaning is not primarily that it is easier for people living in the past to believe than it is for us. The point is that we have different access to the truth than they have. They met truth in history, while the enlightened person struggles to meet truth in and through reason. Thus, if religious truth is related to history, it is because it can be found in history and not because it is itself history. History can help us to see a truth that is founded in reason, but not itself be a kind of truth that is constitutive for the establishment of a religious faith. The religious subject is thus given another footing, and Lessing helps to spell out the presuppositions for this footing in his reconstruction.

Religion consists of more than a truth achieved by reason alone. It involves a broader dimension of the subject, which includes more than its rational faculties. On this basis, it is understandable why Thielicke argues repeatedly for considering the relationship between the truths of reason and truths of belief as complementary, not mutually exclusive. The truths cannot serve as substitutes for each other. No matter what reason alone says, the *testimonium sentiendi* in the heart of the believer remains convinced of the truth.[53] By affirming this, Lessing seems to suggest an idea of the essence of religion that overcomes a mere rationalistic understanding. But what this means in detail must be spelled out further. To this we now turn.

---

53. See Thielicke, *Vernunft und Existenz bei Lessing,* 28-30. We should also note that this way of rooting truth in the "feeling" *(Gefühl)* and thus of identifying the subjective roots of religion in something other than reason corresponds to the parallel rooting of morality in *Gefühl,* not in reason. "Morality for Lessing is based in feeling" (Peter, *Stadien,* 32). Hence the reasonable and the moral are not always identical — a reasonable human being is, according to Lessing, still able to do what is morally wrong. This is a problem that occupies Lessing, and he tries to emancipate morality from reason in a way that for the deists seemed to be a fall back to the belief in revelation, since they identified morality and reason.

The Background for Human Development
in the Treatise on Education

Based on his understanding of truth, Lessing also has to reconstruct the concept of *revelation*. How he does this becomes most clear in the treatise *On the Education of the Human Race* (*Die Erziehung des Menschengeschlects* [hereafter *EdM*], published 1780). Here he depicts revelation as a kind of historical process, "wherein different degrees of insight are produced in various historical communities, each sufficient for the needs of that community." This understanding implies that no single revelation can be seen as having any decisive impact on the understanding of the content of the religious consciousness: "Each is merely a partial adumbration of the truth, more or less obscurely expressed."[54] Consequently, the truth of a religion, as it expresses itself in terms of doctrine and ethics, must be evaluated independently of, but still in relation to its background in, the historical context in which it has its origin and framework of expression.

Thus the treatise serves to establish an interpretation of the history of the Judeo-Christian religion as a history of a revelation that is overcome, and worked over, by reason. Thereby this religion develops into a mature, reasonable religion that serves the development of people's autonomy, and does not oppress them by appeals to a nonrational tradition.[55] Genuine religion serves and contributes to the subject's autonomy. To use Peter Berger's terminology, this means that Lessing reconstructs religion and religious revelation in such a way that it opens up to the heretical option.[56]

Thus we find in *EdM* an understanding of revelation as a maieutic method that is combined with a pedagogical ethos, similar to that of Socrates. Here the historical circumstances give rise to a "dialogue" between itself and the subject that brings into the open what human beings already have innate in themselves.[57] Hence revelation contributes to the teleological development of humanity. But this is not a purely external teleology, as the insights given by the revelation are mediated or internalized in the subject in a way that reveals that this content is already also

---

54. Allison, *Lessing,* 100.

55. Rohrmoser comments on this aptly: "Aus Offenbarungswahrheit soll Vernunftswahrheit werden" and points to how Lessing can do that because he differentiates between religious form and content (Rohrmoser, "Lessing," 126).

56. See the introduction above, 9.

57. See Harth, *Lessing,* 185.

inherent in the subject, that is, given in the constitution of the human beings themselves. It needs the revelation, however, in order to fully develop or to realize its potential.[58]

In developing his position, Lessing wants to avoid the blend of positive and natural religion he found in Reimarus, and let both lights continue to burn separately.[59] Positive religion (as expressed in the historical revelation) is recognized, at the same time as natural religion (given in the human constitution) is also considered important. Hence natural religion is not understood as something sinful, which blurs the pure content of the positive revelation. There is consequently a positive correlation between the two types of religion. But this in turn challenges the understanding of the relation between them.[60]

There is — and recall again what was said in the introduction — in this model an inherent recognition of the provisional character of religious content in general. This corresponds well with Lessing's insistence that we have not arrived at a position where we can be said to hold the whole truth. Lessing has most probably developed this understanding of the historical relativity of truth and the unfulfilled revelation in history in close connection with the concept of truth he finds in Leibniz. "The recognition of the relative truth of each perspective or standpoint is combined with the belief in eventual progress to higher standpoints." This leads to what Henry Allison calls Leibnizian perspectivalism. Here the subject's position in history conditions his or her perspective on the truth of religion. This is a way of thinking that provides Lessing with the background for the rational content or *inner truth* of the Christian religion.[61]

This position has three important consequences for the reflective reconstruction of Christianity:

a. Christianity is no longer grounded in an absolute, universally binding Word of God (the Bible), but has a relative validity as one of the many paths along which the human race can develop.[62]

58. This position, that religion reveals the inner secrets of the human self to the self, can also be found in the early writings of Lessing. For this see Wessel, *Lessing's Theology*, 126-27.

59. Thielicke, *Vernunft und Existenz bei Lessing*, 8.

60. See also the notion of natural rights, noted above.

61. See Allison, *Lessing*, 133.

62. For more on this, see the discussion later in relation to *Nathan*.

b. The position offers a philosophical underpinning for the concept of toleration in Lessing. "Since each religion possesses a relative, and none the absolute truth, each is worthy of respect."[63]

c. Lessing has a notion of divine design and intention in history, but by showing how reason develops, he at the same time contributes to the overcoming of the tradition from which he himself takes the notion of the development of faith.[64]

As indicated in several places above, the position presented here is also interesting because it reflects a teleological reconstruction of religion, where the aim of humanity and what is developing as religion and religious truth have not yet been reached. There also seems to be some freedom with regard to which direction further development will go. However, this also opens up the possibility that no religion we are confronted with is, in its present form, *the* true religion. Development of religion and the further development of humankind belong together. Hence we are provided with a strong argument against any kind of religion that sticks to what is recognized here and now as the ultimate truth. Such forms of religion, static as they are, prohibit further human development, and are consequently inhuman. They stop us on the way toward truth, as this can partly and by means of certain perspectives be recognized by reason. Allison writes on this:

> A purely rational religion, although not that which was postulated by deism or neology, was for Lessing the ultimate truth. *However, rather than the original religion of mankind, of which the positive religions are subsequent distortions, it is now seen as an ideal toward which the human race may strive, but which [it] can never completely realize.*[65]

Now, it would be wrong to assume that this reconstruction leads to a merely negative view of the past. It also opens us up to seeing the previous stages in the development of the history of religion as valuable stages toward where we are now. This will become clearer in the next section.

---

63. Allison, *Lessing*, 134.
64. For the last element see Peter, *Stadien*, 30.
65. Allison, *Lessing*, 134.

The Relationship between Natural and Revealed Religion

Lessing sees in all positive religions the expression of the way along which human reason has developed and still can develop in the future (see 8:489). Hence he holds that the religions are intimately connected to the development of humanity, and that religion will itself develop as humanity develops (see above).

This opens one up to a historical understanding not only of humanity, but also of religious subjectivity. Religious subjectivity is not a static phenomenon, but develops under the influence of other elements in history, in and by which it also expresses itself. At the same time, any *positive* religion can be seen as an expression of religious subjectivity. This way of reconstructing religion has two implications. First, religion is not first and foremost something given, to which the human should connect or adhere. Religion is basically subjectivity; it is an innate faculty in the human being. This innate and reason-based faculty is supported by elements in human history, but these historical elements cannot in themselves prove the truth of a universally valid positive religion (see 7:465; see the previous section).

Second, and historically most fatal in terms of the later development, this understanding of religion as first and foremost an expression of subjectivity clears the way for the critique of religion found in Feuerbach and Nietzsche. If religion is a human product, why should we judge it to be something more than human? In Nietzsche's words, is it not only human, all too human, and consequently something we should do away with? I will not follow this line of thought further here, but want to point to its systematic relation to the reconstruction of religion to be found in Lessing (as well as, later, in Schleiermacher).

Now, this also seems to challenge the relationship between natural and positive religion. In a fragment from his unpublished work, Lessing discusses how subjectivity and religion are related. He claims that the essence of natural religion is the struggle for a clear notion that can help us understand and know God and take this knowledge into consideration in thought and action. This struggle, and thus the content of natural religion, is something that determines every human being (7:282).

Because human beings differ, they also modify their religious expressions (of natural religion) in different ways. In order to make religion function in society, they have to agree on certain conventional notions and practices, and give them the same importance and necessity that the "original" truths of natural religion (based in subjectivity) have in themselves. This is necessary in order to establish agreement and coherence in a society. By doing this, natural religion is enhanced into a positive religion. Lessing compares the relation between them with the relation between natural right and positive right (7:282, 283; see above). As we are always confronted with religion in a positive form, we have to reckon with the fact that it has contingent elements and expressions. These are due to its cultural and political context, and it is thus possible to do without them. Hence the differentiation between positive and natural religion here opens up to a more critical and differentiated evaluation of positive religion that also includes some of its sociological functions.

On this basis, Lessing can say that every positive religion is equally true and equally false. It is false insofar as the conventional and contingent elements threaten to eliminate the essentials of religion or push them into the background. It is true insofar as these conventional elements contribute to the unity of society, probably because this can be seen as a rational aim. What is of importance, however, is that Lessing also offers a criterion for what is the best revealed or most positive religion: the one that can exist with as few conventional additions to the naturally given (religion) as possible. Thus it restricts the natural religion as little as possible (7:283). The upshot of this argument then seems to be that positive religion is acceptable insofar as it offers elements that contribute to social utility,[66] but that it also seems to restrict or distort natural religion. Hence the criteria for estimating religion critically are directed against positive religion. There is, in Lessing, no corresponding development of critical criteria for the evaluation of natural religion. This should be noted, as it gives a clear indication of the positive anthropology we find in the Enlightenment reconstruction of religion in general, and in Lessing in particular.

We can now understand what Lessing says on the relationship between revealed religion and the religion of reason. Revealed religion does not *presuppose* a religion of reason, but itself *contains* it. If the religion of reason were a presupposition for revealed religion, revealed religion would be impossible to understand without the other. This is not the case. By en-

---

66. See ibid., 78. On the recognition of the potential social utility of religion recognized by Enlightenment thinkers, see Gay, *Enlightenment*, 154, et passim.

tering into the framework of revealed religion, we can also come to a greater understanding of what the religion of reason is like (7:464).

Lessing actually used this last point against Reimarus. We should note here especially his reluctance to posit a religion of reason or a natural religion over against revealed and positive religion. There is an inner connection between the two that cannot be ignored or overlooked. This relationship is linked to the fact that human beings live in and under historical conditions with their religious subjectivity. These conditions provide the social and cultural framework by which religious subjectivity has to express itself. By reconstructing a framework for understanding this, Lessing clarifies his own position, in a way that is consonant with what he says in his unpublished papers on natural and revealed religion (see above).

On the Development of Religion and Religious Subjectivity in Christianity and Its Background

The reconstruction of the development of religion in *Die Erziehung des Menschengeschlechts* is directed toward a new historical understanding of the roots of Christianity. The interpretation this treatise contains is more favorable to the Jewish roots of Christianity than the contemporary interpretations that it seeks to replace, but also interprets the historical development in typically Enlightenment terms. The rise of Christianity is at the same time the rise of a more enlightened form of religion, where the core of natural religion is expressed more authentically than in previous forms.

Here I interpret the work not so much as a reconstruction of the development of religion in general, but more specifically as a treatise on the development of religious subjectivity. Implicit in this description of historical development is, of course, also a notion of how the religious subject can mature as time goes by. Lessing himself anticipates this line of reading, when in the first paragraph he says that the education of the individual is just like revelation for humankind in general.[67]

This statement requires a special concept of revelation. Here also

---

67. See §§1-3, 8:490. In the following, if nothing else is noted, I refer to this treatise only by paragraph number.

we immediately face one of the problems in the interpretation of the treatise. In §4 Lessing states that education does not give the individual anything else than what she could have got by herself. It only provides faster and easier access. I take this to say that what happens to us, what we experience by ourselves, is identical to what is given us in education. Hence to live in history and have experiences helps to make us what we are, helps to accumulate the experience and wisdom that is otherwise given to us by education. Correspondingly, education is nothing other than the mediation of experience. This accords structurally with what was elaborated above about the two ways to develop religious subjectivity, through either personal experience or mediated reports.[68]

In order to clarify this structural correspondence, we can state the following:

- The subject can know all by itself, independent of education, if it has enough time.
- Humankind can know all by itself, independent of revelation, by developing the insights accessible through reason.
- However, education and revelation mediate what is otherwise given directly in subjectivity and/or humanity's rational insights. Hence the mediated material confirms subjectivity/humanity.
- Knowledge of past history, past revelations, or past secondhand experience is in itself no proof of its relevance for the present. Proof is given only by its correspondence with personal experience and personally acquired rational insight.[69]

By paralleling education with revelation, however, Lessing says something about the capacity for the human being when it comes to "divine things" as well. Revelation does not give humankind anything other than that which could be accessed by unaided human reason and experience — but it gave and gives us these things earlier or faster (§4) than would have otherwise been the case.

Theologically, this is to state an identity in content between natural

---

68. This is important to see in relation to the question of religion as based on either former history or personal experience, as I did in an earlier section of this chapter. A structural parallel here exists that should not be overlooked.

69. Note again, confirming Berger, how personal experience is the important factor.

and special revelation, or between natural and historical revelation. For the understanding of religious subjectivity, this has at least three implications:

- Revelation is not contrary to reason.
- Revelation is not contrary to human freedom and autonomy.
- Revelation basically has to do with morality.

Let me try to explain these implications:

First, that revelation is not contrary to reason has already been stated in the above section, and should not be a surprise. By holding this, Lessing at the same time delimits what religion is about: it is about that which can be found by reason, working on the basis of human experience in history. Hence religion is reasonable, or, to put it another way, the religious subject does not have to depart from reason in her elucidation of the content of religion.

Second, the most important consequence of this is that religious revelation is not seen as a threat to the rational and moral subject. Since religion in principle does not contain anything but that which can be founded on "inner" experience, it is only aberrations in religion that need to be conceived as such a threat. Lessing would probably say that such aberrations can be explained in one of two ways. One can say either that they are necessary at a particular historical stage but will be overcome as soon as one has grown sufficiently in maturity, or that they represent a misuse or a misconception of religion. In the first case, the aberration represents a necessary accommodation of religious truth to a historical and social setting (see Semler's theory of accommodation)[70] and can be seen as being grounded in revelation and explainable by reason. In the second case it is an expression of a group's interest in sustaining or gaining power over others (see the Patriarch in *Nathan*), and is an expression of how a positive religion also uses sources foreign to revelation to shape a specific social structure. Hence positive religion and religious revelation do not necessarily overlap. Positive religion is built on revelation, but also integrates the content of these revelations into a wider culturally and socially conditioned framework. From this it follows that religious subjectivity can have both authentic and inauthentic

70. For this see G. Hornig, *Die Anfänge des historisch-kritischen Theologie.*

expressions. This is most clearly seen in how religion configures itself in morality.

Third, by saying that revelation has basically to do with morality, Lessing states something that is quite obvious from a theological point of view. By herself, the human being cannot (at least not in the Lutheran Protestant tradition) achieve or merit the grace of God. This grace is revealed in the historical revelation of Jesus. This historical revelation is at once reduced merely to an example of morality when it is said to be identical with what the human can find out by herself. According to this tradition, however, what the human being can find out by herself is only what has to do with God's law — not with the gospel. When religion is about basic principles revealed by natural reason in the historical being of the human, this historical element loses its extensive and constitutive meaning for religion. Christianity could then do without history.

Lessing must surely have sensed the problems inherent in this. As a student of theology and the son of a Lutheran pastor, Lessing was well aware that to state that religion can do without historical truth was inconsistent with what his contemporary, church-based Lutheran religion claimed to be the case. This gives perhaps also part of the reason why the basis laid down in §4 is complicated by a later statement in the same treatise, in §77. Much of the scholarly discussion on this treatise deals with the apparent contradiction between these two paragraphs.

Now, instead of immediately contrasting the two understandings of reason that scholars claim can be found in the two paragraphs, it is important first to look at the preceding §76. There Lessing says that it is important to develop the truths of revealed religion into truths of reason, if humankind is to receive any help from religion. Such truths are revealed in order to become truths of reason (8:506). This is why I said above that Lessing's process of religion and religious development is similar to that of the Enlightenment. By integrating these truths into reason, religion develops and becomes more rational. At the same time the human becomes a free being, unburdened by the heteronomies of tradition. Hence we see how Lessing turns the problem of how to establish a modern religious subjectivity into a problem of how to appropriate by reason what is given in historical revelation(s).

In view of this, when reason turns to historical religion it develops the materials given there into more consistent and transparent notions, and offers it a validity that can also be sustained independently of the historical truth of the original circumstances in and through which these truths were revealed (§§76, 77). Reason and reflection make religion more transparent and reconstruct its content in a clearer mode.

This indicates that a religious position could, in principle, be established without relating to historical events. Does this also hold for what is practically possible? The answer to this is somewhat obscure in Lessing's writings. We can see this most clearly when dealing with the alleged contradiction mentioned above.

Lessing raises the problem at the end of §77 (8:507), when he states that human reason is no longer able to reach these (religious) truths. This is totally contrary to all that he said thus far. Why is this so?

First, we note that the truths in question here concern central concepts like the unity and trinity of God, original sin, and the vicarious punishment of Christ (§§72-75).

We should also note explicitly that the subject of the treatise as a whole is the rationalization of religion by the faculties of the human subject. The suggestion for interpretation offered by K. Beyschlag is therefore interesting. He says that the apparent contradiction between §4 and §77 is dissolved if one sees the statements in the framework of the treatise as a whole: revelation is rationalized by reason, and this rationalization leads, on the basis of what is revealed, to some dogmatic statements that would not be possible to reach without this revelation (see §§72ff.).[71]

This suggestion is not totally convincing, however, in that it does not consider the full content of §4. There it is quite obvious that revelation is not needed in order to constitute the content of reason — what is reasonable can be constituted without any historical revelation. Hence we must turn to another attempt to solve the present problem. In his contribution to the clarification of the problem, Helmut Thielicke suggests that Lessing uses two different notions of reason in the treatise: one transcendental, the other historical.[72]

Thielicke takes the notion of reason in §4 to be the subjective side of the objective truth that is bound to history. To relate to this truth is a

---

71. K. Beyschlag, *Lessings Werke*, 3:696; here based on the commentaries to §77 in 8:711.

72. For a short survey of Thielicke's understanding, see his *Glauben und Denken in der Neuzeit*, 145ff.

general faculty and is not restricted to specific empirical elements. The aim of revelatory history is to reach objective truth, as it appears independent of mythos and history; the aim on the subjective side is to reach a state of reason where reason is cleansed of or detached from the historical and empirical. The meaning of the historical process as described by Lessing is finally to release the content of religious traditions from its reified connections in history and to place it with and link it to the subject, thereby contributing to the subject's autonomy.[73] Hence the process of establishing an immediate relation to religious truth can be fulfilled without taking the way of history — a way that Lessing regards as blocked.[74]

This indicates that what Lessing stated in §4 about the content of revelation is not an account of what is given in history, but revelation and reason are described there in their basic and transcendental relation to each other. Their common basis is not constituted by historical elements, but serves as a postulate for understanding the development of human history and reason. Reason left by itself in this sense does not exist in history, according to Thielicke, but is like a Platonic idea, which changes character once it enters history.

Hence it is because reason is inescapably linked to history, because of confusion and plurality, that the end of §77 is written. §77 speaks of the practical impossibility of the self-realization of reason in such ways that it can by itself achieve or attain the objective truths of religion. Similarly, as long as reason is directed toward religion as given in history, it is also in a difficult situation because it does not relate to any "pure" religion but rather to religion as given in and under the conditions of history.

Without the notion of reason in §4, the teleological element in Lessing's thought would have been considerably weaker. At the same time, the notion of a historically bound reason in §77 makes it even more important to have the notion in §4, since it makes the possibility of transcending the empirical realm into something true that is "above" history.

Revelation, as something not yet arrived at its telos, is both partly transparent and partly still opaque to reason. Although it holds the objective truth, the subjectivity of the believer and his or her interrelatedness with the contingencies of history make it hard to spell out what the core of this truth is. The content of faith and reason is also deter-

73. Ibid., 146.
74. See above, 37-39.

mined by the historical situation of the subject. Therefore their truth permanently transcends what the subject is able to achieve. Thus argues Thielicke.[75]

Allison offers an approach that can be combined with this explanation. He argues that Lessing views revelation both as a stimulant for human development and as an anticipation of the same. "It is an anticipation because it contains within itself an implicitly rational content, which is destined to be disclosed, and it is stimulant because . . . it provides the occasion which first leads reason to consider this content."[76]

This apparently reconciles the tension between the two paragraphs. On this basis, it becomes perfectly reasonable "to argue that without this education or revelation human reason might never have actually come to recognize them, just as the slave boy might never have come to recognize the geometrical truths which he apprehended under the prodding of Socrates." The former assertion (§4) is concerned with the logical (or transcendental) structure of these truths, and the latter (§77) with the psychological (and, I would add, historical) conditions necessary for their apprehension.[77]

Summing up, we could say that Lessing combines in *EdM* (1) Leibniz's perspectivism, (2) Spinoza's (or perhaps Semler's?) theory of accommodation of revelation to the standpoint of its recipients, and (3) an understanding of historical development in religion as guided by God's providence.[78] Thus he opens up to a more differentiated evaluation of the content of religion. This evaluation takes the empirical aspects of historical religion into account, and does not proceed immediately to the evaluation of it in terms of some suprahistorical rational and natural religion, as the deists and neologists did.

> From the relativistic standpoint, the apparent contradiction between the emphasis on both the rational and incomprehensible aspects of the "inner truth" of the Christian religion completely vanishes. Since the doctrines of this religion do contain a perspectival adumbration

75. Thielicke, *Vernunft und Existenz bei Lessing*, 33.
76. Allison, *Lessing*, 158.
77. Ibid., 158-59.
78. See ibid., 148.

of the ultimate truth, they may be seen to have an implicitly rational content, but since they are only inadequate, historically conditioned expressions of this truth and not the ultimate truth itself, they inevitably contain elements of obscurity and incomprehensibility, which are merely the necessary concomitants of all finite and limited knowledge.[79]

Plurality without Truth?

In order to understand the Enlightenment pressure for a more tolerant society, one has to consider the most obvious religious background and obstacle to such tolerance, that is, the exclusivist understanding of Christianity.[80] Apart from the religious wars, this is most vividly expressed in the doctrine of eternal damnation. This makes it possible to criticize religion on a moral basis, in a way that makes such a critique plausible and welcome to the public in general. Lessing treats this doctrine, for example in the Patriarch in *Nathan,* with moral indignation. Hence dogma without positive moral meaning seems to have a crucial and often negative impact on both true religion and true morality. It is "not doubt or ignorance but dogma, which if believed ultimately leads to superstition, [that] is the real enemy of both morality and of religion" for Enlightenment thinkers.[81] However, the question of tolerance is present not only in a moral framework but also in the wider framework of the plurality of religions and the discussion of their truth. In this setting the moral element serves as one of the criteria for defining the truth of religion.[82]

Problems with exclusivist dogma are even more apparent in a situation marked by religious plurality. In his treatise on *Cardanus* (7:9ff.) Lessing discusses the accusations against Cardanus, who in his compari-

---

79. Ibid., 163.

80. One should, however, note that even more important than this element is the political element, i.e., the right to say and publish what one wishes. Censorship was not an option only in terms of religious matters, although Lessing was subjected to it on such grounds.

81. Allison, *Lessing,* 18.

82. See Küng's report of the position for tolerance in the young Lessing in the introduction to his essay, "Religion im Prozeß."

son of religions indicated problems with the understanding of Christianity's superior status in relation to the other religions. Such a comparison primarily opens up the question of the truth of religion: If there are many religions, how can only one of them be true? And how do we determine which religion is true?

Now, Lessing affirms that the comparison of religions is not a great threat to Christianity. If one lacks the courage to do it, it is an indication that one's faith is in poor condition (7:18). To support this approach, Lessing offers two arguments:

- Such unwillingness shows that one lacks true faith in the works of the Savior.
- If one were to lose faith due to such a comparison, it would mean that one position had been exchanged for a better one. Hence such an outcome should not be regarded as a loss, but as a gain, since one now holds a better-established position (7:18).

We should note here in passing that Lessing seems to think of this process of comparison as one that has influence only in the rational dimension of the individual. In other words, the arguments he presents here tend to ignore other important elements in religion. He overlooks the impact a specific religion can have on the formation of individual identity. Hence he tends to ignore how scrutinizing one's religion can lead to a possible change in religious position, which will affect the individual's identity in a way that reaches far deeper than the intellectual level.

Lessing does, however, note some of the virtues demanded of a subject who is willing to establish his or her religious position on rational grounds. To be able to carry out such comparisons, the subject must be impartial and open-minded (7:18, 21). Hence Lessing suggests that we should use the pluralism of religions to establish an attitude toward religion in general that is honest and open-minded.

If "enlightenment" means to establish distinctions and contribute to differentiation, this is exactly what Lessing attempts to do here. He shows that although Cardanus seemed to reject that the Christian religion is much better than another, this does not indicate that he is an atheist. Thus the first distinction drawn here is between atheism and theism.

There are, however, different forms of theism. The "core" in Lessing's distinctions concerning religious pluralism bears on the distinction between natural and positive religion. If the "truth" of natural religion is connected to the promotion of charity and other virtues, then there seems to be no trouble in accepting doctrinal differences. Hence a second distinction appears between a theism based on natural religion and a theism based mainly on the doctrinal content of a positive religion. We shall see below how this works out in *Nathan*.

I should add that to compare religions is neither dangerous nor threatening as long as one believes in both reason and natural religion as sufficient tools for achieving insight into the divine. This "natural core," which is anthropologically, not historically, founded, helps each to stick to his or her own religion. At the same time it serves to relativize the truth claims of the different positions.

There remains a challenge here, inherent in the confrontation with a religious attitude that does not allow for an alliance with critical reason, or one that does not view religion as different expressions of the reason inherent in natural religion. Hence, for example, a traditional position that affirms its own truth versus any other position still has the problems indicated above concerning identity. If, however, religious identity is based on a more general notion of religion, this problem does not have the same impact.

As we can see, the general notion of religion makes it possible to affirm both plurality and truth, and to maintain the moral critique of a traditional exclusivist position that sentences people of other faiths to eternal damnation. The truth is something every religion has in common. It is not something accessible only from the doctrinal specifics of one religion.

Lessing's Mediate Position as a Critic and a Mask Wearer

An ironic, critical position toward traditional religion can serve a twofold purpose: either to destroy religion or to contribute to its further development. No doubt, Lessing opted for the second approach. He was convinced that religion is better off if treated in a critical manner and exposed to public critique. In the same manner he was convinced that Reimarus's critical fragments were better discussed in the open. They would make fewer converts than if they were circulating secretly and not subject to critical discussion (see 8:343).

Irrespective of this, Lessing himself did not come out into the open with his own, clearly distinguished critical position. He usually hid behind a "mask," an adopted persona. When he addressed the problems that challenged religion, it was typical for Lessing to do this by discussing a critic of religion. We see this in his different *Vindications* (Rettungen), as well as in his discussion of Reimarus's fragments. The pattern that develops here is that Lessing does not openly promote his own position. Indeed, it is sometimes hard to see what his personal position is. He uses the different authors he comments on as points of departure for both challenging traditional Christian views and being critical toward the critique itself. In this way, the different authors and opinions he addresses serve as masks as well as for contributions to the public and critical discussion of religion. This is also related to the fact that Lessing never identifies himself as a theologian. It is an advantage for him not to be a theologian, since he can then know and study everything without any public obligation. It also offers him the necessary freedom to develop a critical attitude toward many different positions, while not holding any definite position himself.[83]

As indicated, however, Lessing's position is still spelled out clearly enough for us to say that it is neither neology nor rationalism. Even though it is hard to tell exactly what his position is, from what is said above it is clear that he does not identify religious truth completely with historical truth. This is because religious truth is not founded on historically contingent circumstances but on the ability of the subject to experience it as something present and confirmed by its own personal experience.

One interesting point in Lessing's argument brings out a further problem with a more traditional approach to Christian religion. As understood by proponents of this religion, Lessing attacks Christianity. However, he can state — perhaps ironically — that he subscribes to every statement about Christ found in the creeds of Christianity (see 8:310ff.). Apparently, this makes his counterparts insecure. He is — as a critic, as

83. On the indefiniteness of Lessing's position, see Saine, *Problem of Being Modern,* 214ff., and 237, where he even speaks of Lessing's *irony!* Also in *EdM,* which is "not at all an ironic work, Lessing distances himself by insisting that he is only the 'editor' of the tract, not its author" (Saine, 271).

one wearing a mask — difficult to pin down in a defined position. On the other hand, it is only possible to uphold a traditional position as long as one can exclude the critic — as "not one of us." If he must be recognized as belonging to the same group, this forces the traditional position to integrate and reflect on the distinctions and proposals offered by Lessing. Thus the naive, traditional position is abandoned.

In other words, a traditional position can exist only as long as it delimits itself from distinctions and differentiations that make a more critical attitude possible. As Lessing turns into a counterpart for everyone, he is at the same time offering everyone tools for developing their position toward a more differentiated and well-argued status. This, however, builds on the supposition that his differentiations are found to be acceptable. And as long as he is placed by his opponents in an "outside" position, there is a high probability for misunderstanding, due to the lack of a clear identification of common concerns.

We see all this clearly illustrated in Lessing's controversy with the Hauptpastor Goeze of Hamburg (8:305ff.). Here the irony or mask wearing seems to set things into motion, with no predefined result or direction. By his critique, Lessing brings out Goeze's reluctance to accept the critical differentiations in his writing. Goeze has not entered into a serious discussion of the content of the Reimarus fragments, but only attacked Lessing as the publisher of the fragments by accusing him of blasphemy (305-6). But by doing so, Goeze remains "outside" the position Lessing attempts to discuss.

If a critical position that applies differentiations like Lessing's is really mediated with a traditional position, it leads to the enlightenment of the latter position. As long as Goeze refrains from entering a discussion of Reimarus's position (as Lessing himself actually does), he withdraws from the possibility of enlightenment. Even though there are historical differences, I think we can still often see the same pattern today in the reluctance of some strands of conservative theology to deal seriously with other positions.

Like Socrates, Kierkegaard, and Nietzsche, Lessing does not import any already-finished products of truth. Through their appropriation of what is given in tradition, all the above authors develop their own responsible notions of truth (or mistakes) in what is given. Hence it is hard to "fix" the shape and extension, as well as the actual content, of the positions they hold. Also, this implies that there is always a tension between

57

their own contributions and what is given.[84] This tension is also expressed in their attempts to express irony over against any clear-cut position. In doing so, they do not commit themselves to any particular point of view.[85]

Pluralism in opinions and critique of tradition(s) thus open up for new ways of establishing a religious subjectivity. There seem to be at least three major components that constitute subjectivity in this respect:

- The subject can detach himself or herself from the traditional view presented, since they no longer take for granted that he or she belongs to a homogeneous group.
- The plurality of views seems to make it possible for a critical discussion of different points of view, without involving any point of view that is ultimately possible to identify as the subject's own. The subject is free to wear a mask, hide his face, and change his position.
- What the truth *is* remains uncertain, and the critical discussion itself does not necessarily help the subject in coming closer to it. Hence to be in, or to know, the truth cannot possibly be as important for the subject as it once was. The struggle for truth serves to compensate for this, and also maintains the relationship to truth in religion.

This way of "keeping the truth at arm's length" serves as the foundation for a basically ironic position. Simultaneously, Lessing can try to "save" others in his *Vindications,* by claiming that they hold positions quite the opposite of what they actually say (see 7:47). Of course, this makes it difficult to develop and expound an outline of the critical position he takes. An ironic position does not offer much in terms of a positive stance.

More important than finding Lessing's irony in the *Vindications* is to see that these writings also serve an important purpose in his work as a whole. The aim of these works is to contribute to a public discussion that is not restricted by any power. Such discussion takes place in order to clarify the limits of faith as well as confidence in reason. Without such

---

84. See Thielicke, *Vernunft und Existenz bei Lessing,* 8. The addition of Nietzsche in this list is by me.

85. For their theory of religion, this also means that "the continuation of the process of enlightenment, in which reason still has not reached its identity, also keeps open the question of the truth of religion" (von Lüpke, *Wege der Weisheit,* 64).

discussion, one cannot escape from the prejudices of academic life.[86] The very idea of discussing opinions in the public without addressing them as someone's point of view contributes to such critical discussion. The condition for a modern, critical discussion is also established by the possibility of putting the religious subject holding the view discussed "within parentheses." Hence a discussion of a position need not be experienced as a discussion of what constitutes a person's identity. If I am right in this, however, the question of the relationship between religion and identity is underestimated in Lessing's work (see also what was said on this above). I think we can see this clearly in *Nathan der Weise*.

Relativizing the Impact of Religion — Transforming the Subject: *Nathan* as a Final Gateway to Lessing's Understanding of Religion

In Lessing's most famous play, *Nathan the Wise,* we are confronted directly with how religion functions in framing the self-understanding of the characters. In other words, we see here a discussion of some elements in the problem I have indicated above, concerning religion's impact on personal identity, and how this should be understood in modern terms. The discussion is also well carried out in a way that criticizes a traditional, exclusivist understanding of religious truth. At the same time Lessing offers a different understanding of religion that transforms not only the understanding of the content of religion, but possibly also the self-understanding of the religious characters themselves.

The theme of the play is given in two ways: by the main plot, and by the parable of the ring. This parable, which is told by the main character, Nathan, holds a central place in the narrative, and also serves as a key to understanding the message it contains. In order to get hold of the details of what Lessing suggests for the understanding of religion in the play, it is advisable to look at the parable first.[87]

The ring symbolizes true religion, and the privileges related to that. But the ring is no longer recognizable, for the original owner, the father, has made two perfect copies of it, because he loves all three of his sons.

---

86. See Harth, *Lessing,* 176.
87. For various possible interpretations of this parable, see Boethe, *Glauben,* 98ff.

The father is obviously the one to be identified as God, while the sons are humankind. The three sons represent the three major religions: Judaism, Islam, and Christianity.

The father, according to his love for all his sons, makes it impossible to recognize the true ring (the true religion). Through this, everyone is put on the same level, with no way to find the truth, or with the same lack of possibilities to find the truth.

Lessing does not want to play down the importance of religion in general by setting the stage like this. But the parable itself hints at different ways in which religion may function. Having a ring may make one either absolutize or relativize one's position. In the former case, if one thinks he is the only one privileged with the true ring, to possess it may lead to hatred, struggle, exclusion of others, and separation. In the latter case, if one realizes that there is no way to identify the true ring and that we are all in the same position, ideally, this would lead to charity, recognition of the other, and the establishment of a humane community. There are hints at the end of the parable that a possessor can only prove himself worthy of holding the ring if it leads to the second way of behavior.

As we can see, this way of setting the scene takes plurality in religion seriously. There is no attempt here to reduce the different religions to one common core, but to see them as different expressions due to different cultural and historical settings.[88] But the parable seems to indicate that there are clear criteria for determining what can count as the authentic function of religion. A practice that mirrors the love of the father and establishes human community is the indication of religious truth.[89]

Through this, the notion of religion is transformed, and consequently the self-understanding of the possessors of the ring changes. Religious opinions and positions function as truth in the shape of morality, not as a separate dogmatic truth or worldview. Despite their differences, however, there is clearly a connection between religion and morality. This connection is given in the self-understanding of the subject. Religious self-understanding frames the way in which a subject behaves morally toward a neighbor.

88. This does not mean that Lessing has given up his idea of a natural religion, but only that he is not using it as the basic setting of the play. As we shall see below, there still seems to be enough place for it in the disguise of morality as the true content of religion.

89. See what I said earlier about practice as a criterion for religious truth in Lessing.

When we consider more explicitly the truth of religion, the discourse in the play is founded on the trivial but not unimportant presupposition that there is more than one religion. It also presupposes the possibility of talking about true religion. Hence, implicitly, others may be false. This approach is conditioned by several factors. First, an evaluation need not conclude that one religion is true and another false; for example, Christianity is false, Islam true. It could just as well lead to the conclusion that there are true and false forms of Christianity and Islam alike. Second, the evaluation also presupposes that the different religions can be dealt with on the same basis when it comes to this question. Indeed, such discussion in itself already breaks with the traditional self-understanding of any of the three religions in question.

In the play, the emperor of Jerusalem, Saladin, seems to presuppose that one has to evaluate the truth of religion from the basis of reason when he questions Nathan about what he has to say on the truth of religion. He thus indicates that it is reasons and arguments that make it possible for the wise man to choose his religion. He thinks that the contingent circumstances of birth, race, or location should not determine the wise man in his choice of religion. The wise man should alone determine, on the basis of the insights he has gained by reason, and consequently choose the better of the religions as his own. According to this view, it is reason that makes it possible for us to choose which religion we will adhere to (see 2:374).

Nathan does not accept this approach as being immediately valid. His answer seems to indicate that history, family, localization, and community bonds cannot be ignored by those who have a religion. Religion cannot be chosen. If this is the case, however, the discussion must take a different turn. One has to accept contingent circumstances as unavoidable: not to be overcome but rather to be respected and given an adequate form. This approach implies that we can presuppose, and therefore try to find, the truth in any religion. Lessing here seems to speak through Nathan (2:278). The bottom line is then that one should not leave one's own tradition but rather make sure that it functions in a proper way. In other words, tradition is to be appropriated and reworked, reconstructed, in a way that recognizes the plurality of religions.

The argument given to support this position is interesting. When parents tell a child what to believe, no child doubts his or her own parents. It is inappropriate to accuse one's parents of lying. Lessing seems to

61

indicate that we should all respect our own tradition, and regard the love that our parents have for us as the most important argument for the presumption that they are telling us the truth. People who love others would not lie to them — even to suggest such a thing is insulting (2:278).

Again, several presuppositions are behind this view, and most of them are already well known. Truth is not given as something objective, something that is the possession of one specific religion (2:275). By claiming this, Lessing, through Nathan, anticipates the position taken by Kierkegaard decades later, that the important thing in a religion is not its objective truth but how one relates to this truth. As we have seen, however, for Lessing truth then seems to be almost exclusively related to the practical sphere. It is a question of practicing love and tolerance. If religion contains doctrinal truth, it is to be found in, and ascertained by, its practical and moral consequences.

Hence Lessing's options concerning religious pluralism turn out to be the following:

- No religion "has" or possesses the truth, but
- All religions are expressions of the truth, in that
- All religions can function truly when they sustain love and brotherhood for the other, also for the neighbor with a different belief.
- All three religions are equal in terms of the basic insecurity of their historical and theoretical foundations. Hence they appear as equally probable options.[90]

Thus we can talk of a functional, not a substantial, notion of truth in religion, as it is understood by Lessing. The important element of truth is how religion functions and contributes to human coexistence and our struggle for insight, that is, our humanity, not its substantial content in terms of rites, myths, and doctrine.

In the play, Nathan himself thinks it impossible to detect or disclose the true faith. He leaves that to the Father (God) in a very distant future — the truth is for him alone (cf. Kierkegaard's famous quote from him).[91] In the parable of the ring, the only thing that seems to be a proof of true religion is whether it is possible to transform the people's attitude

90. See Boethe, *Glauben,* 100.
91. See above, 27.

from self-centered love into acts and deeds that support the maturation of humankind in general (2:279-80). By describing Nathan thus, leaving him no traits of a positive religion, with its habits or rites, Lessing makes him transcend what can be identified as Jewish religion and approach a kind of natural religion of humanity.[92]

Thus the realization of the power of the genuine ring or the true religion becomes not a gift but a task, not a fact but a result to be achieved. This corresponds to the teleological view in *EdM*. Moreover, since this task is universal, it is equally binding on the adherents of all faiths, and it provides a unifying standpoint from which the relatively inessential differences of the various religions can be overcome.[93]

One has to ask: Is this way of handling the problem a withdrawal from the whole question? Is Lessing a skeptic hiding behind a mask? Considering what he does, it is not basically religion, but what people make of it, that is in his focus. This is, I suggest, a typically modern way of approaching religion. It is not the question of a religion's doctrinal truth that is the most important, but how it functions in social life and contributes to the structure of society. In other words, the question of its substantial truth is put inside parentheses. This corresponds with a shift toward the subject, its authenticity, and its approaches to the world in terms of how it acts according to rational standards (a shift from objective to subjective truth). Also, this means that the criteria for authenticating a religious position lie in the practice of the religious subject, not in its rationally examinable substantial content or the rational elucidation of this doctrinal content (see above).

The theme of the parable of the ring is more broadly spelled out in the play itself, where all the main characters, despite their different religions, in the end turn out to belong to the same family. Hence the message seems to be that we all belong to the human race. The realization of this insight is the means by which the separation and the division among humans can be overcome. But this also opens up another important issue in the play.

The recognition of "brotherhood" is closely connected to the main

---

92. See Boethe, *Glauben*, 88ff. "Nathan outlives his natural religion of humanity, and is also at the same time self-conscious about being a Jew; because he is the ideal human, he is simultaneously a Jew, the ideal Jew" (93).

93. See Allison, *Lessing*, 144.

theme in *Nathan.* This recognition actually serves as a way of neutralizing the obstacles to human community set up by religion. The Muslim ruler of Jerusalem, Saladin, shows mercy toward the Christian Templar because he resembles his own brother. Thus the recognition of likeness overcomes the religious differences and establishes a new bond of community between them (2:215, et passim). To be able to see a brother or sister in someone who belongs to another faith gives morality a more prominent place than religion in the shaping of the self-understanding of the individual. Hence it also contributes positively to the construction of human bonds, and thus relativizes the differences that religion establishes between persons.

A similar point is expressed when Nathan distinguishes between his friend the Dervish and the officer who comes to borrow money from him on behalf of Saladin. To differentiate the person from his office or his religion is one of the attitudes Nathan exposes when he confronts others. I think this approach is parallel to the one we identified earlier, when we saw how Lessing opts for distinguishing between a person and the opinions he holds or represents.

The relation between a supranatural and a natural interpretation of events and experiences is another important element in the play that has to do with how the understanding of religion contributes to a new shaping of religious subjectivity. Nathan is full of scorn toward any interpretation of the rescue of his daughter as something performed by an angel. What makes things wonderful is not the one who performs the deeds, but what actually happens. To say that an angel caused or performed a deed does not make it more wonderful than if a human had performed the deed. Thus, Lessing says, a supranatural interpretation of self and reality is no better, and does not contribute more to the actual understanding of things, than a mere empirical attitude. Here we can also see a kind of affirmation of the wonderful in the ordinary, and an attempt to make an interpretation of daily life as being religious without recourse to supranatural interpretations (2:214).

This approach has implications in another direction as well. By relating the wonderful deeds of others to the supranatural, one can back up one's own pious feelings. But if this is the sole aim of such interpretations, their moral impact is reduced. Nathan understands such attitudes as a kind of self-centered hubris and as an amoral attitude simultaneously. The main point here is that only human beings are given a richer and better life through our attention toward them — neither God nor the angels are moved toward something better by our piety (2:216-17). Our piety should therefore be directed toward other humans. It has a practical function. Hence Lessing reorients traditional piety toward the framework of morality.

By spelling the opposites out in this way, we see in the play the bipolarity between a traditional religion, represented by the Christian woman Daja, and a religion of human morality striving for community and unity, represented by Nathan. This opposition can also be spelled out along the lines of a traditional piety versus a piety directed toward what can benefit other human beings. For Lessing (expressing himself in Nathan), the traditional piety closes off from seeing and recognizing the fellow human being and his or her needs. Hence a supernatural interpretation also tends to have the same outcome. Being attentive or directed toward the other world (i.e., God) closes us off from seeing the needs of this one. The play even indicates that such attitudes could be regarded as blasphemy. "God rewards deeds done here, while we're still here. . . . Do you then understand how much easier it is to be a pious romantic than it is *to do the good?* How willingly the lazy human piously romanticizes in order — and this, he often is not conscious of — to avoid the duty of action" (2:218). Piety thus becomes an excuse for not taking the moral task seriously. Another way of expressing this critique is to say that Lessing, through Nathan, criticizes a morality that is enrolled in the service of religious interests. Such interests are always partial, and can easily be entertained by someone for his or her own sake. Hence in Nathan we find a person who insists on evaluating and estimating religion on moral terms. If religion supports demands that seem immoral when viewed from the standpoint of common humanity, it should be rejected (2:230-31). However, this attitude presupposes the ability to distinguish between morality and religion, or between the person and her faith or office (see above). In this way Lessing tones down the importance of religion for the way human relationships are constructed.

One can ask critically if Lessing's attitude in *Nathan* leads to the dissolution of positive religion. Distinctions are relativized and toned down so much that religion in the end does not have any valid specific content beyond that which is expressed in universal morality. Thus he seems to neglect the fact that religion and our offices (or better: social roles) also inform and contribute to our self-understanding in a way that cannot be so easily dissolved. His valid contribution, however, seems to lie in his insights into the necessity of distinctions when we describe the functions and the content of religion and religious life. He also points to the need for some kind of common morality if we are to be able to lead a common life in a society consisting of different cultural and religious communities.

Consequently, Lessing is critical toward those who understand themselves as Christians before they understand themselves as human beings. In addition, to be a true human being is to be a rational human being. When "acquired" religion becomes more important than the status given by birth ("descent"), rationality and morality are neglected and superstition takes their place. Hence by giving religion priority, and not seeing religion as something that is framed by and should be brought into accord with humanity, one misunderstands oneself as a human being. It is important to be a Christian because one is a human being. Furthermore, we are not human and moral persons because of Christ's teachings. Rather, this was part of his teachings because it is in this way that humanity realizes itself. Similarly, it is not important to love because Christ said so, but Christ told us to love because to love is one of the conditions for a good human life (see 2:238). Thus Lessing actually evaluates "descent" as a more important and legitimate background for adhering to a religion than a Protestant orthodoxy that seems able to deal with the problems using only categories of assent.[94]

Hence authority is given to that which can count as being truly human, as this is perceived by human rationality and in common experience. Authority is not a status that belongs to a person as such. This reflects the transformation in modernity from personal to material authority. What counts is not *who* says something, but *what* is said. In this way, the individual's own reason is the presupposition for and the counterpart of the message of religion. If religion fits with this reason, including morality, it is acceptable. If not, the message should have no impact, no matter who proclaims it.

As for opinion, Lessing suggests through Nathan that there is no specific demand of anyone as to what they ought to think. The good person knows *how* he or she must think, and this demand stands over and above every religiously motivated demand for *what* to think. To be a good

---

94. For an interesting discussion of religion in terms of assent and dissent, see P. Morris: "Communities Beyond Tradition," esp. 238ff.

human being is to live according to this demand — and in this there are no religiously motivated differences (2:252): "For what does being a people mean? Are Christians and Jews rather Christians and Jews than humans? Oh, if I just had found one more among you, who would be satisfied with calling himself a human" (253). God is not the possession of a special group. God is also not something to fight for — his truth can take care of itself. Rather, all humans are created by and live by the gifts of God (see 263). In stating this, the play stresses the importance of an ethic based on the common descent of humankind, rather than contingent elements such as a particular faith, linked to where one grows up.[95]

Thus Lessing repeatedly underscores the dissonance between religious particularity and moral universality. He underscores how religion based on particular interests easily ends up as inhumane, for example, in the execution of heretics, and the indifference shown toward people of other faiths (2:298-99). This contrast serves as a basis for Lessing's critique of religion: religion is wicked and narrow-minded as long as it does not let itself be enlightened by the reason that founds morality. Both reason and morality offer the criteria for what a sound traditional religion is like.[96] He can also recognize, however, the positive elements in a given individual religion.[97] The individual religion is not to be sublated (*aufgehoben*) into some kind of abstract, natural religion.[98]

95. Against the prejudices that rise out of the belonging to a specific nation and religion in *Nathan*, see von Lüpke, *Wege der Weisheit*, 148-49.

96. "When Lessing was confronted with the phenomenon of Christianity and its historically founded faith, his appropriation of it could only lead to a 'reinterpretation of the Christian content into the natural worldview of the moral reason'" (Wessel, *Lessing's Theology*, 20). For the emphasis in Lessing on the practical scope of religion, see also von Lüpke, *Wege der Weisheit*, 41-42.

97. However, this must not be taken to imply that Lessing on such a basis would recognize one religion as being profoundly better than another in every respect. Again, the decisive question is of practice. Hence one can say with Cassirer (*Die Philosophie der Aufklärung*, 256-57) that Lessing wants to rescue religion through an understanding and reconstruction of its history, but this true, absolute religion is the one that can contain all the historical appearances of religion in itself. In this process, Cassirer thinks that the individual religion does not become lost, but is seen as a contribution to the understanding of the truth.

98. The ethical foundation of the claim of the absoluteness coming from revelation does not lead to questioning any particular form of religion. Moreover, the moral task of the believer is fullfilled under the concrete conditions of his religion. By making himself perfect, the meaning of the actual religion is fulfilled. See Schultze, *Lessings*

Of course, this position is possible only on the basis of Lessing's double notion of religion. On the one hand, he talks of natural religion, uncontaminated by particular customs and contingent interests. (In *Nathan*, this type of religion is most clearly contrasted in the characters of Daja and the Patriarch.) Expressions of this religion accord with reason and are not subjected to the same kind of critique as the positive religion(s) that makes an absolute out of specific customs, such as eating habits. (Cf. the words of Saladin, the Muslim: "Nathan shall experience that he will be allowed to raise a Christian child without the taste of pork!" 2:308.)

At the same time, what is common and in accord with reason is in *Nathan* expressed as that which constitutes the core of the religions. That which makes one person a Christian and another a Jew is the same thing, even though they both perceive this common core to be something particular and special to them: namely, the act of love for the neighbor (see 2:317). What makes the difference between religions, and causes tensions and conflict, is the particular. Conflicts arise when this particular is addressed as the constituent element in religion (317).

Interestingly, or perhaps ironically, in the last scene neither the traditional and confessional Daja nor the extremely tolerant Nathan is present. At the risk of overinterpreting this, I take their absence as something that can be understood along the following lines. From their different positions they have made the participants see that they belong together, and that their differences are less than what they have in common. In this reestablished community of different religions, however, neither a traditional exclusivist position nor a humanistic-agnostic position has a place. They are "outside" the unity between different religions. One could also see in this that Nathan's way of approaching the other has now become internalized in all of the other characters, so that his mediating presence is no longer needed.

Lessing thus says that the relativizing attitude toward religious particularity is the basis for entering a dialogue with others. This attitude makes one realize that there is a common morality that is more funda-

---

Toleranzbegriff, 75. Schultze points out how this is related to the fact that even if natural religion is the philosophical definition of the essence of religion in Lessing, it still must be realized in the concrete, individual, and historical shape of a specific religion (ibid., 76).

mental than the particulars based on contingent religious customs. As long as the core of religion is seen as morality, dialogue can realize the underlying morality as that by which we evaluate the other. But this dialogue can only function on the supposition of a clear conceptual distinction between positive religion and morality.

Concluding Remarks

In many ways Lessing can be seen as a representative of the Enlightenment approach to religion. Religion is still desirable, but only on certain conditions. This conditional approach to religion has at least two implications. First, religion is not immediately acceptable on its own terms, but has to be scrutinized by the critical subject and evaluated according to the subject's own experience. Second, this means that religion is perceived as a problem, as something that is not easily integrated into the common stock of goods and values in modernity. Thus religion does not automatically serve the cause of reconciliation among people or their search for the common good. Instead, it is understood as a potential troublemaker.

The only way to overcome this seems to be to reconstruct a normative concept of religion that puts most weight on its moral content, with a corresponding downplaying of its substantial doctrinal content. This approach lends more weight to the functional side of religion in society, although, as we have hinted at, it still tends to ignore the formative impact of religion on personal and communal identity. To point this out is also to say that the reconstruction of religion on Lessing's basis has specific consequences for the constitution of religious subjectivity. Subjectivity now consists of the development of moral (and thus functional) elements, and in the search for what is common for humankind. The identity of this subject is then mainly shaped by the realization of what is common, not by what is the distinct and what is idiosyncratic in different religious traditions. Hence the task of critically appropriating what is given in tradition is in Lessing mainly a task of using what this tradition expresses in terms of the common values of humanity, more than that which distinctively belongs to a specific tradition.

It is tempting to add here that this mode of understanding religion is echoed in Nietzsche's conflation of religion and morality as two sides of the same coin. Nietzsche and Kierkegaard receive the reconstruction of religion that Lessing expresses in quite contrary ways. In Kierkegaard the emphasis is not, as in Lessing and Nietzsche, on the common morality, but on the individual and the more idiosyncratic shape religion receives in the subject. What all three have in common, however, is the relatively low importance they give to the appropriation of the historical content of Christianity. When Lessing deals with this (see above), it is in terms of emphasis on development and an inherent, maturing rationality.

In Lessing the reconstruction of religion functions normatively as well, in the sense that it serves as a critical tool against exclusivist and intolerant forms of religion, which cling to substantial dogmatic content as being determinative (and constitutive of difference) for their actual appearance and shape.

An important — and to me still valid — point in Lessing is his insistence on the historical dimension of religion and its expressions. This insistence leads to two important insights: (a) the anti-absolutist position following from the recognition of the contextual shaping of every religious position, and (b) the criticism of a mere outward relation to history (a criticism that Lessing shares with Kierkegaard and Nietzsche). Such an understanding enables many of the conceptual distinctions he draws, and makes it possible to see religion in terms of the further development of self and humanity. By underscoring this dimension, Lessing not only opens up a critical evaluation of the static and repressive forms of religion as they function in the sphere of human conduct and development. He also creates a basis for sustaining the further development of religion in the historical forms that are most adequate for the contemporary world.

Considering the many conceptual distinctions presented and analyzed in the material above, we can generally say that the use of such distinctions opens up possibilities for development of self and humanity. In Lessing's reconstruction of religion there is a close connection between true religion and personal (moral and human) development. This functional framework is that which provides the legitimacy of religion in the present. In Lessing's eyes, religion then serves the purpose of the advancement of humankind. It is as a tool for the development of the religious subject that religion still has meaning and value, and it is on these terms that it has to legitimize itself in a modern setting. Thus Lessing underscores on his own terms both the constructive and the developing element in human subjectivity. It is not given what we are to become — this depends on how we use reason and develop our moral skills. In Lessing, however, a normative concept of the human operates. This concept is a standard, common to all humanity, that can function as normative when we are to evaluate the outcome of human development. This standard is the anthropological basis for his reconstruction of religion. It combines both a teleological and a plural element. Any kind of heretical imperative that is fulfilled is to be evaluated according to this standard.

One problem remains in Lessing, however, that is paradigmatic for any form of critical subjectivity that relates positively to religion after the Enlightenment. This is what I, with Thielicke, call the problem of double consciousness. It can be defined like this. If I do not acquire and appropriate for myself a coherent and valid understanding of a tradition that I hold to be valid, and integrate it into my own critical mind, then I divide my consciousness into two separate parts and let go of its unity.[99] This is a problem for any enlightened mind that wants to affirm the truth of his times, while at the same time being rooted in a tradition from which he has no desire to depart. As Thielicke points out, this is a problem with which Lessing, and later Schleiermacher, works, but for which Lessing has no solution.

The actuality and contemporary relevance of this problem is seen when we examine some typical religious constructions that cannot solve the problem. For example, a fundamentalist approach, which claims the truth of the Bible over against science, separates faith from the suppositions of a (post)modern world, whereas a postmodern relativist position gives up any claim to truth at all. The challenge is how to adequately combine the expression of historically rooted religious truth and openness to its revision with a responsible attitude toward the results of reason and the scientific world. In doing this, it is hard to say a priori that any notion or position should have any more privilege or determining power than any other.

I should also add, however, that the process of enlightenment, to which Lessing contributes, is based on the recognition of the dignity and freedom of the individual. This recognition implies that subjects who are themselves willing to be recognized in this way are obliged to offer such recognition to others and to the life forms and institutions that will secure this freedom for them in the future.

In conclusion, we can say that Lessing poses some important issues for the type of Christianity that seeks to confront the Enlightenment and

---

99. Thielicke, *Vernunft und Existenz bei Lessing*, 42.

take its content seriously. This position is followed up in two diametrically different ways by Kierkegaard and Nietzsche. Here I will give some provisional indications of these two ways. They will be discussed in more detail in the following chapters.

- In Kierkegaard we find an emphasis on the subjective basis of religion, where the subject constructs his or her world of faith almost independently of history. However, he appears to side with Lessing in his emphasis that appropriation of a religious position seems to lie in the development of the subject's potential, and by means of that, the actualization of the past in the present. This leads to a corresponding emphasis on this selfsame religious subjectivity. Paradoxically, this does not exclude that Kierkegaard's reconstruction of religion involves the affirmation of a relatively orthodox position in terms of the content of Christian religion. Whereas Lessing emphasizes plurality and the common behind any given religion, Kierkegaard ignores the whole problem of plurality, because everyone has a religion that is basically his or her own personal one.
- Existence in the truth is thus possible also in other religions than Christianity. This corresponds with Kierkegaard's relatively slight emphasis on the role natural religion plays in this construction, and consequently also with his emphasis on the individual. He takes the historical relativity of religion to be an argument for its absoluteness, subjectively speaking. This points to a problem that is still relevant and necessary to discuss in a more comprehensive way. Is it defensible to reconstruct Christianity in a way that ignores or underestimates the historical dimension in that religion, and tends to ignore its specific historical character? Can a Christian religious subjectivity do without some reference to, or constitutive elements coming from, the specific history of Jesus Christ? Furthermore, I find that Kierkegaard is relatively ignorant of the moral element and its bearing on the formation of religious subjectivity.[100]

100. This is a statement that needs further qualification in the light of Arne Grøn's work on "Kierkegaards 'zweite' Ethik" (Kierkegaard's "second" ethics), where he points to how in Kierkegaard's devotional writings there are elements that I claim are ignored. I do not develop this here, however, as it demands a more extensive investigation into Kierkegaard's work than can be offered in the present context.

- Nietzsche turns in the opposite direction. Here we find a total dissolution of a substantial subject and a critical stance toward any kind of religious content that contributes to the shaping of such a subject. In addition, religion is distilled down to morality, and morality is subject to destruction. Here differentiation and critique have become self-consuming. This means that the critical reconstruction of religion in Nietzsche is part of a more comprehensive project of criticism of both traditional and Enlightenment forms of thinking and belief. This position is important, since it throws light on the detached, aesthetic, experimental, and constructivist attitudes toward religion that we find in postmodern culture, and offers radically alternative ways of seeing the relationship of religion, ethics, and subjectivity.

These preliminary observations are substantiated in the following chapters.

• *Chapter Three* •

KIERKEGAARD

<hr>

*Irony and the Struggle
for Authentic Appropriation of Religion:
Anticipations of Postmodern Attitudes,
Insights, and Problems*

According to the Danish philosopher Johannes Sløk, Kierkegaard's work is held together as a coherent whole by his examination, from every conceivable angle, of the problem of how the human being is to live a genuine or authentic existence.[1] My task here is to disclose some of the philosophical elements that determine how Kierkegaard understands religion from these different angles, and to provide a framework for the understanding of how religion contributes to fulfilling this task. One central thesis is that we can understand his position in an adequate way only if we are able to grasp some of the basic features presented already in his 1841 dissertation on irony. That work offers a fruitful approach to the identification of issues in Kierkegaard, which can be seen as anticipations of later, and more recent (indeed postmodern), attitudes toward religion.[2]

1. Sløk, *Die Anthropologie Kierkegaards*, 13.
2. Any treatise on Kierkegaard has to make clear how it relates to his use of pseudonyms. In the following, I view the pseudonymous writings as Kierkegaard's attempts to elaborate different opinions and modes of existence. I then take it that they need not (and cannot) be merged into one coherent position. By this mode of writing Kierkegaard

Kierkegaard's Dissertation on Irony
Read as a Prolegomenon to Postmodernism

*"Irony is a qualification of existence, and thus nothing is more
ludicrous than regarding it as a mode of speech" (10:181).*

The ability to distance oneself from a certain position, and not be totally
attached to it, is crucial for understanding how modernity configures
new forms of religious subjectivity. As we have seen in the introduction,
the heretical imperative, as Berger puts it, is backed by the awareness of
the possibility of choice — of taking a different stand. To keep this possibility open is part of what can be called an ironical position. Of the three
authors that we are discussing, Kierkegaard has dealt most extensively
with what irony means for the human subject, as well as emphasizing
how important choice is in the constitution of the subject's existence.

One of the reasons why it can be fruitful to start with Kierkegaard's
academic treatise on irony is that we indisputably confront Kierkegaard
himself in that work. It is not written by any of his pseudonymous characters. In the work he presents two main ways of understanding irony.
The one that he presents most extensively is Socratic irony, which is obviously the one he has most sympathy for. The other is the type of irony
found in romanticism. Kierkegaard seems to regard this second type as
being very similar to that of Socrates' opponents, the Sophists.

Irony is a motif that can be understood as the Kierkegaardian parallel to the negative in Hegel. Irony delineates that which cannot be positively stated, that which appears through the limitations given by a specific position. Hence irony is connected to the recognition of the
provisional in any position. Kierkegaard, however, takes great pains in
trying to show how his understanding of irony is not a moment in a systematic development of a positive position. Irony is a dialectical way of
approaching thoughts and positions in a questionlike form, without the
aim of achieving a positive result (see 1:109). On the contrary, irony consists in the idea of establishing a limitation to all that is, and showing
how it cannot be seen as absolute. Hence irony and the finite element in
knowledge seem to be two sides of the same coin. This finitude corre-

---

simply exhibits what we can see as anticipations of a more experimental way of exploring existence, without any need for appearing as a coherent subject.

76

sponds to the limitations of the finite subject explored by Lessing, when he says that the final truth cannot be reached by a person living in historical circumstances where things may develop further.[3]

Thus irony contains the idea of a limit, a boundary to a position (1:201). The ironical element keeps the problems "floating," so that they never are able to settle finally on firm ground (see 1:162). By already pointing out this basic feature of irony as a possible approach to intellectual issues, Kierkegaard makes clear how an ironic position could indicate problems with a religious attitude and for establishing a religious subjectivity: as he himself constantly illustrates in his writings, a truly religious position consists in affirming an absolute relation to the absolute. But this is not, and indeed cannot be, gained by the ironical approach, since irony, as I have just said, seems to leave no room for absoluteness. Hence irony threatens to dissolve a committed position. In other words, one could say that there is a basic tension between a religious and an ironical approach to self and world in Kierkegaard.[4] As we shall see below, however, at least one type of irony also serves to open the field for piety.

Socratic Irony

In his description of Socrates and his ironical position and conduct, it is not hard to recognize some of Kierkegaard's own attitudes. He points out the limitations of every point of view, and insists that a person should not be ensnared in some fixed position. This feature points to the variety of pseudonyms and positions that Kierkegaard describes in the following writings. His attempts to describe and reflect on the same issues repeatedly from different angles are, apart from marking the ironical in his own position, also possible to view as anticipations of the postmodern critique of all absolute or "closed" positions.

An ironic stance secures the freedom of the subject as it approaches the other. According to Kierkegaard, however, there is a difference between Socrates and his contemporary "others" in the result of this irony.

3. See above, p. 43.
4. As he says (1:206-7), this position hides in itself a polemic, and turns into a horror for anyone who has found his rest in some finite relation to the deity.

In his dialogues, Socrates liberates the other from any positive presuppositions, and establishes in the other the freedom that he himself enjoys. This freedom consists in the possibility for reflecting once more on the given point of view under discussion. For the other, however, this is a most unsatisfactory freedom, because it is based on negativity, a negativity that is not dissolved by Socrates. Hence this freedom leads to eternal unease instead of comfort, an uneasiness that keeps the subject and her position(s) "floating."[5]

Irony has another effect too. It sets subjectivity in an idiosyncratic form, over against "the other." Socrates then typically becomes distinguishable from anyone else by the fact that he cannot be fixed to a positive position. Kierkegaard here tacitly assumes that Socrates is alone in this project. If there were many who held the same attitude, however, one could ask if this is really a way of establishing a concrete and idiosyncratic subjectivity.

Ironical positions have large potential for criticism. Kierkegaard interprets the accusations against Socrates from that perspective. These accusations can be partly seen as being based on his criticism against the concrete *Sittlichkeit* (morality) of his times (see 1:196-97), in that he challenges it to develop into a more conscious morality. If this is so, the accusation against Socrates can be read as a consequence of his challenge. Socrates led youth astray by weakening children's respect for their parents, that is, he contributed to the dissolution of illegitimate and rationally unfounded authority and tradition. This reading of Socrates makes him fit very well into the "modern" critique of tradition; but paired with the ironical position, it also anticipates more postmodern features. By insisting on the principle of subjectivity, Socrates sets the individual over against these figures, thereby serving the freedom of the individual over against them (see 1:214). According to Kierkegaard, Socrates questions the validity of institutions such as the family, and contributes through this to make the individual stand forth as an individual (215):

> Let us turn back for a moment to the circumstances that gave us the occasion for this investigation: the accusation against Socrates. We can now easily perceive what his crime consists in (from the viewpoint

---

5. 1:206. For Socrates' enjoyment of this position in contrast to his partners, see also 1:212.

of the state). He neutralized the validity of family life, and slackened the law of nature according to which the individual member of the family rests in the whole family — namely, pious respect (1:216).

Several elements warrant comment here. First, the quotation points to what I have already said about the questioning of the validity of the given *Sittlichkeit*. Furthermore, it also states that this questioning has the effect of neutralizing the assumed validity of an authority, so that it can no longer be taken for granted. In addition, it shows how irony is able to depict and criticize the validity of what we see as being naturally given, and tell us that this could be otherwise. The validity and the constitution of the relationship between the individual and the group, state, or family need not be the way it is. Also, the way authority is placed can be overcome or altered.

So far Socrates (and Kierkegaard). A more postmodern reading of this same cluster of phenomena will imply that here, by means of irony, we limit the absoluteness of culturally given forms, and give vague suggestions that (but not *how*) they could be different. This anticipation of postmodern critique is given by the fact that we do not take the naturally given as a valid entity in itself, but realize how the natural is also to be understood as given only in and through our cultural framework. This insight leads to the possibility of departing from any cultural form we have assumed to be natural and replacing it with some other. Nature has lost its naturalness, its innocence. Hence its assumed legitimation of the present *Sittlichkeit* and its validity, once taken for granted, is lost.

Let us then return to Kierkegaard. In his study of Socrates, he shows how irony establishes a hiatus between the personal moral conditions and those of public ethics, as this ethics is "stewarded" by the state. This hiatus makes it impossible to reconcile and unify the two, as irony has as one of its features that it cannot lead to an identification with that which is positively given (see 1:223). In pointing out the lack of possibilities for establishing a common ethic to which an ironical subject could also subscribe, I think Kierkegaard captures a genuinely postmodern experience, namely, the experience of a lack of cohesion between the private and the public spheres and between the cultural and the political spheres.[6] This experience is a consequence of the differentiation and

6. This is today perhaps most clearly stressed in the work of R. Rorty. See, e.g., *Contingency, Irony, and Solidarity*.

fragmentation that followed the rationalization of modernity. We have already seen that Lessing gives a good illustration of this.

Irony also establishes a boundary between absolute power and law, as is given by authority and institution, and the negation of this in the individual attitude. Kierkegaard seems here to develop further the critique Lessing directed against traditional authority, although he does not himself apply this position to religion. He simply takes the critique a step further, by holding forth and making explicit how irony holds every positive position in the grip of insecurity, and thus contributes to the undermining of any authority. Hence it provides for the establishment of a more individual basis for commitment than that which can be given through an external authority.

It is important to point out the new role that the subject obtains through this movement. This role makes it possible for Kierkegaard to formulate what he sees as the possibility of a religious position. As irony detaches from a positive position, sets the negative, and dissolves the given, this implies that a religious subjectivity can hardly function in an ironical framework or on the basis of such an attitude alone. The question is therefore obvious: does religion have a basis at all, when it can be established only on terms and in frameworks that we constantly confront ironically? (Note that this is the typical situation in a postmodern, highly differentiated culture.)

The answer that Kierkegaard finds for this question is what I, lacking any better expressions, would call the dialectic between irony and passion. Briefly and metaphorically stated, this means that Kierkegaard takes everything that frames religion in the cultural, political, public, and social sphere and puts it into the basket of irony (i.e., leaves it open to irony), while he takes the religion of the individual alone, which has no authority or culture as its sponsor, and puts it in the basket of passion[7] (i.e., he links it to individual, subjective passion). Hence he provides for an unrestricted and nonironical religious commitment.[8]

If this reconstruction of Kierkegaard proves to be correct, then some interesting parallels to Lessing appear. Recall how Lessing criticized the cultural form of religion, calling it a contingent element that

7. This will be elaborated in the following sections.
8. There is, however, one exception to this: Socrates, who combines irony and passion. See 1:237: "Irony is in Socrates truly a world-historical passion."

could also partly confuse or distort its truth. On the other hand, the pure and natural religion of humanity could be found beyond these contingent features. Is this not the same pattern that Kierkegaard develops here, on a different, more existential level? Where Lessing opened to criticism, Kierkegaard opens to irony. Where Lessing opens to an eternal truth in religion, accessible by a reason not confused by contingent historical elements, Kierkegaard describes this truth as accessible by the passion of faith[9] (see further on this below).

The evil principle that governed the decline of the Greek polis is the limited subjectivity that we find in the Sophists. Although they joined Socrates in questioning the given *Sittlichkeit,* they fulfilled an illegitimate task, as they expressed a contingent relation to the task of thinking itself. There is no consequence, no integrity, in their work, and hence no commitment for the good. Their point of departure, in fragments of knowledge, differs from that of Socrates as well (see 1:228-29). Socrates' irony consists in that he has no useful knowledge whatsoever. This also gives him a different position. He cannot say with the Sophists that "everything is true," as he does not know this to be so. However, that also provides him with a different basis for his work. He is not an uncommitted and indifferent, detached subject, but he is passionately searching — by irony — for the truth. According to Kierkegaard, Socrates has a passion for the case, for the issue in question, which makes him very different from the Sophists. He then also has a view for the wholeness of the task; he does not carry it out for fun. In addition, he does not offer consolation for the uneasiness of the individual by linking it to the contingent moment of lust and desire. Hence Socrates' reflections are not limited by the conditions of the individual and her contingent interests, but relate to a far more extensive enterprise (see 1:231ff.).

The contrast between Socrates and the Sophists also contains another important element. They relate differently to the infinite. Socrates' continuous negativity contains an infiniteness, and this infinity is for him the positive element on which his enterprise is founded. It is a pas-

---

9. This existential truth can also be described, as E. Mooney (*Selves in Discord and Resolve,* 73) does with reference to B. Williams, as constituting the fundamental projects or commitments that give meaning and point to our lives, but "whose importance rests on something other than an argument that such concerns *must* matter."

sion. This infinity is, however, to be understood as a limit, a boundary, not as a revelation of something positive (see 1:234).

The relation to infinity configures the subject in a specific way. Its internal consequence is a destiny *(Bestemmelse)* that is metaphysical, not only aesthetical or moral. Kierkegaard finds this expressed already in the statement that "sin is lack of knowledge."[10] Sin is a metaphysical notion, not primarily moral. To exist in this position is the basic feature of a religious subject as well as being a Socratic position. In other words, we see here a more negative configuration of the subject's teleological determination than Lessing's, since it defines the sinfulness of existence more clearly as the point of departure for this destiny.

The lack of knowledge linked to sin is the lack of ability to define one's own identity objectively.[11] Hence the freedom that the subject has in and through irony is a transmitted or mediated freedom.[12] This transmission or mediation is due to the negation that irony implies over against any positivity. The interesting element here is that Kierkegaard spells this out as something that involves not only a formal but a substantially defined infinity. Irony leads to freedom, but metaphysically and morally speaking this freedom is also sin, since it involves no positive relation to the positive.[13] Here Kierkegaard seems to be caught up in a Hegelian understanding, where negativity or sin becomes a necessary and mediating element for both freedom and the positive affirmation of the substantial absolute.[14] That there is a link to more Hegelian modes of thinking here can also be substantiated by looking at a later sequence in the dissertation, where Kierkegaard affirms that Hegel also defined Socrates as one who constitutes morality, in spite of his irony. This is because morality is

10. That sin is related to the impossibility of stating a positive subject is the other side of this. This is most clearly elaborated in *Sickness unto Death*. See further below.

11. The true self that subjectivity uncovers is a sinful self — not in affinity to God, but separated from him. For this see D. R. Law, *Kierkegaard as Negative Theologian*, 215.

12. 1:236: "It is the infinite, given freedom of subjectivity that we face in Socrates, but this is exactly the irony."

13. If this is a correct interpretation, Kierkegaard overcomes this theological problem first when he distinguishes between two types of religiosity (A and B) in *Concluding Unscientific Postscript*, and elaborates the distinction by making clear that we talk of a subject constituted either by an immanent or by a transcendent teleology. As long as the teleology is immanent, and not linked to the incarnation and what is given by it, the constitution of subjectivity will be marked by sin. See further on this distinction below.

14. See Hegel's *Lectures on the Philosophy of Religion*, 17:254ff., esp. 259.

based on a subject who is negatively free. For such a subject, to achieve the good can be defined as the task of achieving the infinitely negative, the unconditioned that cannot be stated positively. Although this is not the task for the common human, it can still be defined as the specific moral task for Socrates (see 1:254-55). The reason why this is so seems to be that Socrates possesses the freedom constituted by negativity.

Irony and silence are, in Socrates, two sides of the same coin. The silence of Socrates is important in order to ensure that his irony and subjectivity are not taken as vain, or can be taken seriously (1:238). As stated, the ironical mode of speech provides the speaker with his freedom, because the negativity of irony, which consists in the realization that "he does not mean what he says," leads to the following position: If what is said is not my opinion, or the opposite of my opinion, then I am free in relation to others and to myself, since what I have said is not something that can be taken as my positive position (1:264). Irony thus provides the possibility to transcend the factual social reality established in speech, and expresses that there is something in the subject that is in dissonance (or not in accord) with this reality (1:269).[15] Hence we could perhaps say that irony sets the individual free from the social setting, but that it does so by way of a very social phenomenon, namely, speech.

I think this last point expresses something that is of great importance also for how a (post)modern subject relates to religion. As the present and positive forms of religion are not to be accepted as true or fully adequate expressions of the absolute, irony helps to free the religious subject from the assumption that this is the case, as well as to transcend the positive form it takes in a specific religious community. If a person relates ironically to religion, it is almost a truism, but one still worth stating, that this implies that this subject is not fully able to adhere to the positivity of that religious form.[16]

Moreover, the religious dimension can also be opened up by what Kierkegaard calls contemplative irony, that is, the irony that discloses the *vanitas mundi*. In this, irony functions contrary to doubt. On the one hand,

---

15. See 1:275. Here Kierkegaard states how the ironical subject experiences the given reality as something that has lost its validity, at the same time as he does not have anything to put in its place. He knows only that the present does not conform to the idea.

16. "Even for Socrates, the historically given has surely lost its validity. His point of view is irony as infinite, absolute negativity" (Lindstrøm, *Stadiernas Teologi,* 256).

doubt arises when the subject tries to achieve a positive relation to what is given, but where this given escapes her. On the other hand, irony arises when the positive is given, and the subject wants to escape from it, in order to establish her freedom (1:272-73). Insight into the *vanitas mundi* does not lead the subject to take herself in vain, but this insight saves the subject from her own vanity. Contrary to traditional piety, irony here is not an attempt to nullify the subject and empty the world of its positivity in order to make the divine visible. The task of irony is to secure the freedom of the subject (1:273). The effect, however, is that it opens up to a negativity in the subject that alienates her from, or makes her uncomfortable with, reality (1:274, 275). I think it is worth noting that by depicting this distance to the positively given through irony, Kierkegaard still opens up to holding a distance from a positive religious quality.

The basic point in this seems to be that irony is needed in order to secure subjectivity. Subjectivity needs irony in order to experience its own force, validity, and impact. In being ironical, subjectivity saves itself from the relativity that the given reality tries to bind it to. Hence irony is the first and most abstract definition of subjectivity (1:278). In other words, irony, when it has untied the bond to the relative, opens up (negatively) to relating to the absolute.

When it comes to the further development of subjectivity in line with this, Kierkegaard expresses himself in ways that are similar to more recent statements in the later philosophy of Richard Rorty,[17] who claims that life today is lived most fully when we poeticize our lives. On one point, however, there is an important difference between them that expresses their different religious attitudes, as well as the difference between Socratic and romantic irony. Kierkegaard states that irony leads to a poeticized life, but a Christian is not making poetry of her life; rather her life is made poetry (1:292). To live a life open to being poeticized in this manner is for a Christian to recognize the task of her life. On the other hand, if one does not approach this from a Christian point of view, one runs through many different possibilities, before ending up in nothing (292-93).[18] This nothing is due to the fact that the subject then does

---

17. See *Contingency, Irony, and Solidarity.* I think the similarities can best be explained by pointing out Rorty's and Kierkegaard's common heritage in romanticism.

18. This is also a background for understanding Kierkegaard's own use of different pseudonyms as a way to explore different modes of subjectivity.

not see herself as having a specific identity, a specific task to fulfill, or an origin that determines her task. Hence according to Kierkegaard the very relation to something outside us offers the subject the means for a stable identity. If one understands oneself as someone who has such a background, this makes irony, as well as the task of structuring one's life, a serious matter and not a mere play.[19] This points to a basic distinction that now needs to be elaborated further, namely, the difference between romantic irony and Christian faith.

Romantic Irony and Christian Faith

According to Kierkegaard, irony, as it was understood after Hegel, implies that the past of the subject is of no importance to him (1:291). Hence also reality, as a gift to which the subject relates as his own task, disappears together with the tasks or challenges that this reality poses for him. In romanticism, reality is basically approached as possibility (291, 293). Time is spent on keeping these possibilities open, and to make sure that the person is not defined by one of them. In other words, time, history, and social reality lose their force as determinants for the subject.[20]

This has significant consequences for understanding the romantic ironist as a continuous person with a continuous project. Kierkegaard

19. For this task see also Sløk's excellent formulations: "The anthropological concepts have their center in the thesis that to be a human is a task to be fulfilled, and everything that Kierkegaard says about Christianity is in principle based on this presupposition, that the only possibility of fulfilling this task is given in Christianity" (*Anthropologie,* 89). These insights are substantiated by Kierkegaard's own reflective self-characteristic in *Point of View for My Work as an Author.*

20. This is a description that fits well the position that Kierkegaard offers of the aesthetic position in *Either — Or,* part one, as well. On romantic irony Lindström (*Stadiernas Teologi,* 256) points to how Kierkegaard realized that romantic irony "leads to a total subjectivism that negates all historical reality in order to make room for a world created by the subject himself." The difference between the romantic and the Socratic irony seems then to lie in the difference of their understanding of reality as an other — as something given to be appropriated and related to, or as unlimited possibilities for self-realization. Hence I think this distinction anticipates an important difference to be clarified in the understanding of the ethical content of postmodernity as well. For this see further Henriksen, *På Grensen,* 22ff.

explains this by spelling out the difference between being subject to poeticizing vs. poeticizing oneself (see above). One who subjects himself to poeticizing (by God, faith) is already placed in a context that gives his life project a certain form, meaning, and continuity. This is different for the romantic ironist, because he is himself also the author of his context. For him it becomes important to suspend the reality that he constantly collides with in his poeticizing, that is, morality or *Sittlichkeit*. In his poeticizing he is constantly still an observer to the life he poeticizes, and everything exhibits itself to him as something hypothetical that could be, or could be otherwise. The effect is that his life loses continuity (1:294, 295).

Kierkegaard thus argues how an attempt to ground reality solely in the creative powers of the individual leads to the dissolution of this individual, because he cannot by himself establish the continuity necessary for being a continuous self. A person who is not totally left to himself is not redefined every moment by his changing passions or emotions. What happens is also given meaning by being related to a larger context. This is not the case in a romantic attitude. Here irony, in the romantic sense, is coupled with superficiality and boredom (1:296). This is, although Kierkegaard does not say this explicitly, most probably linked to the lack of a larger context within which the experiences can be understood.

In his description of the possibilities in his dissertation, Kierkegaard comes very close to a subject that we meet later in his work, namely, "A" in *Either — Or*. The hedonist aesthetic approach depicted there exhibits the attempt to poeticize oneself, instead of being subject to formation by the reality in which we live. As a consequence, however, we lose sight of the highest enjoyment and eternal blessedness, according to Kierkegaard. This bliss consists in that the subject becomes absolutely transparent for himself, achieves or appropriates himself fully, in religion. This implies that the relation to religion is indeed a personal one, and that the appropriation in question is not to be understood as simply the reception and notification of something externally mediated. The personal appropriation is thus genuinely a *self-appropriation* as well. Religion is a condition for this, since it is in religion that the individual does not have the infinite outside himself, but within himself (1:306-7). As long as the content of religion is not appropriated fully, or held at a distance by irony, the subject cannot achieve full transparency.

86

Conclusion: As a Mastered Element, Irony Creates Reality

In his description of romantic irony, it is obvious that Kierkegaard sees the positive task of irony in something other than being constantly disengaged. He describes this positive function on the last pages of his dissertation, where he states that what doubt is for science, irony is for the individual. There is no true human life without irony (1:328). By being used in a controlled manner, and mastered for specific purposes, it serves a positive function. It does not, as it could seem from our description so far, only point out a negative dimension in everything positive: "Irony delimits, makes finite, delineates, and thereby it also offers truth, reality, content. It demands and punishes, and thereby offers virtue and consistency" (1:328).

Irony can create reality by helping it to have a specific shape and a more clearly defined content, because it opens one up for relating subjectively and passionately to it. The dialectic between passion and irony then not only shows itself in the fact that irony is the start of subjectivity, and thus the start of the life of the individual (1:329). Irony also opens up reality for the individual, and confronts him with it. It represents a critical and reflexive approach to reality that gives depth and coherence. This is only possible if it is not used profligately and romantically, but is mastered as part of a personal project in the search for truth (as in Socrates).

Another and partly different way of posing the same issue is found in *Fear and Trembling*. I refer to it here, since it has some striking similarities to what was just said. Unlike the previous description, the relation to reality is there also described more explicitly by the notion of *faith*. By faith, the subject is able to grasp the depth of reality in a way not possible otherwise (see 5:44, 46). Before this becomes an actual option, however, it must be preceded by resignation. To resign from mastering the challenges, to resign on behalf of oneself, is the final step required before faith can arise. This resignation lets go of the wholeness of reality, but by way of faith the subject can receive reality back in a new form.

It would not be relevant to refer to this here if it were not for one remark that Kierkegaard makes in passing some pages later. There he states that Socrates' lack of knowledge expresses exactly this infinite resignation. In other words, the other side of this coin is Socratic irony (5:64). Although Socrates never reaches faith, the attitude here apparent illustrates how far the human being can advance by his own capacities. In resignation there is only one hope: that God will intervene.

To resign is also to give up thinking. Thinking means mastering reality in a rational way. This is only partially possible according to Kierkegaard. Consequently, he here clearly exhibits traces of the postmodern critique of the capacities of rationality. To give up thinking is then to accept that the subject cannot completely master reality. Fully in accord with this he says, "faith starts where thinking ceases" (5:50).

Consequently, the ironical subject need not be a detached and distanced subject, but can also, by using irony in a constructive and determined manner, be a subject that has capacities for appropriating the content and validity of reality that the subject that lacks irony does not have. This is, of course, not without interest when we try to understand on what grounds we can appropriate religion, and how religion is configured under the conditions that Kierkegaard ascribes to the subject.

Faith, Truth, and History — Kierkegaard's Answer to Lessing

In *Philosophical Fragments,* Kierkegaard writes under the pseudonym Johannes Climacus. This is not only to avoid being personally identified with a specific opinion, but more because he understands direct communication of substantial content regarding faith as a *contradictio in adjecto* (see 6:11, 15ff.). Thus he continues in his own writing to make use of the basic insight he has received from Socrates; that is, that truth has to be mediated in and by the subject itself, more than by a teacher. At this point any similarity with Socrates ends, however, since Climacus is keen on developing a notion of Christianity that does *not* end up in a Socratic mode of thought. The whole treatise deals with three questions that are strikingly similar to a position posed more affirmatively by Lessing: "Can a historical point of departure be given for eternal consciousness? How can this be of more than historical interest? Can one build eternal happiness on historical knowledge?"[21] In the way he poses the problem, Kierkegaard shows that he is informed by Lessing's position. But he also gives the problem he finds in Lessing's work a new turn. First, he poses

---

21. This question is posed on the title page of the work (vol. 6). It must be seen as referring back to the dictum by Lessing that contingent historical truth cannot be seen as a point of departure for metaphysical truth (8:12; see chapter two above).

the problem as a question, and does not state negatively that history cannot be of such importance. He also leaves out any mention of truth and metaphysics. Finally, he states this as a problem about the basis for eternal blessedness or salvation *(salighed)*.

Concerning the first point, Kierkegaard's reluctance to state the problem in an affirmative way can be seen as being caused by the fact that he still relates to a rather distinct or positive Christianity, not to some notion of natural religion, as a point of departure for understanding the relation of history, faith, and salvation. If he had simply accepted Lessing's way of formulating the framework for this relation, he would have given up in advance the possibility of relating faith to something within history, *in casu,* the incarnation of the eternal God in time[22] and history. As we will see, this is an important element in his whole treatment of the problem.

Second, I think that by omitting any mention of truth and metaphysics, Kierkegaard simply tries to avoid the philosophical associations connected to these terms in Lessing. Kierkegaard is not concerned with truth or metaphysics as such, at least not in the way Lessing was. His concern is with existential truth (see further on this below), and this truth is per se to be taken as something other than metaphysical truth, which is derived by a universal or speculative reason. The emphasis on the existential position, and not on any philosophical system, is then also expressed in the third element, that is, that Kierkegaard is concerned with what all this means for the eternal blessedness of the individual, not humankind in general.

If we look at this from a distance, we see that by readjusting the direction of the problem in this way, Kierkegaard turns the interest toward the personal, the theological, and the subjective, instead of the common or general, the philosophical, and the disinterested. However, his understanding of subjectivity is not identical with the Socratic irony or with the autonomous subjectivity of Lessing. His idea of subjectivity is primarily based on how one is interested in his/her own case, not only in theoretical problems posed by modernity toward religion. In other words, Kierkegaard points out that if religion is to have any interest whatsoever in modernity, it has to be related to the existential interests

---

22. "The pure anthropological category of 'facing God' becomes exchanged with the historical fact of 'God in time'" (Sløk, *Anthropologie,* 134).

and passions of the subject. If not, it is reduced to metaphysics and history, and we get (and face only) the kind of problems that confronted us in Lessing.[23]

Such a position, however, does not mean that Kierkegaard tries to avoid the problems presented by Lessing. He frames them in a different way, from a more existential angle. The reason for this is also that in order to solve the problem posed, he sees that subjectivity has to be constituted on other conditions than those offered by both Socrates and Lessing. In both of them, we can see how the insight into truth that they offer is basically an insight acquired through their own reason. In Socrates, self-knowledge and God-knowledge are identical (6:16-17); and in Lessing we have seen how it is that what is acquired unmediated by tradition can confront the individual as truth. As Kierkegaard points out, this also means that any occasion in time is a mere contingent fact, without any real content or meaning in itself. Hence the impact of reports about historical events for acquiring and appropriating truth is actually nonexistent in Lessing's and Kierkegaard's mode of thought.[24]

Just like Lessing, however, Kierkegaard emphasizes the insight into the importance of the historical for the formation of the subject. At the same time he applies this insight to the formation of religious subjectivity in a far more extensive way than Lessing does. Also, he points out how unavoidable such a historical point of departure is for reshaping the subject, so that she can act and live on other conditions than those offered by philosophy. But he does not do this to secure the autonomy of the subject

23. See C. S. Evans, *Faith beyond Reason*, p. 13: "Christianity is concerned with how people can actualise Truth in their lives; it wants to see Truth not merely as propositions to be believed, but as something to be incorporated in the inner life, the 'subjectivity' of the individual." It is tempting here to follow up this remark with a comment made by J. Kellenberger, who points out how both Kierkegaard and Nietzsche are acutely aware of a dimension in religion that modern analytic philosophy of religion tends to ignore: "If the concern with doctrinal truth and the concern with rationality have importance for the life of religious faith, they do so by virtue of the psychological dimension of belief — the side of faith that analytic philosophy is inclined to dismiss as irrelevant" (*Kierkegaard and Nietzsche*, 4).

24. See what I said in the previous section about the romantic as one not being determined by her own past. As now becomes clear, Kierkegaard is criticizing not merely a romantic position, but any modern position that denies any impact of the historical context on the subject. As will be clear below, he advances what he sees as their main points in a way that also opens one up to the typical historical basis of Christianity.

over against tradition and authority. It is more likely that he realizes that he must secure the insight in the necessity of incarnation for upholding the central elements in Christian religion. Whereas philosophy (Socrates and Lessing) tends to diminish and ignore the historical as something more than the mere occasion for setting a relation to the divine, Kierkegaard stresses how everything is based on, and gains importance due to, the meeting that takes place in history between God and the human. This meeting he characterizes as *the moment (øyeblikket)*, that is, the moment in time. Hence Kierkegaard has a relational understanding of the religious subject that makes the issue of autonomy secondary.[25]

By way of a subtle argument, inspired by the willingness to counter a Socratic notion of truth and learning, Kierkegaard shows how God (the teacher) has to offer the human not only the truth, but also the possibility for acquiring it. This is actually an anti-Socratic position, as it implies that the human being cannot acquire the truth about herself by and for herself, without any intervention from God that also implies a change of her natural conditions. That the human is "outside" the truth, and not in a position to acquire it, but exists in "nontruth," is a definition of the basic position that determines the conditions of the subject as an individual who is incapable of escaping this nontruth by her own means. In other words, with regard to God and religion, the individual has no chance whatsoever of acting in an autonomous way. God sets the conditions for acquiring truth.

At this point we do well to remember how we characterized the function of revelation before the advent of modernity, and the establishment of the notion of natural religion. The traditional, orthodox dogmatics could affirm and make use of the notion of natural religion, as long as it could also affirm that this naturally given religious disposition was in need of correction and had to be renewed through the insights given in special revelation. Such correction was needed due to the sinful-

---

25. Moreover, the kind of autonomy where the self is the origin of his or her own ideals and norms, for Kierkegaard is a kind of aesthetical approach that ends up in despair. See Evans, *Faith beyond Reason,* 31, who in discussing D. Cupitt says on this: "According to Kierkegaard, it is not true that the self is autonomous; we are throroughly relational creatures, dependent for our sense of the self on others, and ultimately on some 'power' that is the ground of the self." This relational constitution of the self is also much underscored in the Kierkegaard research done by Arne Grøn, *Begrebet Angest hos Søren Kierkegaard;* and *Subjektivitet og Negativitet,* passim (on this see below, 193).

ness of human beings. Sin proved to darken the faculties of human beings. Thus, from the orthodox point of view, enlightenment had to come from the content of revelation.[26]

With this background, the reconstruction of religion in Kierkegaard's position can be seen as using premodern, orthodox doctrine. From the outset he poses a hiatus between God and human beings, between time and eternity, and this hiatus can be overcome only by God. To do this, God incarnates in time, in history, and in this moment he creates a unity of time and eternity that is the condition for the subject to face the truth and establish a new and more authentic form of subjectivity (6:33-34). Kierkegaard develops how God, in this, is determined by his love for humans, and that this love makes him undergo everything in order to make human beings face the truth about themselves.

There is one important element in this that has to be underscored. The human being does not know by herself that she exists in nontruth. It is the presence of God, the occasion of his appearance, that makes the human realize this (6:20). Hence the presence of God forms the conditions for a new subjectivity, a new self-understanding, and a new self-relation that was not previously possible. By confronting God, the human thus also confronts the truth about herself and the basic condition for her life. Here we have a classical formulation of what *revelation* means. It is to receive something by way of another, and to get knowledge of something that a human being cannot deduce or acquire by her own reason. This is seen most clearly in the understanding of what takes place in the incarnation. The human could invent a fiction where she became like God, or where she made God similar to herself, but humans could not by themselves invent a solution to their own problems where God made himself like us (6:36). Here we see again how Kierkegaard emphasizes the point of departure for revelation outside and independent of human reason.

In postmodern terms, this implies that the presence of God as the other also establishes the condition of a new kind of subjectivity. God appears, not only to reveal himself but also to reveal something that opens one up to a new self-understanding, a new subjectivity. After God has revealed himself as the other, a human being can no longer understand and define him on the basis of what is accessible by reason alone. Theologically speaking, this means that a human being now has to define her-

26. See 17-18 above.

self on new terms, either as being subject to God or as opposed to God. There is no longer any neutral stance — hence the existential seriousness with which Kierkegaard deals with this question.

Kierkegaard spells out mainly in theological language the change in the person after the confrontation with the deity. The person now becomes a *new* human being. Her change is due to a *conversion,* which also causes regret and sorrow. In contrast to a Socratic position, however, here the newborn disciple has received everything due to the presence of and confrontation with the Teacher (Christ), and after this she can forget neither him nor what he has done — the deity becomes the determining factor in her life: "Just as the person who by Socratic midwifery gave birth to himself and in so doing forgot everything else in the world and in a more profound sense owed nothing to anybody, so the one who is born again owes no human being anything, but the divine teacher everything. Hence in turn he must also, because of this teacher, forget himself" (6:23). It is in *the moment* that the human being realizes what the historical appearance of the teacher means for her. This notion, for Kierkegaard, serves as the means of describing how the historical also has an impact in an existential sense, indeed more impact than mere information about what has happened in history (6:24; 6:22). In this, he states what is already expressed in the Lutheran Confessions: "It is one thing to believe history, another to believe what it means for me."[27]

Given this, I think it is fair to say that Kierkegaard takes a far more theological approach than Lessing does to the problem stated initially in this section. By taking his point of departure in an assumed relation between God and the human being, and how they have to relate to each other, he spells out a different basis for framing the whole understanding of appropriation of religious truth. This truth is mediated through the relation in the moment where time and eternity meet, and the content of this moment Kierkegaard describes as the *paradox* (e.g., 6:55). This paradox, the actual coexistence of time and eternity in the presence of the incarnated God, is what alters every already-given condition for understanding the human self and religion.

From this, we can sum up by pointing out the following consequences. In his description of the human subject, Kierkegaard

---

27. Augsburg Confession, art. xx.

- Frames the individual basically in her relation to God.
- Hence she does not understand herself as autonomous, guided only by her own principles.
- Thus she exists by herself in nontruth.
- Also, she has to be offered an external truth that is not possible to mediate Socratically, but must be seen as a paradox according to human reason alone.
- As paradox, the mediated content (truth) cannot be understood as deriving from human reason (see 6:47). It means the end of autonomous, Socratic reason.

The paradox, that the human subject gives up her status as existing in nontruth and at the same time gives up herself, becomes a paradox because it both sets new conditions for reason and gives it another content (6:47). Kierkegaard can also say that the subject now develops a new *passion*. This passion, which is based on a paradox contained in the moment, does not try to escape the paradox that is the content of Christianity, but attempts to bring it into a new relation with reason. Kierkegaard names this passion *faith*. This new relation receives its content through a new definition of how historical knowledge and faith are to be understood. The paradox is not to be understood, but we have to understand that it is a paradox. How is this possible? Kierkegaard describes it like this:

> It occurs when the understanding and the paradox encounter each other happily in the moment *(øyeblikket)*, when the understanding steps aside and the paradox gives itself, and the third, within which this occurs, . . . is the joyful passion that we shall now give a name. . . . We shall call it *faith*. This passion, then, must be that above-mentioned condition that the paradox provides (6:56).

Hence the self-mediation or self-revelation of God leads to the mode of existence described as faith. Without God, paradox, and revelation, there is no faith, passion, and reconstituted and true subjectivity. Thus the contrast with Lessing is clear. There is no internal mediation here, in the sense that revelation makes use of or utilizes already-given elements in subjectivity in order to be recognized as true. Faith is not self-generated, but generated by the moment, that is, by the historical circumstances by which the subject receives a new self-understanding. As we shall see below, this is important background for his understanding of the subject's transcendent teleology in religiosity B.

This means that historical knowledge is important, but when it comes to the central question of incarnation, both the contemporary disciple and a later disciple are in the same position with regard to the actual information they have on the alleged birth of God in history. They both depend on the central witness, that is, the other. Here all potential disciples are in the same position. By pointing this out, Kierkegaard places the problem on another level than Lessing does. It is not depending on historical knowledge as such that is the problem. Every potential disciple has to depend on this. But to relate to such historical records is in itself not sufficient to constitute faith (6:56). From this, Kierkegaard also argues that the contemporary disciple is in no better position than a later disciple, as they are both challenged to relate to the records of that which happened, in a way that transcends mere historical recognition.

There seems to be an underlying assumption in this that is important to spell out in order to understand the argument. The historically given is — in and for itself — characterized by ambiguity. In order to overcome this ambiguity and relate to it as something distinctive, with infinite importance, we have to be given the chance to operate on different conditions. These conditions are found neither in the subject himself nor in the mere historical. They are given by the infinite in the historical — that is, through the paradox that gives rise to faith. Thus it is not the historically contingent in itself that holds the subject from assuming the truth inherent in it (as would be the case in Lessing), but it is that the subject lacks the basic condition for recognizing this historically contingent event as something that is of eternal importance.

As a consequence, humans can relate to historical knowledge in different ways. We can sometimes be eyewitnesses. But to be an eyewitness does not yet make us a disciple, because the knowledge such a witness can have is merely historical. Having pointed this out, Kierkegaard focuses on how we have to relate to the historical in a specific way in order to make it a basis for faith. We have to see *in* the historical moment itself the paradox, and to recognize that the historical is not only an occasion for confronting the eternal, but something that contains the eternal. We then have a relation to the historical that also makes it a basis for faith. As long as the historical and the eternal are separated, such recognition is impossible. If this is the case, we would be back in the Socratic situation (6:57).

From this, it would seem as if Kierkegaard approves when Lessing says that historical knowledge cannot lead to eternal truth in metaphysical matters. The alleged agreement is superficial, however, because Lessing, in Kierkegaard's eyes, is probably an excellent representative of the Socratic position. The Socratic position has no need of an incarnation — it is sufficient to provide an occasion in history for grasping the truth that is already inherent in reason. For Kierkegaard, as we have seen, it is otherwise. The subject has no access whatsoever to eternal truths.[28] But it is not only a question of seeing the incarnation in history as a unity of time and eternity, expressing itself in the paradox of the moment. It is also important how we relate to this paradox. This makes the moment of this relation something that determines our further life:

> But if the whole structure is not Socratic, . . . then the disciple owes the teacher everything . . . and this relation cannot be expressed by talking extravagantly and trumpeting from the rooftops but only in that happy passion that we call faith, the object of which is the paradox. But the paradox unites exactly the contradictories, and is the eternalizing of the historical and the historicizing of the eternal (6:58).

Kierkegaard offers us a framework for understanding faith, by way of a description of that which faith relates to. This framework is, however, strongly theologically biased. Even more so, this framework is already based on specific theological assumptions. We have to notice this critically, because Kierkegaard, in doing this, assumes a position that differs from Lessing's. Consequently, the task of appropriation in the case of religion also turns out to be different. It challenges the subject to relate to the historical as if the contingent historical had eternal meaning, since the historically given contains far more than mere historical information. This very assumption is itself based on faith — it is not argued philosophically.

From this follows, by implication, that the relation to the historical has to be passionate; it cannot be restricted by reflexive or ironic reason, or be fulfilled by means of historical reason alone. The passion is — as al-

---

28. Consequently, Kierkegaard is not in agreement with Lessing: we are limited to contingent empirical knowledge, and have no access to eternal truths. For this see also A. Hannay, *Kierkegaard*, 98.

ready said — called *faith* by Kierkegaard. The subject is thus configured in relation to the historical in a way that is far more differentiated than the possible positions arising from the Enlightenment reservoir of thought. Reason is suspended (not abolished), although it still has its functions when it comes to establishing knowledge of either the historical or the eternal objects of knowledge.

This means, however, that faith is not to be understood as a means for establishing an alternative type of knowledge. Kierkegaard accepts the insight that understanding is either acquiring knowledge of the eternal (the Platonic-Socratic position), thereby excluding the historical as unimportant, or that understanding and knowledge relates to the merely historical. There is, however, no understanding that can grasp the absurdity that the eternal *is* the historical (6:58).

This is important, because it shows clearly how Kierkegaard establishes a position "between" the Socratic and the modern, critical, historical mind in order to create room for faith. This can be seen as a tacit refutation of the mode in which Lessing posed the problem stated at the start of the chapter. Kierkegaard overcomes the "either-or" of historical vs. metaphysical by making use of the notions of faith, moment, and paradox. But he also does something more: he underscores the difference, the total *otherness* that faith relates to, compared to the forms of knowledge that our understanding establishes.[29] This difference is not encompassed by anything that the human subject can establish itself. I take this to mean that that which gives rise to faith cannot be controlled by human reason or understanding. Faith is not motivated by human will, or caused by human will, but is given, together with the occasion for faith, by God himself.[30]

To name the relationship to the eternal in time as faith, and that which faith relates to as paradox or even the absurd, shows clearly how Kierkegaard refuses to establish a common ground in reason for establishing faith. Faith is a personal relationship, not based on conditions acquired by reason, but based on what the believed has provided the subject

29. I take this line of thought to be one of the main reasons why Kierkegaard can be seen as a forerunner for the dialectical theology found, e.g., in Karl Barth. The emphasis on otherness and the inability of "entering" into faith by means of the given natural conditions of humanity are quite parallel.

30. "It is then easily seen, that faith is not an act of the will, for all human will always only be effective within the condition" (6:59). See 6:76.

with, that is, a new self-relation as well as a new relation to the other (i.e., God). Hence the believing subject — when it comes to the point of departure of the existence of faith — cannot understand herself as holding her destiny in her own hands. She is totally in the hands of that which from now on determines her existence.

From this it follows that faith itself becomes paradoxical, since it is established neither through historical justifications alone nor on metaphysical grounds (see 6:61). The transmission of the basis for faith is given with the Teacher, who himself becomes the object of faith. By underlining how personal or existential relationship is the basis for any religious subjectivity, Kierkegaard emphasizes quite different elements from those found in the Enlightenment approach. As I have already hinted, Kierkegaard abandons the notion of the individual's autonomy when it comes to faith, and the self-constituted subject is eliminated in order to provide space for a self constituted by the object of faith. At this point we find in Kierkegaard a position quite similar to that of Hegel, who argues for another approach to the constitution of the subject than the one found in Kant.[31] In one way or another this seems to be the only way to rescue religion from the risk of being understood as a product of human subjectivity — a risk that Lessing's approach also runs.

By developing the relation to the historical in such ways, Kierkegaard has to explain how he understands the relation between faith and doubt. Is doubt the lack of ability to see the eternal in the historical — or what is it? In the context of *Philosophical Fragments*, Kierkegaard explains faith and doubt simply as two opposite passions, as he recognizes neither of them as having faculties for acquiring (empirical) knowledge. Faith is simply the sense for becoming something other than what one previously has been through the meeting with the historical. By contrast, doubt is a protest against any kind of inference from the immediately given in sensation and understanding to some eternal sphere.[32] As already indicated, both the first-century believer and the later believer, who bases his faith on the records of others, are challenged in the same way to make such an inference from the immediately given in history (or

31. For this see W. Pannenberg, *Metaphysik und Gottesgedanke*, chap. 3.
32. See what was said above, 83-84, about doubt as arising when the subject is trying to achieve a positive relation to what is given, but where this given escapes him. One can say that that is what happens when the inference from the factual to the eternal is not established; then the real content of the given escapes.

the records of others on history) to that which can be said to be the implications of this history for their own existence (6:77).

Thus the divine reality, mediated through the historically given — which Kierkegaard names *the absolute* — is the object of faith. But this must not be understood in a way that accentuates the historical as being most important, that which determines the individual (6:90). Kierkegaard seems to indicate (a) that the historical is more than an occasion for the genesis of faith, but also (b) that the merely historical is unimportant, theologically speaking. The most important is the absolute that is given in and through the historical. Hence the connection between historicity and eternity serves the function of relating the subject passionately to both spheres simultaneously.

The task of the eyewitness is then nothing other than to provide an occasion for the later disciple and his faith, by telling him what he himself has believed. However, this communication is only successful to the extent that the listener understands himself as not being in continuity with the witness, but only in a relation to the *content* of his testimony. Here we are again inside the Socratic framework, as the witness has no other task than to function as the occasion for achieving a new position, as Socrates did. He does not offer the condition for faith; he merely offers an opportunity for the other to receive this condition himself by relating directly to the content of what he says. In this framework the witness himself becomes unimportant, and his trustworthiness is of little interest (6:92). By saying this, Kierkegaard also comes close to later statements by Bultmann, namely, that the most important point is *that* God has revealed himself in a human fashion, not *how* this took place in detail (see 6:93).[33]

This can be taken to mean that on the one hand Kierkegaard insists on the historical as an inescapable condition for faith; on the other hand, he does not emphasize the correctness of every historical detail as being an important element for upholding this faith. But it still serves as a way of formulating an alternative position to that of many Enlightenment thinkers, as it bases the reasons for faith neither in the mere metaphysics of natural religion nor in the provision of historically correct records. This is also well in accord with Kierkegaard's statement that faith is not a mode of understanding.

---

33. For Bultmann's positions here see *Glauben und Verstehen,* vol. 1, passim.

As a conclusion to this section, it is natural to ask in what way Kierkegaard's elaboration can be seen as helpful in understanding a more postmodern climate for religion. First, I think the important element here is that he does not take the facticity of the historically given as something that holds a specific content per se. In order to open up to and relate to the religious, one has to relate to historical facticity in a specific manner, with specific concerns. Hence any kind of "objective" relation is ruled out. We note, however, that Kierkegaard does not do this by way of arguing that it is impossible, but because he finds it of no relevance for dealing with the questions that concern him.

In terms of the basis for a philosophy of religion, Kierkegaard anticipates here the postmodern emphasis on how human relations, interests, and interpretations are important when it comes to depicting reality in religious terms. This is a more specific way of laying bare the general postmodern insight into how human relations, ideas, and interests contribute considerably and constitutively to how reality is shaped or constructed.

As I have already hinted, Kierkegaard is concerned not mainly with the general truth of Christianity, but how the individual *relates* to Christianity (9:18). This should not, however, be taken to mean that he is not interested in discussing the "objective" truth of Christianity. He is. But he holds discussions of such issues, and the result of them, to be of minor importance compared to the issue of how the religious subject configures itself. The historical approach expresses a common concern that is not individually shaped, while he considers it more important to establish an individual concern for this truth. This individual concern has to be subjective, that is, it is something that cannot be offered by another person or tradition, or something that is secured by any safeguarded doctrinal system underpinned by authority or human rationality.

There seems to be both similarity to and divergence from Lessing here. The similarity is found in how they both stress the personal appropriation of religion, while the difference lies in Kierkegaard's rejection of a common rationality as a way to recognize religious truth. I think we see in this how Kierkegaard develops a typically modern position, which he has in common with Lessing. The emphasis on the subjective autonomy on behalf of authority develops into an anticipation of a postmodern skepticism toward the use of the same rationality in all fields or areas of human life. This rationality will also not do in the sphere of religion.

In the way he addresses these questions, we can also see in Kierkegaard a typically modern feature, namely, the refutation of the givens of the life-world in terms of religion. The individual cannot take his religious position for granted, as something guaranteed by what has gone on so far in his milieu: It is a crime against Christianity when the singular individual without further thought assumes its relation to Christendom as something to be taken for granted.[34] The challenge to reflect on the subjective relation to Christianity implies that one overcomes the given life-world, and determines this relation by means of one's own, individual passion, and not by simply noticing the common goods of history, tradition, or any transferred mode of thought. In other words, the individual is challenged to develop his own relation to religion, in a way that is not commonly arguable. This is perhaps most clearly elaborated in *Fear and Trembling*, where Kierkegaard stresses how a genuine religious commitment cannot be spelled out in terms of "the common" *(det Almene)*.

The Religious Mode of Existence:
Subjectivity as Passion for Truth

We can now conclude that Kierkegaard basically operates with two dialectically opposed modes of relating to religion. These two modes reflect two distinct modes of subjectivity: the objective, reasonable, and critical subject, who stands detached and disinterested "outside" the religious position; and the subjective, passionate, concerned subject, who has a deep personal interest in what religion means for her. These are symmetrically opposed ways of approaching Christianity. According to Kierkegaard, their difference also gives rise to their quite different chances for appropriating the truth of this religion.

Much of the difference between these two modes of subjectivity is well known to anyone acquainted with Kierkegaard, and I am not going to retell that story here. But for our task, namely, to investigate how reli-

---

34. In the words of Johannes Climacus: "I have understood this much, admittedly standing on the outside, that the only unforgivable lèse-majesté against Christendom is when the individual, without further (thought) takes his relationship to it for granted" (9:19).

gious subjectivity relates to and influences modern constructions of religion, some elements are important to point out.

Kierkegaard's emphasis on a personal decision is an important element in his understanding of the constitution of the religious subjectivity. But the objective thinker is not concerned with such a decision for her own part. According to Kierkegaard, she lacks the interest for such decisions, because she wants to be objective. This lack causes her to lose sight of what really should concern her infinitely, namely, the task of making a decision that concerns her own eternal salvation. Hence the appropriation of religion in terms of relating to it in an absolute way and giving it the place that it should have according to its own nature is made impossible, simply because any such personal relation is blocked by a scientific, "objective" approach.[35]

Kierkegaard can depict this scientific or objective approach as thoughtless because it lacks self-reflexive subjective involvement. If the person involved in a search for the historical truth of Christianity were eternally interested in her relation to this truth, she would end up in despair, because she would rapidly see that her relation to the historically given cannot offer her full confidence. This is because the historical approach leads her to rest her confidence solely on approximate reasons. According to Kierkegaard's pseudonym Climacus, historical approximations are too narrow a basis for building one's eternal salvation (9:24).[36]

We recognize in this Kierkegaard's version of Lessing's basic problem: What is the relationship between historical and metaphysical truth? But now we also can see how he refigures the problem. It is no longer a question of choosing between a historical or a philosophical/metaphysical approach — either more or less detached from the subject — or options for a neutral subject that has to choose between different approaches in a way that does not affect the basic way he relates to the truth. Kierkegaard instead locates the problem in subjectivity itself. In doing this, he strengthens the *modern* approach to the problem, as he underscores more clearly that the principle of subjectivity is a basic feature in relating to the content given in tradition and the life-world.

35. See 9:23 and 24: "Their understanding wants to be objective, without interest. As for the subject's relation to the recognized truth, it is assumed that when the objectively true is established, then appropriation is a small task; it follows almost by itself, and in the end the individual does not matter."

36. See also what was said in the previous section of this chapter.

At the same time, we see how Kierkegaard is critical toward an understanding of Christianity that makes it into a mere historical entity. Such a historical approach is, for him as well as for Lessing, simply not capable of framing the passionate search for eternal salvation. Nevertheless, he still does not let go of a discussion of the historical content of Christianity, but the aim of this discussion is simply to point out the limits of such an approach. It is not to state its positive contribution to the configuration of the content of Christianity or of the subject itself.

Several things demand comment in view of this. First, I find good reasons to ask whether Kierkegaard is right in insisting that a modern subject relating to religion can and should do so by suspending the historical and critical attitude to religion's historical foundations. Christianity is not something apart from its history, and a critical attitude is necessary to establish a grasp of its content that is at least somewhat more precise than what a mere uncritical approach can achieve.

Second, there are also reasons for asking if his notion of Christianity, as something that has mainly to do with the eternal salvation of the individual, is capable of framing Christian life as a life in this world. By stressing this element, Kierkegaard tends to isolate the individual and his faith from both the life-world and the social dimension.[37]

Finally, it is apparent that an insistence on a passionate relation to the absolute is Kierkegaard's way of attempting to overcome both romantic irony and the blows of historical criticism of Christianity. He is probably right in his insistence that faith has to exclude the other two in some way. But this exposes the problem we touched on in dealing with Lessing: that of the double subject, that is, a subject that is both "outside" and "inside" faith. Neither of these approaches can be ignored. As far as I can see, Kierkegaard does not reflect on this in his discussion of the believing subject, although he is very much aware of the double reflexivity that this subject needs to display in order to take seriously the content of faith as an individual passion. One way of reading him is to say that he actually deals with this problem by exposing different subjective attitudes to religion by way of his pseudonyms. It is important to take all these various approaches into account in order to understand what shapes the conditions for developing a religious subjectivity in a modern or postmodern framework.

37. I think this critique is also paralleled in Adorno's commentary in *Kierkegaard.*

103

If this is the case, Kierkegaard as well would agree that the individual probably has to display some kind of "double" subjectivity — and be at once not only "objective" and disinterested but subjective and passionate. Is it possible in the modern world, based on criticism toward any tradition, only to state: "For faith does not result from straightforward scholarly deliberation, nor does it come directly; on the contrary, in this objectivity one loses that infinite, personal impassioned interestedness, which is the condition of faith, the *ubique et nusquam* in which faith can come into existence" (9:29; see 31). To be a modern mind and still state only this, and say no more, would be to give up the subjectivity that has its point of departure in itself and its own autonomy. We have already seen how this is the case in Kierkegaard. Religious truth, established on the basis of a passionate subjectivity that is moved by something other than itself, is opposed to disinterested, objective deliberation. A direct conclusion from this is that scientific proofs both for and against the truth of Christianity on historical terms are of no relevance for the believer (9:28, 30). We must ask, however, whether Kierkegaard is not contradicting himself here. It is the God in historical time who shows himself in the paradox that faith relates to. If there were no point in history that could reasonably be addressed as the point where God reveals himself in time, what would then be left to support such a position?

Thus there is a dialectical tension in Kierkegaard, one that cannot be mediated, between the speculative (literally, the one who is observing) and objective mind on the one hand, and on the other hand the subjective and passionate mind that is involved and existentially touched by the object of faith. Faith relates the subject to the religious dimension in a way that neither speculation nor irony can. This is because they have a direction that cannot grasp the self-relatedness of the individual in a way that really lets the individual understand himself as *a self,* that is, someone distinct from others, with individual and personal concern for himself. In other words, without the subjective passion there is no basis in subjectivity for a genuine religious relation to self and world.[38]

The way he understands existence is further developed by Kierkegaard in his elaboration of the relationship between objective and subjective modes of thinking. While the objective mode of thinking is in-

---

38. See what was said in the previous section on how confronting the other shapes a new self-understanding or subjectivity.

different toward the thinking subject and its existence, the subjective thinker is interested in her own thinking and exists in it. Her mode of thought is marked by a reflection that has inwardness as its distinctive mark, and through this inwardness the thinking becomes something personally marked by the individual in question, as something that can belong to no one else.[39] Accordingly, her mode of thinking also precludes her from being consumed by what is common, average, or mediocre. Thus she becomes subjectively isolated (9:63).

Consequently, the mode of communication changes: since objective forms of thought are indifferent toward subjectivity, communication can be straightforward. On the other hand, the subjective mode of thinking must communicate itself in an indirect manner, in order to secure the appropriate form of appropriation (see 9:65-66). Kierkegaard speaks of a mode of communication that not only brings about reflection on what is communicated, but also leads to reflection on how the one communicating herself is related to that which is communicated (9:66).

On this basis Kierkegaard can define that what is central is the subjective mode of understanding. The central element is the appropriation in the subjective mode, in order to avoid any form of externality (see 9:68). Such appropriation of what is subjectively relevant turns the existent thinker into the mode of becoming — she is always on the way to her destination, and can, as long as life goes on, not reach a time where she can be said to have fulfilled this task (see 9:74; cf. Lessing). Hence existence becomes a struggle, a quest directed toward the infinite (9:79). Accordingly, existence in the subjective mode is connected to development, where the individual reflects just as much on what she positively is — in relation to her destiny — as on what she negatively is not in the same relation (9:72-73, 79).[40] We see also here, then, a sort of double reflexivity in the subjective thinker — in the believer that understands herself as related to the eternal.

A similar mode of reflection shows itself in the subjective thinker's relation to truth. The objective question of truth makes truth an entity

39. "The concept of inwardness is an important, indeed the central, element in Kierkegaard's answer to the question of what is required of subjectivity for it to grasp 'the' problem of the *Postscript*: the subject's relationship to Christianity" (Hannay, *Kierkegaard*, 128).

40. For this see also Grøn, *Subjektivitet og Negativitet*, passim.

to which the thinker can relate. Reflection is not concentrated on the relationship, but on the truth to which one relates. Subjectively speaking, however, the relationship itself can also be made a theme for the struggle or quest. Accordingly, a subject can be in truth by relating in an authentic way to something that objectively is untruth (9:166). This authenticity is marked by the limitless passion of the subject: a passion that is not limited by the reflection on what objectively counts as truth.

It would obviously be nonsense to say that Kierkegaard holds that a true relationship to the objectively untrue is just as good as a true relationship to what is objectively to be understood as the truth. By stressing the subjective relation being just as important as the question of objective or historical truth, however, he advances the reflection further than Lessing. By stating that subjectivity contains the highest truth for the existing subject (9:169-70), he points out that religion also belongs to another dimension than the historical and objective. We can say that he now locates religion not only in the subject — as does Lessing by his ethical emphasis — but in the relationship to that which counts as a religious object.[41] The religious is then not marked by that which is common to all, but rather by that which is personal and unique for every individual, namely, her relationship toward the objectively insecure.

Given this emphasis on the relation(s) of the subject (toward himself as well as toward the objectively insecure), we can now understand more fully what Kierkegaard means by the term *existence*, or what it means to be in existence. Existence is constituted by *becoming*, by being in development, by the quest for the infinite. To live as an existing being is to be able to take oneself into account in what is reflected on, so that one does not forget the consciousness of oneself as being set apart from the infinite (see 9:80). To exist like this is to accept that one is not a finished subject, but still developing. The other side of this realization is that one is not fully one's own master. There are elements in life that one cannot

41. I think it is worth reflecting on this way of configuring religion in relation to Luther's statement in the *Large Catechism*, where in the explanation of the first article of faith he says that what one puts one's trust in is one's God. Here Luther stresses the relation of trust toward an object, in a way that makes the independent, objective standing of that object secondary in terms of whether it is worth the attention we give a God. It is how the subject relates to the object that makes it an object of religious devotion, more than what the object is in itself. We can see Kierkegaard's way of elaborating the subject as a possible way of following and pursuing further Luther's mode of reflection here.

deduce by rationality and secure for the present a fully transparent subject that controls reality. This is one of the insights by which Kierkegaard anticipates postmodernism.

Faith Shapes the Development of Subjectivity

"The paradox of Christianity lies in the fact that it always uses time
and the historical in relation to the eternal" (9:82).

Kierkegaard states that faith demands a leap that cannot be secured by rationality or any kind of speculative mediation. This leap in faith was just as much a leap for Jesus' contemporaries as it is for later believers (9:84). Thus Kierkegaard tries to correct Lessing by stating that the same effort is demanded from both. This leap of faith, subjectively speaking, can be characterized as the decision (9:85). Moreover, faith depends not only on an objective uncertainty, but also on special subjective dispositions, related to the double reflexivity of the subject, reflecting on both his relation and his objective uncertainty in the same moment.

Hence the insistence of the paradox on the absurdity of faith, of existence as a mode of becoming, and the necessity of a leap of faith all prove to serve as means for avoiding a rational reconstruction of:

- the believing subject,
- the Christian religion as more than a historical phenomenon, and
- the truth of faith.

Only a finalized, absolute mode of thinking is able to make such a rational reconstruction. Kierkegaard, through his construction of the understanding of religion, makes the believing and existing subject a subject that is in becoming. Every becoming precludes the rational reconstruction of religion, since the content of religion cannot be adequately thought of independently of the subject (person) in question (see above, the end of the previous section).[42]

42. See 9:101: "Reality itself is a system — for God, but cannot be that for any existing spirit. System and finality conform to each other, while existence *(tilværelse)* is exactly the opposite."

It seems, then, that Kierkegaard and Lessing have in common the insistence that the development of personal subjectivity is an important element in how religion functions and, consequently, that this also contributes to how they shape their own views of what religion is all about. "The continued quest is the expression of the existing subject's ethical understanding of life. Accordingly, the continuous quest must not be understood metaphysically, as there is no individual who exists metaphysically" (9:104). Kierkegaard tries to avoid any kind of religious thinking that ignores the subjective dimension in the development of a religious relationship. In this quotation, this is understood in ethical terms, that is, in terms that have to do with how the individual relates to and forms his or her own life. This is a concrete project, not an abstract metaphysical task. Ignorance of this leads to two interrelated difficulties that should be possible to understand on the basis of what I said above: first, ignorance about what religion is all about (i.e., about existing in truth); second, ignorance about what a subject is (i.e., not an abstract entity that has finished its quest, but a becoming individual; see 9:105ff.).

Several paragraphs define well the reconstruction of the Christian religion based on Kierkegaard's notion of subjectivity. They show clearly how there is a close interrelation between the two, in a way that substantiates the major thesis of this book. Subjectivity is *the* case, he can say (9:107). To define the case thus is related to two elements already mentioned: the challenge of the decision, and the question of appropriation. To decide for Christianity is at the same time to relate to it in a way that opens one up to how to appropriate it in an authentic way. This authenticity is conditioned by the relation of the subject more than by the objective truth of what is appropriated (see above).

Even if Christianity supposes that the possibility for appropriation is inherent in the subjectivity of the individual, and consequently that the individual can relate to and take possession of this good, this does not automatically imply that subjectivity itself exists in a finished or perfect state, or that it has an adequate understanding of the importance of what it appropriates. Confrontation with the religious object, that is, Christ, sets subjectivity in motion, develops and reshapes it. By focusing on the mere objective or outward elements in the relationship, this dimension is lost. By configuring this as the main point of Christianity, however, Kierkegaard can also say that the purpose of Christianity is that the subject shall be infinitely concerned about himself (see 9:108).

Consequently, the subject has to practice at becoming subjective, and to let himself be involved with the religious object. In *Concluding Unscientific Postscript*, Kierkegaard develops his idea of the eternal task of becoming subjective. This task implies several elements:

- The task shows concern for individuality and individual development.
- It marks religion as being closely and internally linked to subjective development.
- A "detached" relation to religion must be seen as a "natural" point of departure for an individual, but the religious task is to overcome this detachment by appropriating the task that Christianity sets, namely, to become an existing individual.
- Objectivity, and the objectifying mode of thought and existence, is a permanent temptation for the subject, in which he can literally lose himself in the religious relationship.

To overcome the detached relation to religion is to live in faith. Faith is, as Kierkegaard has famously put it, to live in objective uncertainty, to be seventy thousand fathoms deep, and still to believe (9:170). In this, the paradoxical dimension again reveals itself:

- Subjectively, in the passionate relation to the truth. In other words, truth is linked to "qualities" in the subject.
- Objectively, in that the paradox is the truth, although it is at the same time (objectively speaking) defined as the uncertain (9:171).
- Socratically speaking, subjectivity exists in untruth, if it resists recognizing that the subjectivity is the truth, and instead tries to overcome itself by becoming objective (9:173).

Of these elements, we need to concern ourselves further with the last. To say that one is in untruth means that one is not yet where one is destined to be. Moreover, in himself, apart from the confrontation with Christ, the teacher, the subject has not yet become himself. Theologically speaking, this mode of untruth in the subject can be called *sin* (9:174). According to Kierkegaard, however, this is not an essential definition of the subject, although in being born, subjectivity also becomes sinful by not relating appropriately to the transcendent dimension of its own life.

In §3 in *Concluding Unscientific Postscript,* guilt is identified as an important element in existential pathos (199). This guilt makes the individual into a concrete self (200). Consciousness of guilt determines the individual in his totality, and this determination relates the individual to his eternal blessedness *(salighet)* (10:202-3). This is a remarkable way of describing the subject, since guilt — a notion that is basically negative — still proves capable of relating the subject to his positive telos. However, Kierkegaard distinguishes between an immanent and a transcendent definition of the subject in this respect, as consciousness of guilt seems to be based in the immanent dimension, while sin is related to the transcendent dimension of the subject (ibid., 204-5). But guilt is to be seen as a meaningful and serious matter only when it is related to the question of the eternal blessedness of the individual. Religiously speaking, it is possible to know the positive element here through the negative, that is, through suffering (205; see below).[43]

According to Kierkegaard, it is of utmost importance to make sure that the consciousness of guilt remains constant and does not diminish (206). This consciousness is a token of the individual's relation to the eternal sphere. Nonetheless, it marks the distance from eternal blessedness, but in this distance the constitutive element is still the relation to eternal salvation (208).[44]

It is therefore possible to understand consciousness of guilt in immanent terms, while consciousness of sin, by which the individual subject also alters his identity, is something that has to be mediated from the transcendent (10:249-50):

> In the consciousness of sin, the individual becomes aware of himself in his difference from the universally human, which in itself is only an awareness of what it means to exist as a human being. Since the relation to that very historical event (God in time) is the condition for

43. On the relationship between suffering, guilt, and resignation, see further Lindström, *Stadiernas Teologi,* 273ff. On guilt, he writes aptly on how the consciousness of sin enables the subject to deepen his existence in the way that presents the largest possibilities for existence within the limits of immanence.

44. On this basis, we can also say with D. R. Law that "eternal happiness is the *terminus ad quem* of truth. That is, the goal towards which the individual is striving in his quest for the truth is that of acquiring an eternal happiness" (*Kierkegaard as Negative Theologian,* 100).

the consciousness of sin, this consciousness cannot have been there when this historical event had not occurred (10:250).

We can here see how Kierkegaard uses an element from Christian thought in a way that would seem alien to any kind of flexible, postmodern thought. Guilt is a normative notion for how the self is constituted; it is thus also something indispensable, something that should not and cannot be overcome, according to Kierkegaard.[45] Hence the very way Kierkegaard describes the subject and the categories he uses are clearly delineated by a framework where traditional Christian religion still provides the determining interpretation of the self.

To exist also means to know that one is living in untruth, that is, in a state where one has not yet reached one's destiny. At the same time, to relate subjectively to the destiny revealed in Christ also has to do with truth. Exactly the fact that the objectively uncertain is the highest truth for an existing individual shows the double character or the subject's character that Kierkegaard establishes in order to develop his understanding of religion and subjectivity. What is objectively uncertain is acknowledged as such. At the same time, the way the subject relates to this shows to what extent this counts as true for her. She can relate passionately, and thus truly, to this.

This does not, however, exclude the acknowledged uncertainty. Quite the contrary, it opens up for the absurdity of faith. "Det Absurde er netop ved det objektive Frastød Troens Kraftmaaler i Inderlighed" ("It is by way of objective offense that the absurd can measure the power of faith in inwardness"; 9:176). To try to exclude this absurdity by attempting to develop securing reflections on the objective element in faith, and thus to relate by approximations to objective insecurity in order to calculate the risks (ibid.), is an attempt to let go of this double relation that the subject exists in. Any such attempt changes Christianity from being the life and the development of a subject to a collection of doctrines (9:179-80). The more emphasis on objectivity (and thus attempts to secure), the less passion, and the less faith and concern for oneself (9:175).

---

45. A typical statement that shows how he is at odds with postmodern thought in this respect is: as a human subject one can be both good and evil, but one cannot become — at the same time — both good and evil (10:110).

Decontextualized Individuality

Let us take two steps back and try to reflect on what this means. It seems to be a tacit element in Kierkegaard's thinking that he wants to maintain the insecure or unstable status of both the subject and religion as we face them on modernity's terms. The subject is conceived as mastering neither herself nor the world fully. Furthermore, religion is not conceived appropriately if it can be secured by the results of human rationality. This is easily recognizable as one of the elements in Kierkegaard's thinking that anticipates postmodern modes of thought.

In this, Kierkegaard affirms an emphasis on subjectivity, but he also stresses that religion is founded on grounds that cannot be taken for granted, but must be reappropriated. He still maintains, however, the historical element in religion, as there is no attempt to try to escape into metaphysics or universal rational reasons for becoming or being a believer.

We should note one more thing here, which is important if we compare Kierkegaard with Lessing. In Lessing the background for adhering to a specific religious belief is partly due to contingent historical circumstances. Whether one becomes a Muslim or a Christian depends on where one lives and one's cultural, local, and historical context. Consequently, for Lessing there is no point in stressing the differences between different religions, or the uniqueness of one of them. Lessing's perception of the contextual element in religion makes him sensitive to its relativity. This is not at all the case with Kierkegaard. His main and full emphasis is on the subject — and this subject is decontextualized, that is, thought of in isolation from her historical and social setting. Consequently, Kierkegaard scorns any kind of "Kulturkristendom" — a type of Christianity based on some common cultural form. Such forms of Christianity remove the task, challenge, and insecurity with which the subject has to live in order to live passionately in truth. Faith is worthless for Kierkegaard without the passion generated by the insecurity and the individuality brought forth by the paradox. Hence we see how he wants to stress the conditions of a personal and individual mode of existence as a basic and critical point of departure over against any kind of abstract speculation (see 10:9-12).

The conscious, deliberate task of existing in one's individual mode is, however, a difficult challenge to meet. It must be undertaken in its concrete and personal form, since any abstraction from the personal and existential makes the whole task disappear (see 10:15). As we saw above, Kierkegaard can also describe this as the ethical task of the individual. Ethical existence is infinitely interested in how to live, while the contrasted aesthetic mode is marked by a corresponding lack of interest with regard to such issues (10:85).

Ethical "happiness" is the absolute telos that totally reshapes the individual — nothing is excepted from this reshaping. The absoluteness of this struggle can be seen in that there is nothing that the individual would not give up for its sake (10:88). Here the absolute and the concrete (including the ethical) merge.

The challenge or demand for an existential relation to the absolute starts the individual's development. Kierkegaard here uses the word *bevægelse,* "motion." This motion is generated by the link to the eternal. More than this, however, it is the eternal in its concrete form in the life of the individual. In the passionate anticipation of the eternal, the individual partakes in the truth. On this basis what Kierkegaard means with his famous statement that subjectivity is truth becomes more comprehensible. Subjectivity is truth through partaking in this eternity, which is mediated by the presence of God in history (see 10:19). Now, it becomes clear why and how existence, that is, individual concrete *self*-fulfillment, has to be a person's prime interest. It is in and by this mode of existing *(sic)* that reality is disclosed as the challenge for the individual — the ethical challenge (10:21). "The only reality there is for an existing person is his own ethical (reality); all other reality he only has knowledge about, but genuine knowledge is a translation into possibility" (10:22). Since the existing individual is infinitely interested in her own existence, this possibility interests her more than everything else. By being thus interested, she becomes real, and in this sense we can talk of the disclosure of reality. On the other hand, a speculative or abstract way of relating to truth only considers the content of knowledge as one possible reality, and is correspondingly less interested in translating it into personal existence.

Consequently, faith shows itself in an interest in a reality that is not one's own. In this, there is a difference from the ethical, since in the ethical sphere one is primarily interested in oneself (10:28). But there is a common core between the religious and the ethical in the subjective quality of being interested (29). From this framework of understanding, it becomes clear what Kierkegaard considers to be the "core" of faith. This core can be described as:

- The reality of the other.
- Not a doctrine (as a basis of intellectual, knowledge-based relationship).
- Not a teacher who teaches a doctrine (as this would again make the doctrine the most important concern).
- The reality of the Teacher, including the affirmation of the existence of the Teacher. This includes the passionate affirmation of God existing as an individual human being, as an existing human being, and not as something abstract and speculative that can be understood and made intelligible by common reason.

The object of faith is therefore God's actuality in the sense of existence. But to exist means, first and foremost, to be a particular individual, and this is why thinking must disregard existence, because the particular cannot be thought, but only the universal. The object of faith, then, is the actuality of God in existence, that is, that God has existed as an individual human being (10:31).

Accordingly, faith must be understood as a sphere or dimension in the subject that is constituted by the relationship to a sphere or dimension defined by faith. Since faith relates to and confirms the reality of the Teacher, this reality is prior to any form of reflective doctrine (10:31). Faith is first and foremost a relation to the communication of the mode of existence provided by the Teacher, a communication that cannot be separated from the Teacher himself (10:76; see above).

I think this is an important element if we are to understand what Kierkegaard means when he says that subjectivity is truth, and links this to the statement that subjectivity is reality (10:45). The previous discussion has been directed toward the importance of showing how the existing thinker must be understood in her difference from the abstract speculation that has no subject. Subjectivity and reality are linked, because they disclose a mode of reality that is unattainable to any kind of subject-free speculation about the mere possibilities of existence.

The statement that Christianity is not a doctrine but a communication or mediation of a mode of existence should not be taken as a direct negation of the doctrinal content in Christianity. It does have such a content, but this content is mainly related to personal and individual existence, not to what can be spelled out in paragraphs resulting from mere speculative thought (10:76).

The best way to understand Kierkegaard's relation to Christian doctrine is perhaps to compare his position with Schleiermacher's. In Schleiermacher's opinion, doctrine is secondary to the religious subject's self-consciousness. It is this that forms the basic dimension of faith.[46] Hence the primary movement is from faith to doctrine, and any attempt to go from doctrine to faith neglects this basic constitutional element of religion in subjectivity.

In many ways, this seems to underscore how Kierkegaard develops an understanding of Christianity that is mainly based on inward-directed subjectivity (see 10:78). Thus he not only stresses the paradoxical, but also the difficult or tough task of becoming a Christian (80, et passim). To become a Christian one then not only has to relate to specific circumstances in history in a specific way, but is also challenged to relate in a specific and self-reflective way toward oneself. In this inwardness, the individual expresses her relations to herself *in God*, and this must be seen as a mode of self-reflection of the subject that constitutes religious subjectivity (see 10:124).

Since God is the absolute other, adoration is the most adequate relation to him, because this expresses and maintains the difference between God and human (10:104). This way of formulating the relationship is interesting because we can see in it how Kierkegaard finds a subjective quality that does not mediate God into the human sphere of rationality, but lets God be God. Adoration consists also in passion, in being interested, and in the recognition of (God's) otherness.

To give God adoration is an appropriate way to relate to the absolute. Kierkegaard can say that the task for the human being is to relate in an absolute way to the absolute and to relate in a relative way to the relative (10:112, 119). Adoration is the mode in which this is done. This once more stresses that the human task is not theoretical but practical. It is characterized by forsaking the relative in order to relate to the absolute (10:120). Hence to act religiously and to struggle for this relation also mean to suffer (10:120). Suffering implies letting go of the immediate and the relative of this world. To live accordingly becomes a quest of overcoming immediacy — because the worldview of immediacy is related to happiness (10:121).

However, this is not a question of seeking or provoking suffering.

---

46. See *Der christliche Glaube*, §3.

The religious individual need not, and should not, search for suffering in order to secure or confirm her worldview. Rather, it is a question of realizing that one exists in a state of suffering, religiously speaking (124), that is, one exists in untruth.

Suffering seems, for Kierkegaard, to be a distinctive and continuous element in the life of the religious subject. It is a permanent state of existence (10:131). He can thus also describe suffering as dying away from immediacy (10:146, 163). Since this suffering is marked by its inwardness, however, it has a permanent mode that need not always express itself in exterior forms (10:177). Hence the ordinary life of a religious person can seemingly be identical with the life of anyone else. The difference, however, is to be found in the reflexivity of the person — a reflexivity that mediates the relation to the absolute telos in and through the ordinary life.

Kierkegaard describes how the subject proceeds on the way inward in a manner that mainly serves the purpose of defining the function of religion in how it constitutes the self or a certain mode of subjectivity. This formative, or even disciplinary, function is without doubt very important. But it also has its costs: both historical and doctrinal elements are overshadowed and play a secondary role. Still, his reconstruction of religion and subjectivity on this basis cannot totally do away with or simply ignore these elements. What he states would be nonsense without the information provided by the historical knowledge of the foundation of Christianity (see above).

Different Modes of Religious Subjectivity

As is well known, in his *Concluding Unscientific Postscript* Kierkegaard distinguishes between two types of religiosity, A and B. I will not discuss this in detail, but will just take up the elements in this distinction that prove to be most important for the development of our topic.

Being dialectical and paradoxical, that is, being based on something external to the subject (10:225), marks the specific type of Christianity (religiosity B). Religiosity A, a less specific mode of religiosity, is marked by being directed inward, but in this mode the relation to the individual's eternal blessedness is not conditioned by something specific. By contrast, what characterizes the Christian mode of religiosity is exactly that something outside the subject offers the determining condition for acquiring this blessedness; accordingly, an important question is how to appropriate this. This appropriation does not take place by way of reflection or thought, but by using the paradox contained by the God in history as a motivation toward a passionate existence (10:225). Correspondingly, this type of religiosity is, as we have already seen, related primarily to the communication of a mode of existence, more than consisting in the adherence to a specific type of doctrine (10:226). In Christianity, however, this is linked to facing God as the other.

From this, we can also see more clearly how Kierkegaard defines the paradox of Christianity in its relation to us. In religiosity A, we find a rather unqualified relation to the eternal. In religiosity B, however, we find a relation to eternity that is mediated through time — because we here find a subject that relates herself to an eternal person that exists in time. Hence the mere relation itself is defined and established within the horizon of time. This is contrary to all thought and is therefore a paradox (10:237).

The main point here seems to be that for the paradox-based form of religiosity (B), there is no immanent point of departure for the individual's faith. "Immanent" here means that which can count as reasonable on the basis of the capacities of the subject alone. The point of departure for faith is not in some kind of common humanity, but in a revelation in time that has its origin outside time (239). This differs from Lessing.

In one respect, however, one can say that Kierkegaard follows the Enlightenment trend of defining religious content more in terms of practice than of doctrine. But both his insistence of the reflexive or dialectical mode of religious life and his reluctance to define religion in terms of morality show that he does not follow this path all the way. He seems to think more in the vein of Schleiermacher, who struggled to maintain distinctive room for religion in the human sphere.[47]

Another element that is easily identified in Kierkegaard is the romantic insistence on passion. The passionate seems to form a device for keeping the subject "on the right track" in her continuous development. To the extent that the historical content of Christianity still matters, it is

---

47. See Schleiermacher's position as it is spelled out in *Reden über die Religion*, Rede 2.

defined in terms of providing us with categories such as "the paradox" or even "the absurd." Kierkegaard makes a virtue out of this, in order to keep the subject clear of all merely historical foundations of her mode of existence. One could then perhaps say that Kierkegaard actually follows Lessing in making the subjective, not the historical and objective, the most important (but not basic, in terms of origin) point of departure for developing a mature religious subjectivity. Unlike Lessing, however, the subjective in Kierkegaard is not countered by any insistence on the common human rationality or natural religiosity.

The paradoxical mode of being a Christian in Kierkegaard is consequently addressed as living in faith, without any reasonable ground. The Christian uses her reason in order to make sure that she believes against reason (10:235). In using her capacities for reason, however, the subject is still able to distinguish between pure nonsense and what is incomprehensible. It is toward the incomprehensible that the believer relates in faith, against reason (10:236).

Religiosity B is polemical against any other, alternative condition for salvation than the one offered by God in time. Here as well Kierkegaard makes a virtue of that which is perceived by Lessing as a problem: that only that which is given in time can be a basis for eternal salvation.

To be a Christian is to live in such a transparent manner that one cannot condone the aesthetic dialectic of existence, which lets the individual be for others in a different way or mode than he is for himself (10:275). Accordingly, there is a kind of integrity in being a Christian that does not exclude reflectiveness or irony, but at the same time the Christian mode of existence seems to exclude a fully aesthetic mode of existence. Hence we are now challenged to look a little bit more into what Kierkegaard thinks of the problems connected to the aesthetic and ethical modes of existence.

As is well known, the three basically possible modes of existence are described by Kierkegaard as the aesthetic, ethical, and religious stages. We have already dealt to some extent with different ways of establishing the religious mode. The reason Kierkegaard excludes metaphysics from this list is that no human being exists metaphysically. Metaphysical modes of life show themselves only in abstraction from the concrete mode of existence (8:266).

The aesthetic form is marked by *immediacy*. Hence a typical statement by the aesthete is that "a love affair is always threatened by the third party, namely, reflection!" (7:35). The immediacy of the aesthetic attitude expresses itself in the categorical imperative he sets for his life: "Enjoy!" This attitude relates to what is, not to what should or could be (7:68).

However, the uncommitted life of the aesthete is also characterized by despair, by lack of continuity (see above). The only way to overcome this is to leap into a more committed form of life, where one has to stand for something specific, and take up the responsibilities that life offers. Kierkegaard writes: "Falling in love is marked by immediacy, marriage by reflection and decision" (7:93), thereby making us attentive to the difference between the aesthetic and the ethical.

Ethically speaking, the individual has his telos in himself (3:252-53). It is a concrete telos, related to the individual's own life. The ethical is marked by a demand. This demand, however, is so strong or absolute that it always leaves the individual in a state of bankruptcy. Hence the ethical stage is a stage of transit, where the highest expression is regret, as a negative action (8:266). Correspondingly, the religious stage is the stage of fulfillment, where the regret has "made infinite place for the possibility of lying at seventy thousand fathoms and still being happy" (8:267). In the development from the ethical to the religious stage, the subject has to take fully into account the need for a double relationship to himself. He can and must resign himself, but in this resignation (which is, I would add, provided by self-reflection), he at the same time opens up to a new form of existence, which is not based on what he is in himself, but on what he relates to in terms of his existence.

Kierkegaard deepens the description of religious self-reflection in *Sickness unto Death*, where self-relation is essentially defined in relation to despair — a despair that comes into being because there is no reconciled relation between what the subject is and what he is not. The basic definition of the sickness unto death is itself spelled out in terms of subjectivity, that is, the self-relation. This sickness is due to

- despair over not being conscious of having a self,
- desperately not wanting to be oneself,
- desperately wanting to be oneself (see 15:73).

The second of these options, not wanting to be oneself, is described elsewhere in Kierkegaard's work as the aesthetic mode of existence. But the first form is also tacit in this mode of life. We can read this interpretation of the aesthetic mode of life in the papers of B in *Either — Or;* the outcome of this life is — exactly — despair (3:191). Kierkegaard can also say that immediacy has no self, it cannot recognize itself. Neither does it know itself (15:109).

This corresponds well to what we find in *Either — Or.* We face in the first part of this work a person who lacks any lasting commitment, any substance. He is moved by his impulses and sudden ideas and fantasies, and creates reality as he likes. There is no religious dimension in this life. What is lacking here in not only a commitment, but also a life project. But in order to establish such a project, immediacy has to be overcome. As an option for developing this, the ethical way of existing presents itself. But as we saw, this is a transitory life stage on the way toward a fully developed religious subjectivity.

In the development of religious subjectivity, the notion of God has a special function. Once the notion of God enters, sin becomes the defining way of stating despair: either to be one's self desperately (against God) or to not be one's [true] self (also against God) (15:131, 148; my comment in square brackets). This corresponds well to what I have already said above about the transcendent basis of sin. Hence Kierkegaard can, in good Reformation terms, state that the opposite of faith is sin (15:136), as faith is that which lifts the subject outside himself, and relates him to something other than himself in which he can be confident and put his trust. Accordingly, the central issue in Christianity is the consciousness of existing before God *(coram Deo)* (15:138). One could say that this is the point of departure for Kierkegaard's development of reflections concerning religious and Christian subjectivity.

In *Sickness unto Death,* Kierkegaard also defines the spirit as the self. Spirit is the self, and the self exists only when it is aware of its own existence, and hence is able to relate to itself (15:73). When despair is rooted out, the situation of the subject is the following: to relate to itself, and in wanting to be itself, the self has to relate to, or ground itself in, the power that lets it become what it is (15:74). This power is apparently God. Hence God constitutes the subject as spirit, as he makes it possible for the subject to relate to his true self, that is, a self unmarked by the inherent tension of existence described above (i.e., not wanting to be oneself). Kierkegaard can, in full accordance with what is said above, describe this relation to the power of God as *faith* (15:180).

As faith is basically a relation to God in time, that is, to Christ, Kierkegaard can also say that "Christ" is only accessible by faith — not by mere historical reasoning (16:36). Christ helps the human to become his own self and live in truth. To be a self is thus to have a choice for oneself, to have *freedom* (16:155).[48] This freedom is not unconstrained, but is fully realized only in the subjectivity of the individual. Kierkegaard says that the person has a kind of double existence, determined externally by history, but internally still free and self-determining (3:165). If we are to understand this theologically, it must imply that the historical conditions of Christianity that determine the subject release his subjectively based freedom. In other words, God becomes the condition for human freedom.

In *The Concept of Dread* Kierkegaard appropriates the traditional doctrine of sin and, by way of his understanding of the individual's existence, develops how Christianity, also through its doctrine of sin, contributes to shaping the individual's concrete life form and subjectivity. Of special importance is how he says that dread *(Angst)* expresses the possibility of freedom (6:234) and, related to and shaped by faith, contributes to the formation of the subject. Hence it reflects the self-relation of the subject in terms of the possibilities of his freedom. Correspondingly, there is a close connection between dread and sin, as sin implies failure to become oneself. Angst can also be the angst of becoming a self.

Conclusion: Religion and the Quest for Self-Formation — a Postmodern Interpretation

I now try to sum up and conclude this analysis of Kierkegaard by asking how it has contributed to our understanding of how he reconstructs religion on modern terms while anticipating some issues that are relevant in the postmodern context.

I have hinted several times that it is possible to interpret Kierkegaard's religious understanding of the self in two different ways. An understanding of the self could either be developed from the perspective of an immanent teleology (as in Socrates, the ethical person, or religi-

---

48. The religious implications of this freedom are described more in detail in *Concept of Dread.*

121

osity A), or from the perspective of a transcendent teleology (religiosity B).[49] In the first instance, the self develops itself on the basis of that which is inherent in it; while in the second case, the self develops on the basis of that which is offered it by confronting God in history. Here God is seen as the one who overcomes the limitations of the self and offers new, not immediately accessible conditions for self-fulfillment.[50]

The problem with religiosity A (the immanent form) is twofold:

a. It is based on an assumption that the individual possesses the conditions necessary for a relationship to the eternal and the relationship both toward God and the truth that it entails (in our context, this would be a likely description of Lessing's position, although it is more frequently used as a description of the Socratic position in Kierkegaard).[51]

b. It seems to empty history, time, and what happens there of any importance in terms of what is of interest for the subject.[52]

In religiosity B the individual has to live with the uncertainty that is inherent in the paradox of the object of faith. As Law puts it, uncertainty is the mechanism by which an individual's faith is both

49. For the use of the distinction between immanent and transcendent teleology in this way see H. Schultz, *Eschatologische Identität*, 245ff., 402ff.

50. See Kellenberger, *Kierkegaard and Nietzsche*, 9, who points out how faith in God, religious faith, for Kierkegaard completes us as human beings and fulfills the potential our lives have for meaningfulness. As we shall see in our discussion of Nietzsche below, it is exactly this relation between self-fulfillment and the meaningfulness of life that is not recognized in him, and makes it hard to realize how he can see self-fulfillment as a meaningful project at all. This anthropological reconstruction of religion in Kierkegaard is perhaps most clearly expressed in Sløk's reformulation of his position in *Sickness unto Death:* "What finally makes the human being human, and an individual, and what makes human existence a serious matter, is God as the measure of humanity, and God as the measure of humanity is the final and decisive deepening of human self-consciousness" (*Anthropologie,* 102).

51. See 10:240.

52. This is a point that Kierkegaard elaborated already in *Philosophical Fragments,* and he restates it in *Concluding Unscientific Postscript,* 9:25 n. 1: "Christianity is something historical . . . and will exactly as historical have a decisive impact on one's eternal bliss." See 10:255, where Kierkegaard affirms how one has to become a Christian *in time;* hence the existence in time, in a certain instant, related to God in time (10:250) is important for the constitution of a truly Christian subject.

sustained and deepened.[53] This is an interesting position, as it is an interpretation of something we can today see as an element related not only to Christian faith but also to knowledge in general. Uncertainty places before all of us the choice as to on which grounds we are to live our lives, and there is no final answer to this question. Kierkegaard uses this insight, however, in order to show how this uncertainty, contained in what constitutes the "object" of Christian faith, can contribute to the development of a more reflective and pious subjectivity. In order to relate to this objective uncertainty, however, some elements in human life experience enable religion to contribute to human self-development.

Despair is the common human experience that opens us up to the realization that something outside us is needed in order to mature and develop. Human despair, and the self-relation inherent in that despair, lead to the insight that we cannot become what we are meant to be only by our own capacities. This experience arises out of the human condition itself, and is the framework for what makes the religious task utterly meaningful — and permanent[54] — for the subject.[55]

Hence one can talk about a coincidence in the task set forward by religion and by the modern agenda in Kierkegaard. They are both directed toward making the subject become a subject. Hence they aim at developing a free, self-determining, and autonomous individual. This is a telos that, for Kierkegaard, is only possible to achieve through the appropriation of the historical conditions offered by God in time (Jesus Christ). The paradox here is that human freedom thus seems to be conditioned by something external to the human being, and only by entering into a specific relation that appropriates what is offered by and through this relation. Thus it seems correct to say with Joachim Ringleben that religious objectivity only as subjectively appropriated is what it is, and that the appropriation of religious content also expresses the constructive mode of the subject, in which it appears as religious. On this background we can see the active and constructive appropriation as the way in which

53. Law, *Kierkegaard as Negative Theologian*, 159.

54. This permanence is stated by J. Ringleben, *Aneignung*, 109, where he points to how this must be understood as a lifelong process.

55. W. Schulz summarizes this: "Becoming a human self as a concrete, existing individual . . . becomes the essential and only theme of interest for Kierkegaard as a thinker" (*Philosophie in der veränderten Welt*, 277).

the religious subject is able to handle and make the religious objectivity her own.[56]

Ringleben indicates two points here that should be noted. First, he affirms that religion receives its proper role only by the function it has for the subject, and has no meaning whatsoever in terms of the mere stating of some kind of historical information. Hence the affirmation of the necessity of appropriation of traditional content serves as a means for giving religion this function. It is by being appropriated that religion reaches its aim. Ringleben thereby also confirms the importance of this appropriation as a central factor in the development of religious subjectivity. This appropriation can thus also be seen as a function of the heretical imperative noted above.

Moreover, this appropriation is also important in terms of freedom.[57] It is through this appropriation that the subject overcomes the heteronomy of traditionalism or dogmatism and integrates and forms (configures) traditional content in a way that makes it her own, through her own reconstruction. This personal acquisition of religious content neither makes religion purely subjective nor pushes it into the dimension of objective dogmatism: the process itself develops the result, which lets the content appear as something that is truly the subject's own. Hence the "subjective way" is essential for how one relates to the results of this appropriation. It is by means of this appropriation that the subject is able to enter into the reality, within which the result has true meaning for her.[58]

Hence we are not only faced with the affirmation of insight into the way as the goal, and the necessity of acquiring religious content in this way in order to maintain freedom and avoid heteronomy. Here is also a radical insight into the processlike character and the provisional in the religious mode of existence. The truth is the way, Kierkegaard states (16:196). This affirms the insight formulated and reworked in our present, postmodern cultural context that the subject is vulnerable, fragile, in a process of change, becoming, and potential despair (we ignore here how a postmodern approach tends to dissolve the idea of truth). Hence there

56. See Ringleben, *Aneignung*, 99.

57. In Ringleben's words: "Successful appropriation is thus also the success of freedom" (ibid., 122).

58. Ibid., 106.

is no fixed point, no position where the individual can be said to be already at the goal of her quest. Simultaneously, this makes the historical present of the individual the main object of her quest, since it is the present, personal, and individual acquisition in her own life that is in question, not some distant past in and for itself.[59]

In other words, what Kierkegaard does make clear is how the self or subject by way of the resources of religion is able to enter into a relationship with herself that is not immediately given by way of some immanent teleology or inherent substance or essence. But religion does not work without conditions in the subject. As he shows in *Concept of Dread*, anxiety discloses that the subject is not a self, and that there is something that still remains in order to become a self.[60] Thus anxiety functions in the same manner as despair. It is a part of human experience that opens one up to an understanding of what religion can contribute to the subject.

Hence the subject cannot be understood as something already there, something fixed and finished. In his dissertation on Kierkegaard, Arne Grøn has developed this along several lines, which indicate how Kierkegaard, on certain conditions, can be said to anticipate the postmodern understanding of the subject as decentered. He says that when the subject in Kierkegaard must be perceived as decentered, this decentering implies an existence in relation to itself, that is, the subject is still outside herself, she is "also on the other side." To be a subject is thus problematic for the individual or, in other words, it means that one is aware of one's own double status of both being and becoming someone.[61] Moreover, the problem is to *become* a subject. This is possible only

---

59. See ibid., 130, et passim. This is also the condition for freedom, as the past here is not a heteronomous instance determining the subject, but something "taken up" in the life fulfillment of the subject. It is the objectifying mode of relating to the past that excludes the subjective appropriation that makes the subject's self-actualization possible. Only the fact that the subject is someone who is going to be someone makes this relation to the past understandable in religious terms.

60. This is underscored at several places in Grøn's works on Kierkegaard; see *Begrebet*, 52. See ibid., 76, where he points to how anxiety tears the individual apart from the context that she risks losing herself in. This consciousness of being other and more than what one is usually defined as is the consciousness of being a person. Hence anxiety opens one up to the experience of being a person.

61. See 15:87. Grøn describes this by saying that, as a self, the human being is on the way, becoming, even on the way to herself (*Begrebet*, 90).

if the individual overcomes the state in which she initially exists when confronted with this problem.[62]

Grøn also points out that the self or subject becomes aware of herself as a problem by becoming aware of, or conscious of, herself as an other. Hence he points to how it is not as a substance (immanent) but as a relation (to the transcendent) that the subject develops. Self-consciousness is conditioned by the possibility of experiencing oneself, and this experience opens one up to the possibility both of affirming or recognizing oneself, and of perceiving oneself as a problem.[63]

Grøn here points at two important elements. First, he shows how the subject must be understood as being basically receptive in her experience of herself. This receptivity becomes the basis for any kind of development of subjectivity. Hence the subject cannot be said to construct herself only on the basis of will or reason. Second, Kierkegaard here adds psychological depth to the understanding of subjectivity found in idealism. This contributes to the understanding of religion in this formation process as well. Religion makes thematic, articulates, and relates to how the subject exists in a mode of becoming, and the different modes of religious existence (religiosities A and B) are different ways of configuring this process. This is due to the fact that in the experience of being decentered, the individual also experiences herself as not "being her own master" — an experience that she receives (sic) through the attempt to be just that![64]

Hence the subject receives this negative experience through forms such as anxiety or despair. Through this experience she finds out that she is not what she wants to be, and it is this experience that is the phenomenological or personal and experiential basis for Kierkegaard's reconstruction of religion. Hence we see in Kierkegaard as well how he makes personal experience a basis for the reconstruction of religion and its functions. But as a Christian thinker in the Lutheran tradition, Kierkegaard maintains the insight that what is given in the individual by herself is not enough to provide the means for the development of a true subject, or to guarantee that she will develop along the lines wished for.

Kierkegaard's reconstruction of religion thus serves as a basis for how he approaches the subjective mode of existence in a way that

62. See Grøn, *Subjektivitet og Negativitet,* 51, 169, et passim.
63. See ibid., 70.
64. Ibid., 170, with reference to Kierkegaard, 15:123-24.

makes this, that is, the changing character of existence, the inherent vulnerability[65] of it, and its decentered character, transparent. At the same time, he affirms both the productive (constructive) as well as the receptive side of the subject in her relation to positively given religious content.

On this background, Kierkegaard's much-noted critique of immediate communication of existential truth is highlighted not only as a consequence of the necessity of a personal appropriation, but also as an affirmation of the processlike fashion of the same.[66] The problem of communication is thus also related to the open-ended character of existence, which excludes any kind of systematic formulation of existential truth.[67]

We now have a background for understanding Kierkegaard's reconstruction of religion. The *framework* of the understanding of the subject is either an immanent or an external teleology. The common *point of departure* for this reconstruction is the negative experiences that point to what the subject is not (anxiety, despair, etc.). The *form* most adequate for stating a religious position is that of irony (mediateness). Religious *experience* is then, in Kierkegaard, nothing other than the subjective reworking of the self, facing all life's challenges. Ringleben formulates this in the following statement: "Religious experience as 'the work of devotion' — that is not only the short-term for the theme of 'receptivity and constructivity,' it also places the concept of experience in relation to a central motif in Kierkegaard."[68] Hence experience also becomes the foundational basis for Kierkegaard in his reconstruction of religion. Experience represents the unavoidable authority of reality, it is immediate and personal, and it confronts the subject with elements that are new and repre-

---

65. Grøn states in the conclusion of his dissertation that the fact that the human being in her innermost self is vulnerable, exposed, is the deepest reality of the human being, and it is by means of this possibility that human subjectivity must be understood (*Subjektivitet,* 416).

66. E.g., Hannay, *Kierkegaard,* 57: "By transferring ownership of the works and their prefaces to fictitious authors Kierkegaard has acquired a combination, so to speak, of the reporter's freedom from having to answer personally for the views he passes on, and of the fiction-writer's freedom to create the persons (and perspectives) of whom (and which) the views are expressions. The advantages of this for someone who wants the views to take effect without consideration of their author's real intentions are obvious."

67. See ibid., 146.

68. Ringleben, *Aneignung,* 435.

sents something other than that which is already given in the subject's established sphere.[69] In addition, experience has an "objective" or external side that makes the truths of experience, once appropriated, not merely subjective, in terms of having their origin only in the subject. Read on this background, the accusations against Kierkegaard for being a mere subjectivist are unsubstantiated.[70]

In other terms, religion contributes to the transparency of the subject, or better: constructs a more transparent subject, by the resources it provides for the development of inwardness *(Innerlichkeit)*.

Given this, it also becomes clear how and why Kierkegaard answers Lessing's question about Christianity's relation to history in the way he does. In *Practice in Christianity*, Kierkegaard states that for the subject in its relation to the absolute, there is only one mode of time: the present (16:70). Hence existence as a contemporary and appropriation of the religious "object" turn out to be two sides of the same coin: "The one who is not contemporary with the absolute, for him it (i.e., the absolute) does not exist" (ibid.). One can therefore say that this contemporary existence is the outcome of the appropriation of the conditions offered to the subject, since the subject cannot relate to herself in any other way than by living in the present, and making out of the absolute what it means for her in this presence. Hence Kierkegaard tries to solve Lessing's problem of the relation to the historical by introducing the notion of contemporaneous existence.[71]

It would be a mistake to say that Kierkegaard, in his reconstruction of religion, tries to make it easier or more accessible for "the man on the Copenhagen omnibus" to become or live as a Christian. Quite the contrary, he emphasizes how Christian existence always is on the threshold

69. See Ringleben's development of the different elements in experience, ibid., 442ff., which is very relevant for describing how experience and personal development are linked also to elements "outside" the subject's control, and hence something not only originating in or generated on the basis of what is given already. This is important in a comparison with Nietzsche, who reduces everything to the manifestations of the will to power. In this, Kierkegaard seems to have a much wider and much more appropriate concept of experience, and also of religious experience, than the one available to Nietzsche.

70. For the same conclusion see Law, *Kierkegaard as Negative Theologian*, 122-23; and Ringleben, *Aneignung*, passim.

71. See Law, *Kierkegaard as Negative Theologian*, 189.

of scandal or offense. Hence what he offers as a modern reconstruction is not an easy accommodation, but a sincere challenge for a subjectivity that realizes that something in life is more important than other things, that it is worth living for in spite of scandal, and cannot be taken lightly (see 16:110-11). It also involves, as I have indicated, the possibility of suffering (see 16:186).

Now, in closing this chapter, I just note that Kierkegaard's interpretation of the conditions of religion seems to have some concerns in common with Lessing, in terms of the discussion of the appropriation of historical content and its meaning for a religious position. At the same time, Kierkegaard is not totally alien to the problems that surface in the context of nihilism.[72] We shall see in the next chapter how Nietzsche also deals with these issues. Moreover, Kierkegaard takes a far more radical turn in describing positive religion's relation to, meaning for, and challenge to the subject. Thus he presents a radicalized reconstruction of Christianity that makes him an opponent to both the "liberal" position of Lessing and the radically negative position of Nietzsche.

72. To point this out is one of the important contributions of Gregor Malantschuk's research in Kierkegaard. See Malantschuk, *Frihedens problem i Kierkegaards Begrebet Angest.*

Chapter Four

NIETZSCHE

---

*The Deconstruction of Religion
as an Expression of Powerless and
Self-Deceptive Subjectivity*

Who Is Nietzsche — and Where Is He?

Nietzsche not only reconstructs religion on modern terms, but his construction also serves as a means for a more radical task: to deconstruct religion as a humanmade device to maintain our picture of reality, and to cope with it in the way we find best or most suitable for ourselves. Nietzsche relates to the conditions of modernity, but his main task is to overcome and criticize them. In his understanding, to overcome modernity and to overcome religion are two sides of the same coin. Hence he offers a different approach to religion in modernity than Lessing and Kierkegaard. He is probably the most articulate critic of modernity and of religion that we can find in the history if ideas. This alone is sufficient to include him in this book.

As with the other writers I investigate in this book, we must ask to what extent we can know, or be sure of, what Nietzsche means, what his opinions are. Although there is no "pseudonym" problem in Nietzsche, as in Kierkegaard and Lessing we cannot be quite sure that Nietzsche always stands behind his own texts, that he is willing to admit that what was once stated in his writings is still his own point of view. There are two reasons for this. The first is that Nietzsche changes his mind over time, and this affects what we can call his "writer subjectivity." The disseminating analytic critic he was in his first period as a writer is not quite the voice we meet when we read his last, more "prophetic" writings. There is, however, no reason for saying that Nietzsche simply contradicts himself; it is more as if he explores his project in different directions, using different voices. Hence he is also able to confirm the idea, common in postmodernity, that no position is given once and for all. He combines this idea with an affirmation of radical plurality and a sharp critique of the modern idea of subjectivity. In his recent book on Nietzsche and religion, Tyler T. Roberts expresses this well: "The dynamic of Nietzsche's thought is one that continually prevents us from holding too tightly to any perspective, any ideal, any meaning. Some of the most profound suffering in human life arises for Nietzsche precisely in confronting the fact that any definitive meaning of life continually escapes our grasp."[1] Hence Roberts indicates how this is not only an arbitrary trait in Nietzsche's mode of writing, but one linked tightly to his own ideas and method. The mask he wears as an author makes a change of perspectives possible — the author need not be identified with his text.[2]

The second reason is linked to the fact that Nietzsche admits that he sometimes "wears a mask," that is, he uses positions and figures of speech that are not necessarily his own, or that reflect all he has to say, in order to make some point or to explore some concern. This is why Nietzsche, like the two other writers, sometimes seems to evade capture. His thoughts are hard to integrate into one coherent system. Just like the others, Nietzsche is no "Systemphilosoph" (systematic philosopher). He is difficult to synthesize.

Nietzsche's self-understanding in regard to the problem discussed here can perhaps be best identified in some passages from *Beyond Good and Evil*. There he states that every deep spirit needs and makes use of a mask. To develop such a mask need not be an act of conscious purpose for the one wearing it, but Nietzsche seems to think that this is usually the case. But why the mask? He explains his reasons for this in a vein similar to Kierkegaard in his dissertation on irony. The mask develops due to the social position of the deep spirit. He is constantly exposed to a pic-

---

1. T. T. Roberts, *Contesting Spirit: Nietzsche, Affirmation, Religion*, 14.
2. See the same point expressed in Foucault's essay "What Is an Author?" in *Foucault Reader*.

ture of himself (a mask) that is developed by others, a growing mask that surrounds him, because others (his friends) understand his words in a superficial manner and interpret wrongly every sign he gives.[3] But the spirit might have moved on from where they think they see him.

By the metaphor of the mask Nietzsche indicates that he knows that any coherent understanding of him — what he says and does — is in danger of missing the point, and does so. Thus it is not possible to obtain access to the depth, to the real person who is a deep spirit, who remains hidden. In a later aphorism in the same book, Nietzsche expressed his skepticism toward the possibility of achieving such access: "The hermit does not believe that any philosopher . . . expressed his real and final opinions in books. Does one not write books in order to conceal what one harbors? Indeed, he will doubt whether a philosopher could possibly have any final and real opinions."[4] Here Nietzsche seems to question the possibility of giving any final grounds for a statement, and indicates that the philosopher must always go on searching. That is why every philosophy also conceals another philosophy. "Every philosophy also *conceals* a philosophy, every opinion is also a hideout, every word also a mask."[5]

As we shall see later, this way of understanding the results of philosophical reflection is closely linked to Nietzsche's understanding of the relation between language and reality. Words can never be an adequate expression of what is. The world itself "moves" on while words remain stiff and static. Consequently, words, language, present us with a problem not only in terms of communication but also in terms of how we relate to and understand the world.

If we read these statements as something that also provides us with some elements of Nietzsche's self-understanding, we need to comment on at least two implications of this. First, it is important to note that he makes use of the differentiation between appearance and depth (or language and reality) — a distinction that is also important for stating his critique of religion and religious subjectivity. We should, however, also be aware that he often criticizes the reasons behind these distinctions, although they are necessary in order to develop and express his tools of critique.

---

3. See *Jenseits Gut und Böse*, §40 (*Kritische Studienausgabe* [hereafter: KSA] 5:57-58).
4. Ibid., §289 (KSA 5:234).
5. Ibid.

Second, as the mask is socially conditioned, Nietzsche seems by way of this metaphor to offer a critique that breaks down the assertion that there are any possibilities of real communication in terms of stating things "of depth." This is an inherent contradiction in much postmodern theory as well, which challenges strongly the possibilities of real communication. Thus Nietzsche here seems to state that he does not have any secured conditions for communicating what he communicates or for making sure that it is understood. This pragmatic self-contradiction contains a paradox that also blurs the conditions for a critical discussion of Nietzsche, who he is and what he really states. Nietzsche lacks the notion of indirect communication found in Kierkegaard, but much of what he writes can fruitfully be read in the same vein as Kierkegaard, that is, as challenges to develop our own, authentic understanding of the subjects treated and criticized.[6]

As a conclusion to the question posed in the heading of this section, we can say that Nietzsche is, and is not, where his texts guide us.[7] We cannot be sure that any text says all there is to say about the subject treated, and we should always look for other angles and points of view. We need not, however, assume that this fills his work with contradictions that present us with many unsolved riddles. Most of what he writes can be seen as explorations of different modes of critique; his work is, like Lessing's, more a critique than the development of a single coherent system or position. In this critique, however, it is still possible to reconstruct some main features of how he — as a critic — understands religion and religious subjectivity. Hence behind the mask there is a constant project of erosion that in our context can be interpreted as a perpetual striving to deconstruct all the positive reasons for the construction of a positive understanding of religion in the modern world.[8]

6. A third comment, here only to be stated in a footnote, is that this can also be seen as Nietzsche's attempt to explain to himself and others why his work did not receive the attention and lead to the kind of debate that he had expected. The statements about the "deep spirit" are then about a mistaken and disregarded writer who is still convinced about his own greatness.

7. This is a point that Walter Kaufmann makes often in his book, *Nietzsche: Philosoph, Psychologe, Antichrist*, e.g., 492-93.

8. See Roberts, *Contesting Spirit*, 96: "Nietzsche's genealogies, whether historically accurate or not, serve as vehicles for imagining different possibilities to the extent that they defamiliarize and open to reconstruction concepts and values we think we know so

Thus Nietzsche's critical approach to the thematic of religion is intimately linked to his views on many other traditional philosophical subjects. This means that he is critically directed not only toward religion but more generally toward the mode of thinking that provides means and reasons for relating religiously or metaphysically to reality. This implies that when we examine his critique of religion, we find a deep and thoroughgoing critique of many elements that are usually counted as the content of the Western tradition of thought. Nietzsche's critique of religion can thus be seen as an expression of his general philosophy and understood in the light of his critical approach to other issues as well.[9] In her book on Nietzsche, Margot Fleischer says:

> Nietzsche's critique of metaphysics is not only directed against one philosophical discipline among others, and not only against the form that Western philosophy has taken on since Plato, but also against the human self-understanding in the European tradition (to which Christianity has made an essential contribution). Already for that reason is it closely linked to Nietzsche's critique of morality.[10]

Critique of Language as a Constituting Element of Subjectivity

Nietzsche is critical toward any understanding of the subject as an autonomous entity constituting itself through means with a rational character. In this, he is a clear antithesis to Lessing. In an aphorism in *Beyond Good and Evil*, Nietzsche suggests that there is perhaps no other reality than that given by our drives, passions, and desires. If this is so, thought must be understood as being generated from how these drives relate to each other. On this basis, he asks if this is not enough to understand the so-called material world and our relation to it. This would have as a consequence that we need to ask critically to what extent our will really has

---

well. To think with Nietzsche is not only to render philosophical judgments about the validity of his methods, but to find ways to think differently about self, community, and history."

9. This thesis I have developed more extensively in my revised and published M.Phil. thesis, *Religion og vilje til makt (Religion and the Will to Power)*.

10. Fleischer, *Der Sinn der Erde und der Entzäuberung des Übermenschen*, 8.

an effect and can function as a cause of events. Finally, he challenges us to consider if we can understand the totality of the life of the passions and drives as differentiated expressions of one thing, that is, *the will to power:*

> Suppose that all organic forms could be traced back to this will to power and that one could find in it also the solution to the problem of procreation and nourishment — it is *one* problem — then one would have established the right to determine all efficient force univocally as the will to power. The world viewed from inside, the world defined and described according to its "intelligible character," would be "will to power" and nothing else.[11]

There are several important elements in this quotation. First, this is one of the rare cases in his published work where Nietzsche actually uses the will to power as an explanation of human behavior, and identifies it as the basis for all other human passions or drives. Also, we find here a naturalistic approach to human behavior, where he attempts to explore the possibility of understanding human action using one principle only. That this must be read as an exploration in the more naturalistic vein is clear since he here grounds all action and behavior in human bodily functions, not in intellectual capacities. This hypothesis also leads to an understanding of the more rational faculties of the human as epiphenomena. They are based on, and are at root only expressions of, the naturally given instincts, drives, and passions. Hence Nietzsche can criticize any understanding of the human being as a rational subject that originates from rationality and thought because he can offer an alternative "explanation." He can also talk of the *Scheinexistenz* (chimerical existence) of the subject,[12] thereby indicating that he stands critically over against any attempt to make the function of subjectivity an autonomous and independent dimension in human life.

In Nietzsche the most developed strategy we find for dissolving the subject as an independent entity can perhaps be identified via his understanding of language. In order to relate in a reflexive way toward oneself, and thereby establish the kind of self-relation we call subjectivity, language seems crucial. Moreover, language is also a tool for the con-

11. *Jenseits Gut und Böse*, §36 (KSA 5:55).
12. Ibid., §54 (KSA 5:73).

struction of self-understanding and is essential for the social communication that establishes a distinct understanding of oneself as an individual person.

As already indicated, however, Nietzsche is highly critical toward the abilities of language to offer access to the truth of reality or to depict how things really are. His position has been aptly described as "semiotic nihilism."[13] We can find the reasons behind this characteristic in how Nietzsche refuses to understand language as either containing truth or offering a picture of reality. Consequently, he is skeptical toward any utterance whatsoever with regard to the extent to which it contains truth or should be understood at face value. This is not simply a kind of consequent skepticism: it is based in a deep and profound mistrust of the possibility of any authentic communication whatsoever.

Language is primarily a means for ruling, controlling, and shaping the world *(Weltbeherrschung)*. It serves as a means for ordering the chaotic reality that the human being is part of. In doing so, however, it immediately sets the subject and her understanding of the world apart from the world as it is "in itself." Language divides reality in two parts; it creates a position of relative stability and an illusion of endurance, from which one can relate to the world and maintain one's feeling of being in power and having control.[14]

Hence language is also the origin of metaphysics, because it serves to sustain the world of such stability and gives one access to another mode of relations toward the world than the immediate relationship. As language overcomes immediacy, it also sets other conditions for human existence and for human self-understanding than those offered by the immediate flux in which one finds oneself as an existent.

In his *Genealogy of Morals,* Nietzsche develops his understanding of how the subject must be understood in terms of its contextually given conditions, and how these conditions determine the subject's ability to perceive and relate to the world. Hence there is for him no "pure subject" of knowledge, with neither will nor pain, no one undetermined by the conditions of time. To make demands for this kind of subject is to de-

13. See I. Houmann, *Nihilismen,* 40, et passim.
14. "The significance of language for the development of culture consists in, that by means of it, the human being can pose a world of its own beside the other, a stance that he can cling onto so hard that he can shake the other world out of balance and make himself its master" (*Menschliches, Allzumenschliches,* 1:11 [KSA 2:30]).

mand that the subject give up her own power, her own perspectives and interests. Hence there is no objective approach to the world (and, I would add, toward religion):

> There exists *only* a view based on perspective, *only* an understanding from a perspective, and the more feelings we allow to express themselves on a specific issue, the more eyes, different eyes, we allow ourselves to see the same issue with, the more comprehensive becomes our notion of this issue, our "objectivity." To eliminate the will totally, and to place outside all the feelings, given that we could do that, would that not imply a *castration* of the intellect?[15]

Before commenting on the content of this quotation in relation to other aspects of Nietzsche's position, I note that he here seems to be in accord with Kierkegaard, at least superficially, because he emphasizes the personal framing of all knowledge, and how the passionate play of human interests is involved in the way we relate to the world. By doing this, he also makes a point out of how there is always a subjective element — a self-relation — involved, tacitly or expressively, in our relation to the world. Hence also in Nietzsche, objectivity seems to be at odds with the powers of life and self-development.

Another way of putting this is to say that to eliminate the will to power, lust, and emotion is to do away with that which makes up subjectivity. It represents an attempt to take away that which constitutes the subject's creative powers and its world relation and replace it with something that diminishes its power.

Reflecting on what this means for the understanding of religion, I note first that every kind of religion is linked to a symbolism and rites that depend on being communicated through language in order to make sense. As Nietzsche seems to criticize the very basis for any truth in such communication, he offers reasons for sustaining mistrust in religion as a container for truth or stable meaning.

Moreover, Nietzsche seems to offer a radical contradiction to Christianity in particular, since language, words, logos, and the self-expression of God here are understood as being intimately connected. "In the beginning was the Word, and the Word was with God, and the

---

15. *Zur Genealogie der Moral,* Third Essay, §12 (KSA 5:365).

Word was God" (John 1:1) is a statement Nietzsche flatly contradicts. For him the origin is the will to power, and language is the means of this will to power. Every kind of "divinization" of language is met with suspicion: they only represent new attempts to make divine what are merely tools of the subject in establishing herself and to make the tools for this establishment legitimate. We look further into this issue below.

Accordingly, Nietzsche seems to think that language is more a means for control than a means for acquiring knowledge. By establishing a world "in itself," language easily creates illusions. When human beings think that they control the world by means of language, it is nothing more than their own understanding of this world, as fixed in language, that they control. We cannot control the world through language, since the world is always developing and changing.

One can then easily see why language is important for the constitution of subjectivity. It gives the human being a sense of control, of subjecting the world to herself. But this is mere appearance. This subjectivity is an illusion, because what happens is not that the human "really" subjects the world to herself. What she controls is her own picture or construction of the world. This is usually neither acknowledged nor made transparent. The human being is not, in any way, aware that this is the case and seldom makes the reasons and interests behind this experience transparent to herself.

Not only the distinction between subject and object becomes blurred in this framework. It also becomes unclear to what extent we can talk about a subject at all. Since language no longer expresses reason, taken as the independent and transparent basis for action and understanding, but as a means of and an expression of the will to power, it is itself also an object. Hence what is usually seen as a constituting factor in human subjectivity "in reality" is not adequately understood as such.[16] There are things hidden behind it, which need to be uncovered in order to get a clearer grasp of what it means to be a "subject." Nietzsche's position here is structurally similar to that of Foucault, who admits that the subject *is* a subject, but in terms of being *subjected* to something else, and

16. The use of quotation marks here and in the surrounding text is, when it is not with explicit reference to Nietzsche's own text, in order to indicate that he is constantly questioning our use, and the conditions for our use, of such concepts as those put within the quotation marks.

thus as being created by forces not immediately apparent or transparent to itself. In the following, I try to elaborate this structure more extensively.

We cannot know the world as it is in itself. There seems to be no guaranteed correlation between language and reality in Nietzsche; hence all his statements about the world as will to power, and so on, are based on a paradox. Once one postulates anything about reality as something "outside" reason and language, this statement is about something *in* reason. We schematize the world with our concepts and words. The world does not exist without such schemas, but how we schematize depends on our will to power — what we want the world to be (see below). This is an important general point that Nietzsche also develops as a means for his critique of religious modes of relating to the world.

Nietzsche stresses how we need to develop language in new situations, if we would attempt to relate to the ever-changing reality that surrounds us. This also implies that "old" words need not contain any truth for us. Language cannot contain any lasting truth, but can hinder us in reaching for what we want. It becomes more and more an expression of prejudice as time goes by. When he writes "Each word is a prejudice,"[17] he indicates that sticking to a picture of reality in language when the world goes on only makes larger the difference between language and reality, and thereby makes the inadequacy of language, as well as the lack of truth in it, more apparent.

The limits of human understanding and the changing character and historicity in everything understood are not in themselves reasons for denying that there is understanding and knowledge at all. The point is more that there are no absolutes and no common measures in the understanding established. Hence we cannot assume that our reason gives us access to any eternal knowledge *(ewige Tatsachen)*. Moreover, our understanding does not establish a content that can be seen as permanent, as valid once and for all. In a late note from his *Nachlass* Nietzsche writes:

> The character of the becoming world as impossible to formulate, as "false," as "self-contradictory." *Understanding* and *becoming* exclude each other. Consequently, understanding must be something else: it

17. "Jedes Wort ist ein Vorurteil," *Der Wanderer und sein Schatten*, §55 (KSA 2:55).

must be preceded by a will to make understandable; a mode of becoming must create the delusion of being.[18]

Several implications from this need fleshing out. First, this means that language can suppress, because it lets the person remain in a position based on false ideas about her relation to the world. This is eminently so for metaphysical and religious language, as these forms of understanding are strongly oriented toward the permanent and lasting structures of reality (assuming that these exist). The will to power, in its undistorted forms, is not served by such language, but is best satisfied without metaphysics and its language.[19] The religious interpretation of reality is thus an attempt to castrate the intellect.[20] Religion delimits the human will to knowledge and to power, and it restricts the corporeality of the individual by creating an illusion of reality where power and control are not only a task for humans, but also for God. The concept "God" represents, in itself, a challenge for anyone who wants to develop a different and alternative interpretation of reality based on human autonomy and self-realization. God threatens this interpretation.

The consequence of this critique of language and its metaphysical implications is a large dose of skepticism not only toward language in general, but also toward any truth contained in metaphysical and religious language. If we elaborate on this a little, making use of notions not much employed by Nietzsche, we can say that what he does here is to dissolve any reason for adhering to the lasting elements in one's life-world and tradition. The immediately given cultural context of the person, as it expresses itself in language, forms of understanding, religion, and values, is addressed critically. Nothing given can be taken for granted. Thus Nietzsche radicalizes the critical subjectivity of the Enlightenment to the extent that this can even mean the self-dissolution of the content of the subject herself. As long as religion is part of the life-world and traditions of the person or the community to which she belongs, Nietzsche's critique of the functions of language has severe consequences. Its ultimate conclusion is that we have to give up the idea of God as inadequate, since any philosophical notion of God as *causa sui* reflects utter stupidity.[21] In his study on Nietz-

18. KSA 12:382 (*Nachlass*, 1887).
19. It is worth noting the inherent self-contradiction here.
20. *Zur Genealogie der Moral*, Third Essay, §12 (KSA 5:365).
21. See "Die Vernunft in der Philosophie," §4, in *Götzendämmerung* (KSA 6:76).

sche, A. D. Schrift puts this clearly, also noting how this is linked to, and can back up, Nietzsche's critique of traditionally derived values:

> God, the ultimate foundation of those values requiring revaluation, is revealed to be linguistically derived: God appears as the doer who is added to the deed of the world, the great author to whom philosophers faithfully attribute responsibility for the creation of the cosmological text that we call the "world." And as long as we all continue to believe in grammar, in the metaphysical and epistemological presuppositions concealed within the language which lead us to attach substantive agents to actions, we will continue to believe in God.[22]

Schrift here alludes to the famous dictum by Nietzsche that we will not get rid of God until we have gotten rid of our faith in grammar,[23] that is, before we have given up all attempts to ground our knowledge in structures marked by stability, being, and the generally acceptable. Nietzsche seems to offer a good reason for taking leave from everything offered in tradition in the way of resources for understanding oneself as well as the world. He suggests that we should meet every attempt to say something about what the world is with suspicion, and be aware of the possibility of power working in such attempts. As far as language is concerned, what it expresses must itself be seen as a reflection of the altering historical circumstances that link the will to power to its idiosyncratic historical expressions.

By this, Nietzsche suggests that language, and thereby the subject using this language and trying to establish an understanding of him/herself by it, is radically historically situated. The subject is not above history, or developed on common grounds, but is intimately linked to specific historical conditions and circumstances. If we recall Lessing's attempt to ground the subject in a kind of common reason, or at least a reason toward which everyone could develop, we see that this is not at all the case in Nietzsche. In him, everything is grounded in, and thus also changed by, the course or flux of history. This also has great importance for his understanding of plurality and perspectivism, since there are, in his understanding, no common conditions in history that all of human-

---

22. Schrift, *Nietzsche and the Question of Interpretation between Hermeneutics and Deconstruction*, 142.

23. "Die Vernunft in der Philosophie," §5, in *Götzendämmerung* (KSA 6:78).

ity can relate to and that can act as some kind of common denominator in forming our understanding and evaluation of the world.

Perspectivism and Plurality

Since Nietzsche determines the understanding based on language as an interpretation of the world, he comes close to claiming that language inherently creates fictions. Language has itself a fictional character, as the interpretation it offers and the perspective it expresses in its way of shaping reality are the final elements in what determines what we know and how we know it. We are now going to take a closer look at his view by addressing the notions of Explanation *(Auslegung)*, Interpretation *(Interpretation)*, Fiction *(Fiktion)*, and Perspective *(Perspektive)*.

Nietzsche claims that there is an infinity of forms and possibilities in the development of knowledge that is correlative to the plurality we can find in possible interpretations. However, his insistence on this plurality has also an ethical and religious meaning that becomes apparent in how it determines the way the subject relates to both herself and the world. This insistence on the maintenance of plurality is necessary to avoid the redoubling of the world that he thinks is the basis of religion. As A. Moles writes in his study of Nietzsche: "To be fixed in reverence of a person is to hold fast to a point outside oneself."[24] It is this continuous reference to something "outside" the person as an ontological determination of how the subject understands herself that Nietzsche wants to dismiss. The most prominent expression of this "outside factor," this "otherness," is, of course, God. But this is also no more than a consequent development of the Enlightenment critique of authority and tradition.

The changing flow of the world thus gets its epistemological correlate in the fact that it has to be interpreted from different and changing perspectives. Knowledge and understanding must be based on a perspective because the human being herself exists in the middle of this flux. We cannot determine anything independent of, or "outside," such perspectives. The human being cannot raise herself above her own position and take a look at the world as it is *sub specie aeternetatis,* even though religion creates and sustains the illusion that this is possible.

24. Moles, *Nietzsche's Philosophy of Nature and Cosmology,* 41.

143

This is a different way to the same result as we saw earlier, namely, a restriction on the traditional assumption that we can have some kind of universal, always-valid knowledge. Because all knowledge is based on perspectives, nothing is more than a mere perspective on what is. From a religious or theological view, this implies that one perspective on the reality of God can be delimited by others, who with equal right can set forward their interpretations of reality. Nietzsche's perspectivism thus offers a basis for criticizing the exclusive character of the Christian religion in terms of defining reality: "one demands that no *other* perspective is allowed to have more value after one has made one's own sacrosanct with the names 'God,' 'Redemption,' 'Eternity.'"[25]

This perspectivism functions as a strong argument for Nietzsche's understanding and criticism of the function of subjectivity in relation to religion. His understanding of language's functions gives reasons for viewing every kind of "double-world construction" with suspicion, as they dissolve the possibility of understanding the relation between self or subject and world in terms of a subject-object relationship. According to Nietzsche, however, this is not a restriction of the possibilities of the human. On the contrary, it must be seen as a natural consequence of the fact that the perspective-based understanding of the world is the only "world" to which we have access. Accordingly, it is important to understand his use of the notion of perspective and other related notions without the use of an assumption that there is a reality independent of this perspective or that fiction. Reality changes according to our perspectives and fictions, and they can succeed each other. Also, perspectives and interpretations are not something we have to subject ourselves to, passively. They are themselves results of creativity and human effort.[26]

The radical character of Nietzsche's position cannot here be overlooked. It takes the subjectively based experience of the world as a basis for all there is to say. Since there are no experiences or modes of under-

25. *Der Antichrist,* §9 (KSA 6:175). This is also in line with S. Houlgate's opinion that Nietzsche's critique of religion is based on his understanding of how the Christian deity cannot tolerate any rivalry or opposition against its authority. This leads to Christianity imposing "an exclusive, unchanging set of values on its subordinate worshippers and condemns alternative sets of values as 'evil'. . . . Such a forcible reduction of possible human viewpoints to one exclusive perspective represents for Nietzsche a violation of the essential plurality and diversity of life" (*Hegel, Nietzsche and the Criticism of Metaphysics,* 40).

26. See KSA 12:382 (*Nachlass,* 1887).

standing that are not framed on such a basis, there seems to be no possibility of reconciling the subjectively framed experience with any kind of religious understanding that assumes that there is more to say about what frames our understanding of the world. Thus Nietzsche develops the modern insistence on experience as a basis for human subjectivity in a manner that no longer frames religion, but excludes it.

Consequently, there is also no possibility of uniting all knowledge that has been derived from different perspectives into one final type of meta-knowledge that is above any kind of perspective. Again, we face the consequence of the fact that there is no common "other" to whom humans relate.

Hence there are no limits, no restrictions as to what we can know, think, understand, and develop concerning figures of thought. There are no "objective" limits imposing criteria of adequacy or inadequacy. All perspectives are equally valid, or equally false, because none of them operates in a room where it makes sense to subject them to some form of evaluation by some "external" norm. This opens one up to an infinity of ungodly ways of interpreting reality:

> Moreover, the world has again become infinite for us: to the extent that we cannot refute the possibility that it contains infinite interpretations in itself. . . . But who wants to make this horrendous and unknown world divine again at once? And to pray to this unknown as *the Unknown?* Behold, there are so many nondivine possibilities of interpretation contained in this unknown.[27]

The element of critique of traditional Christianity implied by the concept of perspectivism is here clearly expressed. Nietzsche's theory of knowledge not only gives rise to but also argues for one or more atheistic interpretations of the world. We can say that for Nietzsche it is more natural to be ungodly than to be pious when facing the unknown. This is not only due to his understanding of religion as an empty and world-denying construction, but also due to the framework offered by his own "theory" of human knowledge.

Consequently, this does not imply that it is impossible for Nietzsche to evaluate different interpretations in their relation to each other. But such evaluation always depends on the kind of interpretation one has as a

27. *Die fröhliche Wissenschaft*, §374 (KSA 3:627).

starting point. For example, it is quite obvious that his own evaluation of the religious way of interpreting the world is critical, because from his perspective religion means that one turns away from reality as it should be seen (i.e., as Nietzsche sees it), and hence refuses to face the truth. However, the argumentative basis for such an evaluation is in no way common to different perspectives. This is a postmodern feature in Nietzsche: he does not believe in the uniting and reconciling power of reason.

In one way, this is a radical affirmation of plurality and perspectives that we also find in postmodern modes of thought. The insistence on plurality functions in the same way, offering the human being the freedom of understanding herself and the world in any way she wants. By taking leave of religion, however, Nietzsche also seems to be forced to take leave of any modern notion of the subject. There is, on the basis of what is described above, no possibility of establishing an authentic subject with an enduring character. Hence the dissolution of this mode of subjectivity and its correlate in religion go hand in hand. What is here the chicken, and what the egg, is not easy to determine. But the main reason for this can probably be seen in Nietzsche's affirmation of a historicist perspective on reality, where nothing abides forever, and everything is intertwined in the processes of history and nature.

Affirmation is thus a central element in Nietzsche's critique of religion and behind his ideals for a subjectivity that wants to dispense with religion. Nonetheless, his main idea on religion seems to be that religion does not enable a positive affirmation of the experienced reality. Hence he — in a typically modern way — uses experience as the normative factor on which religion is measured. This is stated most clearly in *The Antichrist*, which depicts Christianity as arising from hatred of reality.[28] Roberts writes on this:

> For him, the problem of affirmation becomes the problem of how we affirm a life without the hope that the negative — evil and suffering — will slowly wither away to nothing. To affirm life only in the hope that we are able to end suffering — or to affirm life only from the perspective of that goal ("it was difficult, but it was worth it") — is not to affirm *this* life.[29]

28. *Der Antichrist* §§18, 30 (KSA 6:185, 200-201).
29. Roberts, *Contesting Spirit*, 14-15.

We see clearly how this affirmative element is also connected to Nietzsche's critique of the relation between religion and subjectivity in his attack on the idea of *sin*. "His affirmation of will to power and egoism are crucial components of the view that there is *no* absolute power, that human beings are finite, vulnerable, and of limited power."[30] Thus he indicates that no one except the human being herself is capable of judging her life.

This critique is not the only way Nietzsche formulates his affirmation of reality, including its darker sides. Most enigmatically, we also find this expressed in his idea of the eternal recurrence of the same:

> For the affirmer, the thought of recurrence is divine, not demonic, but, as *Zarathustra* indicates, this thought only becomes divine in the process of plumbing its abysmal depths. To say "Yes" to recurrence is not simply to say "Yes" to joy, but also to "every pain." To understand the link between suffering and affirmation in Nietzsche, it is necessary to examine the idea of eternal recurrence.[31]

The concept of perspectivism, when developed along the above lines, not only undermines the character of knowledge as being eternally valid and normative, but also leads to an affirmation of the finitude of all knowledge. When all knowledge is based on a contingent perspective, then it is also provisional, possibly incomplete, and delimited by other modes of establishing perspectives. We face infinite possibilities for understanding the world, because we operate on the basis of finite and perishable ideas. This opens one up to interpretations without any claim for normativity, but more important, to interpretations with quite another character than those usually based on religion or metaphysics. Revelation is here ruled out a priori, as it has no chance of establishing itself in a way that implies some privileged type of normativity or authority in general.[32]

To develop an understanding like this is impossible without also de-

---

30. Ibid., 74.

31. Ibid., 170.

32. Moles puts this nicely: "For Nietzsche, what is absurd is not having a set of beliefs, but insisting that they are final and true" (*Nietzsche's Philosophy of Nature,* 36). This comment is interesting, since this seems to imply a development in something we found already in Lessing's parable of the ring: the notion that we, as humans, with the given, finite character of existence, cannot comprehend or get access to the truth. In Nietzsche, however, the notion of truth is abolished, as it is linked to the hope that we should, or could be, in another position than we actually are.

scribing someone or something that interprets the world and lets it become part of some perspective. This "subject" is only one of several possible points in the flux of the world. It finds its identity by being different from something else, and by not seeing itself as the sole result of any other interpreting point. On the basis of what is said above, the "subject" that interprets is not a subject in the modern sense of the word, but a quantity of the will to power. It can be localized at a certain time and a certain point in the flux of history, and develops its own perspectives on the world.

In this context it is impossible to avoid the problem of self-reference. To say that everything is a perspective, and not only a perspective, but *someone's* perspective, is difficult without assuming some of the elements that Nietzsche attempts to dissolve. The best way to look at this is to do as I have suggested earlier: to see Nietzsche's statements as hypothetical explorations of possible points of view. In this way, he need not be totally consistent, but he still has to admit the paradoxical status of such explorations. What he states when confronted with the fact that his understanding of the all-comprehensive interpretative action of the human being is itself based on a certain interpretation or perspective is typical for how he would answer. "Gesetzt daß auch dies nur Interpretation ist — und ihr werdet eifrig genug, dies einzuwenden? — nun, um so besser ("Given that this also is only an interpretation — and you would be eager to object to that — well, the better!").[33] In other words, he is not willing to admit that one point of view can be delimited by some other (see above), and thus he insists on a plurality of perspectives, where one sometimes needs the content or assumptions of one perspective in order to express a different perspective.

We can say theoretically that this is an attempt to maintain in practice insight into the *hard pluralism* to which the will to power leads. The notion of "hard pluralism" should here be read as pointing to the existence of different perspectives on reality, which are impossible to reconcile in some kind of "higher order."

As an outsider who disagrees with Nietzsche, I am tempted to make the comment that it seems hard to avoid such pluralism and such problems of self-reference as long as there is nothing given, nothing "outside" or independent of the subject's will to power, no "other" that can establish some common boundary or some radical difference. I develop this

---

33. "Von den Vorurteilen der Philosophen," §22, in *Jenseits Gut und Böse* (KSA 5:37).

further below, but here I just want to make the point that if everything is determined by myself as a local manifestation of the will to power, then the problem of self-reference will inevitably arise again, as the resources for saying anything will be — myself. A Christian theology of creation is constructed on the basis of the faith and the experience that this is not so, that there is something before and independent of myself, and that this also forms some of the presuppositions of and limits to my existence. I now turn to how Nietzsche reworks this problem.

Annihilation of the Metaphysical World, Consequently: Dissolving Radical Otherness

It comes as no surprise, based on what has been disclosed so far, that Nietzsche does not view the empirical world as created and originating from the metaphysical world. The opposite is the case. He has developed a clear understanding of the history of Western onto-theology in a passage in *Twilight of the Idols*, entitled "How the 'true world' finally turned into a fable."[34]

In the first three sections of this text, Nietzsche describes the successive development of the "true world" from a world attainable for and lived in by the philosophers, via its existence as a promise for pious Christians, to its final stage as unreachable and ineffable, but still thought of as comforting, and as the origin of human imperatives.

From here on, the description he offers takes another form: the realization of the true world is seen as a problem, since it is both unattainable and unknown. This awareness of the problematic stance of the other world indicates the first early sunbeams from the Enlightenment, because the true world thus also loses its functions as comfort, imperative, and promise of salvation. From this position, the way is short to the realization of this idea as being redundant, and thus dispensable.

The final, and for Nietzsche rather important, stage in this development is how the annihilation of the so-called true world also leads to the annihilation of the so-called apparent world. This world also disappears! How are we to interpret this? First, it should be taken as an expression of how we can give up any understanding of the world that is based on any-

34. KSA 6:80-81.

thing other than subjective experience. The experienced world is the only world for us. The annihilation of a "true" world is thus also the radical expression of modernity's emphasis on experience and subjectivity. Any such world is a contradiction of subjective experience, as it appears, immediately given. This also means that we can no longer evaluate our experience from the vantage point of some externally given norm, or something "other." The notion of radical or distinct otherness is rendered impossible by Nietzsche's understanding of human existence.

When we then use these frames more specifically as a point of departure for a critique of religion, the outcome is obvious: there is no place for either any notion of something given beyond the world as it appears to us, or the realization of otherness as something delimiting our existence. This is a point that Nietzsche elaborates further in his critique of the concept of God (see below). Roberts notes correctly the value implications of this construction, in a way that also links them to what we have said earlier:

> When he uses the term *metaphysics,* Nietzsche refers to a philosophy based in the dualistic conviction that things of the highest value have an origin altogether distinct from the origin of the things of lower value. This dualism draws this absolute distinction in values in a particular way: things of the highest value are unchanging, unconditioned, eternal, and harmonious, while things of lower value are changing, conditioned, transitory, and dissonant.[35]

Thus the development of metaphysics mirrors the human need to overcome the world in which one suffers. The longing for something different arises when humanity suffers — and this is the background, the genealogy, of metaphysics.[36] Hence the more one is unable to endure the present, the more one needs the world "beyond," reflecting values that are more positive than those implied in that negative experience.[37]

35. Roberts, *Contesting Spirit,* 30.
36. See Fleischer, *Sinn,* 9.
37. Nietzsche's moral thought seems, however, to be in a certain tension with its construction of values. This tension is formulated aptly by Kellenberger: "If all values are created through human invention, then there are no discoverable values that exist independently of our creation. If there are natural values, then some values are discoverable and exist independently of human creation. Nietzsche seems to want it both ways" (*Kierkegaard and Nietzsche,* 83).

If the world "beyond" has any implications of importance for how and why we live here, and tells us some clear and distinct truths about this life, it would have some legitimacy, according to Nietzsche. But as this "beyond" is denoted "true," this is hard to claim. If that "world" is dissolved, then it makes no sense to talk of the present world of experience as mere appearance *(Schein)*. As the basis of such dichotomizing disappears, the reason for saying that this world is anything definite at all disappears as well.

I have already mentioned that when reality becomes divided into two different parts, one of those parts becomes more valued than the other. Such a way of conceptualizing the world leads to humanity's self-deception:

> The "reason" is the cause of our falsification of the evidence of the senses. In so far as the senses show us the becoming, the passing away, the change, they do not lie. . . . But Heraclitus will be right for all eternity, that being is an empty fiction. The "apparent" world is the only one: the *true* world has only been added by lying.[38]

We note here how Nietzsche without hesitation views the invention of the "true world" as a human product. This is almost tautological: if it were not a human product, it could not have been described in this way. Accordingly, the fiction here discussed is a deception, since it is an attempt not only to conceal the ever-changing and unstable character of the world as it is, but also to escape from this world. The plausibility of Nietzsche's conception here can derive from the all-too-human fact that the one who needs to lie about reality is the one who is not able to endure it as it is.

Consequently, Nietzsche reduces the content and structure of the traditional onto-theology to anthropological elements, and sees it as a special mode of human subjectivity. Additionally, Nietzsche here also states an ontological position that has large but tacit importance for the understanding of how the religious subject is constituted. The religious subject lives in the delusion that there is something "beyond," something that lasts. This is not so. Any such idea is our invention, reflecting our need for stability.

38. "Die Vernunft in der Philosophie," §2, in *Götzendämmerung* (KSA 6:75).

I think it is appropriate to say that here Nietzsche criticizes religion in a way that reflects the typically modern situation captured in Marx's famous phrase, "All that is solid melts into air." The experience of change in all dimensions of social and cultural life amplifies the understanding of reality as something constantly changing, and as something that seems to have no stable content.[39] The modern era is the most prominent example of this. The presupposition for developing this experience into a basis for a critique of religion is that religion is defined as something that is unable to cope with, affirm, or positively reflect social change. I think Nietzsche here makes his case too simple. There are many indications to the contrary in the history of religion. I return to this issue in the last section of this chapter, when I deal with how Nietzsche understands Christianity's relation to the transitory character of this world.

Nietzsche thinks that the experience of change and of relativity also serves as a basis for the destruction of absolute morality. This deconstruction results in the affirmation of the plurality of possibilities for morality, and for underscoring the conditioned, relative elements in this morality.[40] Furthermore, according to Nietzsche, no relative morality can serve as a means for arguing in favor of religion and religious content. Hence he views the moral argument for a religious position as blocked off by the experience of change and relativity.

The Concept of God as an Expression of Human Subjectivity

In one way it seems possible to claim that Nietzsche exchanges the concept of God for the notion of the will to power. The will to power is the origin and source of the world as we experience it. But the will to power is pluralistic: there are different wills to power, of differing strengths, and consequently with different interests. Thus this notion cannot have the same type of unifying function as the concept of God, or serve as a guarantor for any kind of common rationality. Viewed on the basis of the no-

39. For an elaborate and extensive reflection on this typically modern feature, see Berman, *All That Is Solid Melts into Air.* Although he does not deal much with the question of religion, his analysis is relevant for the understanding of religion's social conditions in modernity.
40. See Fleischer, *Sinn,* 17.

tion of the will to power, the way we understand God becomes intimately linked to how the will to power configures human subjectivity. Nietzsche's philosophy is an attempt to clarify the background of this notion, and hence to elucidate the way the notion of God expresses the inherent self-relation of the subject.

Approaching religion more specifically in Nietzsche, Roberts notes, like most authors today: "Religion in Nietzsche's text is multivalent — both with respect to the meaning of the concept itself, and with respect to his judgments about the value of particular religious traditions and figures."[41]

In *The Antichrist* we find some statements that are of great interest in several respects when it comes to the actual estimation of the qualities of a religious subjectivity. These statements do not seem to express a merely negative evaluation of religion. While the tendency in *Genealogy of Morals* is toward making religion a function of resentment in the psyche of the weak masses, we find here a more open and generous understanding of religion, despite the fact that it is still rather critical. The point of departure for this expression of generosity is that religion is seen as a function of humanity's positive self-esteem. In a quite Feuerbachian vein, Nietzsche describes how, by worshiping deities, people actually worship the conditions for their own well-being and the virtues that they find acceptable. This implies that religion is the projection of the lust and feelings of power into a being that can be an object of gratitude, a gratitude that basically originates from these feelings and powers.

Hence religion expresses the surplus powers of humanity, and is at the same time a means for the consumption of this surplus. "Wer reich ist, will abgeben: ein stolzes Volk braucht einen Gott, um zu *opfern*" ("The one who is rich wants to give; a proud people needs a god in order to *sacrifice*"). On such terms religion is simply a form of gratitude toward the life conditions on which one lives. The gratitude for oneself expresses itself in the need for having a god.[42] As long as the deity is constituted inside such a horizon, it is ambiguous. It is for help and for harm, friend and foe, and is an object for admiration with both virtues and vices. According to Nietzsche this is a *natural God*, that is, a God that reflects human life as it is and represents no attempt to reduce it in any way.

God appears here as an expression of the surplus in the human will

---

41. Roberts, *Contesting Spirit*, 48; see 61ff.
42. *Der Antichrist*, §16 (KSA 6:182).

to power, and as a means for a nonreductive and nonmoral[43] self-affirmation. This understanding of the development of human "theologies" serves as a critical tool in two directions. First, Nietzsche is clear over how this God is a human product, or better, a product of the will to power. Second, this background for notions of the divine can also be used normatively against other, less life-affirming ways of understanding God — and thereby oneself: "The *anti-natural* castration of a God into a God of the merely good would be beyond what is desired here. One has as much need for the evil God as for the good one."[44] This is a way of relating to the divine that Nietzsche finds clearly expressed in the theology of antiquity, but it was, according to him, possible to maintain only as long as people were strong enough to grow and develop themselves further. According to Nietzsche, in the moment when a community starts to deteriorate something also starts happening with its understanding of the divine. When the trust in the future and in freedom disappears, submission becomes the most prominent virtue. This is because such submission to others is now the condition for survival. The understanding of God also reflects this change in position: "He now becomes a dissembler, timid, modest, counsels 'peace of soul,' no more hatred, forbearance, 'love' even toward friend and foe. He moralizes continuously, he creeps into the cave of every private virtue."[45]

The way the notion of the divine reflects the understanding of people's life conditions and attitudes is in one way strikingly similar to the central figure in Lessing's *EdM*, where he described religion as a reflection of the stage of cultural development in a community. But the evaluation of the direction of the development is the opposite of what we find in Lessing. Nietzsche sees the understanding of God emerging in the later stages of development not as an improvement but as a deterioration. Also, Lessing still maintains that there is some reality behind the development apart from human interests, lusts, and will to power. Thus the

---

43. The notion "nonmoral" must here be understood as a relation that involves no grading of reality, but affirms it with all the experiences that it makes room for.

44. Ibid. See the striking comment by F. Wagner, in *Was ist Religion?* 100, that Nietzsche's critique of religion does not have its focal point in the suspicion that it is expressing projections of the self, but in the question what kind of function the taken-for-granted projection of the divine being has for the maintenance and further development of human life.

45. *Der Antichrist*, §16 (KSA 6:182-83).

similarity between Lessing and Nietzsche is to be found only in the way they imagine that the understanding of God has developed through history, and the actual direction this development has taken (we could say: in the direction of a more *humane* God). In addition to this realization — and theoretical utilization — of the historical development, they also, as a consequence, share the insight as to how the understanding of God is contextually based, and should not be viewed or evaluated apart from its contextual conditions.

For Nietzsche, that God no longer reflects the aggressive and bloodthirsty power of a specific community, and is changed into "the good God" who presumably cares for all, but most for the weak, is a reason for approaching the development of this understanding of God not only with skepticism but with contempt. Either the gods express the will to power in its genuine and strongest form, or they reflect some part of the community's lack of power. In the first instance, the gods can be gods for all the people, but in the second instance they are *functionally* only the gods of those with less power, in spite of the attempt to disguise this in a notion of "the good God is the god for all." Nietzsche explores further how this understanding of the functions of the divine is expressed in morality in *Genealogy of Morals,* showing how this is actually a way to compensate for lack of power by means of morality.

Nietzsche seems to agree with Feuerbach on how to evaluate the background for the development of the understanding of God. But there are also striking differences between them. Both see the understanding of God as a projection of inherent possibilities in the human, but as Nietzsche clearly differentiates between different groups or communities, he is able also to make a distinction as to how this understanding actually functions. The god of the weak is different from the god of the strong. In the strong community, the understanding of God reflects all possibilities that the group has, good as well as base, and not only some specially chosen in order to cope better under the power or rule of others. When one has power, God is also powerful, and the God in the strong human's existence is an objectifying function of all the lusts, virtues, and life conditions that this human finds in her own life. Thus this notion of God serves the human, as the reification contributes to exhibiting the actual resources and possibilities of that person.

As long as one is strong enough to have a comprehensive notion of God, and the powers and skills to cope with all sides of reality, any such deity will also be "beyond good and evil." The actual differentiation of reality between good and evil surfaces in the moment when the reality of the human being is interpreted on the basis of lack of power, and thereby lack of ability to cope with reality, to say *amor fati* to herself.

Here is also a tacit element that I am going to develop further below, namely, that Nietzsche is able to recognize some positive elements in religious attitudes — but on certain conditions. A notion of God that leads to the affirmation of reality in its totality is considered to be positive.[46] This must be seen in line with Nietzsche's "program" for qualifying reality as a whole in a positive way, based on a vitalist or naturalistic understanding. A notion of God like the one here in question does not represent a hindrance for such a program. If this is the case, however, this God must not be lacking anything, since such inadequacies will be a reason for making a differentiation in the understanding of reality between normativity and facticity. God needs to have all power, and if he has, then it is possible for the will to power to express itself in all that is. But such a God only serves those who are themselves powerful enough to cope with and realize all parts of life without restriction and without giving ontological preference to any part of it on behalf of some other.

This understanding of God, of course, makes him into nothing other than a human construction. Nietzsche realizes this. He is not clear, however, as to what extent he sees this understanding of a deity in the past as one of his own constructions, serving as a means for making a critical alternative to the theology and religion of his own times. We can thus conclude so far that the main point in Nietzsche's critique of religion is not that God is a projected image of human ideas. Rather, his main focus is on the critique of the conditions that lead to the formation of a modern understanding of God. Hence Nietzsche's critique is a powerful challenge to Kierkegaard's and Lessing's development of religion under modern conditions, since he seems both to identify and to evaluate these conditions in quite a different way from them.

The notions of the divine on which Nietzsche develops his construction clearly have many anthropomorphic traits, and they are easily deciphered as expressions of the human will to power and human attempts to cope with reality. However, the actual notion of God that he

---

46. For one of Nietzsche's attempts to make a distinction between true and false Christianity, see *Der Antichrist,* §39 (KSA 6:211ff.).

criticizes is not so much anthropomorphic, but rather based on moral terms. These terms intimately link together Nietzsche's critique of religion and morality. Hence he can also say that the moral God has been the main target of his critique. This is because he thinks that Christianity needs a moral God in order to sustain its function in our culture,[47] an idea that I think he is quite right in holding. Let us take a closer look at how this idea of God functions, according to Nietzsche.

First, we still have to accept that this notion of God is a projection, like any other notion of God. But it is more than this. In a way not transparent to anyone, this notion is also an expression of the inadequate abilities, capacities, and skills in humans. At the same time as there is a reduction in people's power, the understanding of God becomes more and more a container and a collection of those elements and concepts that weak people need in order to uphold the idea that there is a discrepancy in reality, a discrepancy between what the world actually is and what it is meant to be.

Nietzsche's analysis here is quite remarkable, as becomes clear from the following. By establishing such a discrepancy by means of moral concepts, one obtains at the same time the opportunity to harmonize reality so that it can appear as being in accord with the quantum of power one still has at one's disposal. Hence morality actually appears as a means of controlling and altering reality in accord with one's will. This also makes it possible to understand the basis of morality as will to power, but we are talking here of a will that has no hope of being all-powerful. The actual amount of power expressing itself in this will is then not the one we find in the will behind amoral notions of God, as described above.

Consequently, this also leads to a denial of those elements in the conception of God that could have offered reasons for the human being to experience herself as weak, or as the source of her own weakness. That God is strong and the human weak fits perfectly with the fact that we can experience ourselves as strong when we "have God on our side." God is still the one that creates and offers the good life, when the human no longer has the power to maintain the idea that it is itself the one able to do this.

I have already commented on the parallels with Lessing in how both he and Nietzsche use historical and contextual consciousness as a basis

---

47. See "Streifzüge eines Unzeitgemässen," §5, in *Götzendämmerung* (KSA 6:113-14).

for understanding religion. Now, it should also be possible to see clearly how they both use the conditions of human experience as a means for understanding the notion of who or what God is. Once again, however, we see how rapidly they part ways after this formal similarity. Nietzsche does not see that the experience of the difference between human beings and human experience enriches common humanity or provides a chance for developing a broader understanding of the role religion can play in human life. He dichotomizes humanity according to the basis of experience they share. Hence we can also see how some people *need* religion more than others. On the one hand, strong people do not really need religion, but it expresses the surplus of power they develop in their experience of the world. On the other hand, weak people seem actually to need religion in order to cope with the world. Hence to express a need for religion is to admit or reveal an understanding of oneself as a person that needs to relate to oneself and the world in the terms offered only by morality and religion. These terms fit their actual amount, or lack, of power.

Nietzsche thus offers an understanding of religion and morality that is intimately linked with the evaluation and interpretation of the religious type of human subjectivity. Religious and moral notions serve to construct a type of subjectivity that is not able to reflect on itself. It represents a subtle form of self-deception, where — for the skilled interpreter — it becomes possible to read the concept of God as an indication of how the person is able to cope, or not cope, with herself *and* reality.

There are obvious psychological elements in Nietzsche's interpretation of morality. For example, a person who has problems coping with another's aggression will evaluate such elements in human life as evil or base. Thus moral evaluation not only serves as a means for suppressing unwelcome feelings, but also as an element in how we understand God. Aggression does not belong to God — or only to how God relates to the aggressive.

The interesting thing here is that Nietzsche turns the self-understanding of the believer into a critical interpretation. In this, he exhibits his skills in the hermeneutics of suspicion. As the believer understands herself as different from others, from nonbelievers, Nietzsche agrees: she is different. What makes her different, however, is not her belief but the reasons behind it, the basis this belief has in the will to power. As long as the believer remains such, she is unable to make this construction of her subjectivity transparent, but once it becomes transparent, actual devotion and trust disappear. The nonbeliever is actually the one who is able to see and realize the genuine common ground and difference in humanity. The common ground is that every subjectivity expresses basically some element of will to power, but this takes different shapes and is given different configurations according to the actual amount of power the person can access.

In a notice from his *Nachlass* Nietzsche also reflects on the advantages the Christian "moral hypothesis" offers. This illuminates how what is said above is linked to a rather nuanced interpretation of morality and religion and its functions for human subjectivity.[48]

First, it offers humanity an absolute value, in contradiction to the "smallness" and arbitrary character of all that becomes and disappears. This is, of course, an important element in upholding strong self-esteem when faced with the lack of meaning and the injustice taking place in this world. Second, this interpretation gives the world a meaning, and makes it possible to maintain an idea of God as perfect in spite of all actual incompleteness. From this interpretation, the absurd and the evil could obtain some meaning as well. Third, this interpretation offers the idea of absolute values, an idea important for establishing adequate knowledge. Finally, it makes it impossible for humans to despise themselves as humans and regard life as not worth living. Hence it serves as a means for sustaining the human being, and for not confronting her with the theoretical and practical nihilism inherent in the opposite position.

The notion of nihilism that surfaces here should in this context be read as a contradiction to all that religion offers. Nihilism disclaims all kinds of values and serves as a negative stance from which all that religion offers can be critically evaluated. Nihilism is based on the conviction that life has no meaning or value, and that all there is to it is what we make out of it. It is based on a deep mistrust of previous interpretations of the world, and is at the same time an attempt to affirm reality as it is, without saying anything definite about its character. We can read the following statement as a positive affirmation of this nihilistic attitude:

> What alone can our teaching be? That no one *gives* a human being his qualities, neither God nor society nor his parents and ancestors, not *he himself*. . . . *No one* is accountable for being there, and that he is like

---

48. See KSA 12:211 (*Nachlass*, 1886-87).

this or that, or for living in such and such circumstances and environment. The fatality of his essence cannot be disentangled from the fatality of all that has been and that will be.[49]

The actual, nihilism-based, and fatalistic enlightenment of such backgrounds for belief can thus serve as a critical means of overcoming religion and religious self-deception. Nietzsche is surely right to insist that religion, in many cases, can serve as a means of self-deception. Moreover, the critical question that should not be forgotten when we discuss his position is this: To what extent does religion originate from the self-deceptive forces in humanity? Is it possible to think that it does not have its original source there, and hence not in human subjectivity alone, but also in the historical and contextual conditions of humanity? If the latter is the case, we can also ask to what extent religion can be interpreted more positively as a means to make human life more transparent, to increase coping with reality, and to develop types of subjectivity that are both self-critical and critical of religious expressions. If religion has its source also in events in human history, and not merely as an interpretation of elements in human subjectivity, this also challenges us to ask more critically what these historical elements are, and how they should be interpreted in human life experience.

Merold Westphal has reflected on this issue in a broader context. He argues for a Christian hermeneutics of suspicion, based on the criticism exhibited by Jesus and the prophets against established forms of religious life found among their contemporaries. This hermeneutics seems to have a common cause with Nietzsche in the challenge for continuous self-criticism, critique of the immediateness, insistence on reflexivity, and against any kind of immediate self-assurance, as well as a careful avoidance of judging others in an excluding manner.[50] In this, Nietzsche sides with Christianity when religion presents "high-sounding stories unmasking the lowest of motives."[51] He continues: "While Freud, Marx, and Nietzsche share a deep hostility to biblical religion, Freud and Marx, as sons of the Enlightenment, retain a faith in an essentially secular Reason, whereas Nietzsche sees Reason as an ersatz God through whom the

49. "Die Vier großen Irrtümer," §8, *Götzendämmerung* (KSA 6:96).
50. *Suspicion and Faith: The Religious Uses of Modern Atheism*, 251; see 288, where he argues that the need for this also arises from the insight into human sinfulness.
51. Ibid., 220.

modern secularism seeks to salvage as much of God as possible."[52] I include the last sentence of this quotation in order to remind us that Nietzsche is not an Enlightenment optimist on behalf of reason, but sees the Enlightenment understanding of reason as an attempt to give a new underpinning for the functions that earlier belonged to God. As long as this understanding also involves a self-deception based on reason, however, this is only a different form of the nihilism involved in religion.

Nihilism has a positive side as well. It expresses the attempt to affirm how the world, in its developing, emerging character, should be perceived as innocent. This innocence is not to be taken as a moral concept, but as a notion that states how this world can be considered as being neither good nor base. "This innocence of the becoming" ("Unschuld des Werdens") offers a fatalistic approach to human experience, where every attempt to interpret it in terms of evaluative concepts is abolished since there is no weakness making it necessary. The world, as it appears to human experience, no longer has any foundation in metaphysics, morals, or religion. As a consequence of this innocence, the notion of God is no longer needed: "The concept of 'God' was until now the greatest argument *against* reality. We deny God, we deny being accountable for God, and thereby we are redeeming the world."[53] From this, it becomes apparent how Nietzsche continuously sees the notion of God in its actual forms (not in its reconstructed, ancient forms) as a counterpole to the world that should be affirmed in its pure facticity. The more reality is ascribed to this God, the less possibility there is for affirming this world as it is. One can ask if this is not, in itself, a way of overcoming the inherent nihilism in Nietzsche's position, as such an affirmation seems to necessitate that the world, as it is, is worth affirming. In this, Nietzsche does not seem quite consistent. If we see this kind of critique mainly as an attempt to explore ways of understanding human experience and morality on immanent terms, however, it still makes sense. It is because it makes this project more complicated that it is refused so strongly. In Nietzsche, then, the ethos (if we dare use such a word) is to face reality as it is:

> Once the concept of "nature" had been devised as a concept antithetical to "God," "natural" had to be the word for "reprehensible" — this

---

52. Ibid., 226.
53. "Die Vier großen Irrtümer" §8 in *Götzendämmerung* (KSA 6:97).

entire fictional world has its roots in *hatred* of the natural (the reality!), it is an expression of a profound discontent with the real. *But that explains everything! Who alone has reason to lie himself away from reality? The one who suffers from being there.*[54]

Summing up, we have seen how the understanding of God can have two different functions. On the one hand, it can serve as a full projection of the existing reality, in its good as well as base elements. It then expresses the will to power of the strong "subject." Nietzsche can compare this idea of God with a dream that reflects all that is. On the other hand, the notion of God can result from a subjectivity that does not have strength to cope with reality as it is. Instead of relating to the contingent flow of history, one here attempts to secure existence in nonhistorical, transcendent elements that do not fully reflect the historical realities, but differentiates between them on the basis of evaluations that stem from a lack of power. If this is the case, we do not stand before a case of pure reflection or affirmation, but a forgery, a deliberate attempt to describe reality as something other than what it really is, and should be, for human experience.

The Death of God

Nietzsche's proclamation of the death of God is his most famous and discussed statement. We are right in seeing it as a consequence of the idea that the will to power is the primary condition in all reality. When "God" is no longer seen as a constituting part of human reality — indeed, *the* constituting part — one can face reality as it is. This also means facing oneself as one is: not as a creation of God, but as a bundle of energies, lust, and

54. *Der Antichrist,* §15 (KSA 6:181-82). Note here Nietzsche's own italics. This offers a reason for countering the view of R. Bucher, who reads Nietzsche as a challenge to a modern conception of God and sees his thinking as a means for the formulation of a more adequate understanding of God. Hence he develops the thesis that the God who Nietzsche attacks is not the real God, but "ein Phänomen der décadence" (Bucher, *Nietzsches Mensch und Nietzsches Gott,* 3). Bucher suggests that there is a difference between the concept of God that Nietzsche criticizes in his published works and his own idea of God (17-18). This strategy comes close to the one Bucher himself criticizes in the postscript to his book: "the basic problem in the theological reception of Nietzsche is its implicitly presupposed theology" (431).

will to power. We can see the basis for this in his unpublished notes: "This world: A horror of force, without beginning, without end . . . , this my *dionysic* world of eternally creating itself (Ewig sich-selber-schaffendes). . . . *This world is the will to power — and nothing except that.*"[55] Here also the existentialist vein in Nietzsche's thought becomes obvious: the world creates itself — forever. Hence it can be perfectly well understood without metaphysical notions, including the notion of God. The death of God is thus mainly an expression of how he has become less and less important for the understanding of the world, and finally has lost his functions altogether.

Although this is the ideal description — or construction — of the situation, the idea of God remains as a shadow over Western thought. Consequently, it also still has some influence on how human self-understanding develops, and how humanity has to understand its own conditions after the declaration of the death of God. This implies that we can find some elements of ambiguity in Nietzsche's evaluation of religion, because he sees that it has had some important functions for humanity, and now, since it has lost credibility, poses some challenges for us.

In *The Gay Science* Nietzsche states that it is Christian morality that has finally won the victory over Christianity. By contributing to the development of a sensitive conscience, and its unconditional demand for intellectual honesty, Christian morality is itself the main reason why we can now depart from a Christian way of interpreting reality, and ask if reality has any meaning whatsoever.[56]

It is interesting to notice how Nietzsche affirms that the origin of his own critique of religion lies in that very religion itself. As I have remarked already, this is in itself a reason for asking whether his understanding of Christianity is fully adequate, and if there is not more potential for self-criticism in that religion than he allows.

The important point here, however, is how he can criticize religion for having created an idea of the meaning of reality that is based on the notion of God. As the notion of God becomes untenable (see above), or only makes sense for the weak, it is useless in Nietzsche's own system of

---

55. KSA 11:610-11 (*Nachlass*, 1885). I do not quote the whole note here, as it is rather well known. It provides a good basis for the understanding of Nietzsche's notion of the will to power. Similar expressions can be found also in the published work, e.g., in *Beyond Good and Evil*.

56. *Die fröhliche Wissenschaft*, §357 (KSA 3:600).

values. That is why he can declare religion as indecent, the result of cowardice, feminism, and lies.[57]

To use Christianity against itself, however, is not only a way of showing how it can serve the double purpose of being a means for deception and for uncovering truth. This double purpose also gives us a clear indication of what Nietzsche himself can affirm as the positive functions of religion. In two well-known parables in *The Gay Science* he elaborates his thought on this:

> As religion disappears, we are facing good times, possibilities of new dreams, but also for threatening and dangerous times. When God is no longer setting the horizon for human existence, and when we no longer have any solid ground (there is no ground left at all), when we are totally left to ourselves, then also our freedom is something we have to develop and carry forth on our own, without any assistance.[58]

Using metaphors like this, Nietzsche clearly states how religion once had a function in giving the human a sense of belonging, and of offering a home. Now this home has disappeared. That is why the elimination of God can be a dizzying experience for those who want him dead as well. In *The Madman (Der tolle Mensch)* he develops this theme further from two angles: first, the madman who comes to proclaim the death of God arrives too early; second, he declares that God's murderers are those that have no passion for or interest in what it means that God is "gone."[59]

That Nietzsche sees the untimely in the proclamation of the death of God is not only an expression of how he experiences his own personal fate. It is also an expression of how long he thinks it will be before this event is really taken into the self-understanding, morality, and life interpretation of those who do not believe in God. Even these people will use much time in realizing the consequences of this event. As he says somewhere else: "The greatest event in modern times, that God is dead, that belief in God has become unbelievable, already starts throwing its first shadows over Europe."[60]

Remaining with this last metaphor, we can say that as only the twi-

---

57. Ibid.
58. Ibid., §124 (KSA 3:480).
59. Ibid., §125 (KSA 3:480-81).
60. Ibid., §343 (KSA 3:573).

light is already noticed, full darkness is yet to come. The question is what such darkness means. In *The Madman* the major figure is the only one who notices how the cold dark night is drawing in. With the sun as the image of what God was, he asks: "What happened when we tied loose the sun from the earth? Is it not turning colder? Are we not falling, upward, downward? Is there any direction upward and downward any more?" Posing such metaphorical questions exhibits the ambiguity of religion already mentioned: belief in God offered the experience of solid ground. The loss of this ground leaves humans without direction and the ability to orient themselves. As life then grows harder and colder, we can say that this is an experience that is connected to declaring God to be dead.

Let us reflect further on the title of this aphorism. By means of this title, Nietzsche is able to establish distance from any prophecies of doom implied by it: it is the *madman* who expresses the implications of the death of God, that is, the one who does not count expresses himself. Still, his message also makes an impression on those who listen to him, even if they, as is clearly stated, do not believe in God. Hence Nietzsche shows how the practical atheism of his own contemporaries contains unrecognized, implicit theoretical conditions and elements. Nietzsche's own critique of what he takes to be the intimate links among metaphysics, religion, and morality is an attempt to uncover these presuppositions. Hence he is criticizing not only Christianity, but also indirectly the atheism that does not realize how it builds on, and lives by, the heritage received from Christianity, when it comes to questions of a solid foundation for morality as well as science.

A final point to address in this famous aphorism is how the madman declares that *we* have killed God. The practical atheists are included in this "we" as well. We have seen above what this killing means in terms of depriving God of all functions. This statement is ambiguous, however, in that it also means that God once had a very important function. The "shadow" he still casts over the world is the remnants of the way we used to think of the world and ourselves. "God" offered a framework for which a replacement has not been found. It is the combination of this function, and the still remaining framework of religion, that makes it sensible to talk about the death of God. This declaration is thus a statement about how far Nietzsche considers that the process of secularization in Europe has come.

This process can apparently not be understood as complete. Typical of this is how he can say, "I fear we will not get rid of God because we still believe in the grammar."[61] God is intimately linked to the constructive and stabilizing function of language (see above). To overcome him will demand several phases of deconstruction.

Nietzsche can describe how that which was initially a cold message of darkness in the long run implies a freedom and the development of quite different qualities for those "free spirits" who have looked forward to the death of God. Nietzsche talks poetically about how this death in the long run implies "light, luck, relief, cheerfulness, encouragement."[62] In other words the lack of normative concepts tied to truth, justice, and rationality will provide means for constructing reality in quite different ways than hitherto. This also implies that the social structure maintained by and related to religion now alters. In his sensitive study of Nietzsche, Roberts writes:

> After the death of God, in other words, there is no longer anything to hold us together, or hold us in place, and so circumscribe our world as a meaningful one: Where will one find meaning? What shall we value? If we view religion as a force for stabilizing social meaning, the death of God as Nietzsche describes it would mean the end of religion.[63]

But by referring to Victor Turner and insisting that religion holds cultivating and creative forces, Roberts argues that religion can also invent and anticipate new meanings, values, and social structures. It is this element that Nietzsche neglects or ignores.

The linking of religion and morality, both evaluated as mistaken psychology ("eine Psychologie des Irrtums"),[64] results in the dimension they represent in human experience and relation to the world no longer having any legitimacy, but being seen as a result of human productivity (see above). This is important to realize, since it implies that Nietzsche removes an important presupposition in Christian apologetics: one can no longer point to moral phenomena in the world as an argument for morality or religion. Since morality and religion are not recognized as genu-

---

61. "Die Vernunft in der Philosophie," §5, in *Götzendämmerung* (KSA 6:78).
62. *Die fröhliche Wissenschaft*, §343 (KSA 3:574).
63. Roberts, *Contesting Spirit*, 10.
64. "Die Vier Grossen Irrtümer," §6, in *Götzendämmerung* (KSA 6:95).

ine phenomena of human subjectivity, but as deviations and deceptions of what reality actually is, this is one more way of arguing from morality to religion that Nietzsche has precluded.

Relating to History:
The Productivity of Life in the Subject

In the third of his *Untimely Meditations,* one of his earlier works, Nietzsche presents his critique of different modes of relating to history. This critique is important for two reasons. First, it is partly related to how Nietzsche sees how Christianity deals with history; second, it tells us something about how he himself regards the importance of history for the subject. Given that Christianity is a historically rooted religion, there seem to be perspectives from this work that can throw light on how Nietzsche would regard the importance of this history for the presently living subject. Hence I find sufficient reasons for reflecting on the importance and meaning of this critique to include a section on it here.

Nietzsche is critical of the development of all historical knowledge for its own sake. History should contribute to life here and now, and not overlook the perspective of the present. This is clear already from the first page of this meditation.[65] Hence one looks backward in history in order to disclose the meaning of what is looming on the horizon of the future, or to understand better what is happening now (see KSA 1:255). Historical knowledge that is known only as past is dead knowledge, and contributes nothing to the development of culture and life (KSA 1:257). We note here a point of view that both Lessing and Kierkegaard have already developed in different directions, more directly related to religion.

History belongs to life in three respects, according to Nietzsche. As active and striving, history belongs to us as *monumental;* as confirming and adoring, we relate to it as *antiquarians;* and as suffering and in need of freedom, we relate to it in a *critical* manner (KSA 1:258). The service that history offers a people or a human being is always one or more of these, dependent on the present situation, with its aims and needs. To ignore

---

65. See *Vom Nutzen und Nachtheil der Historie für das Leben,* part 1, §209 (KSA 1:245). If nothing else is stated, the quotations and references in the following are from this work, and will be indicated only by numbers in parentheses in the text.

this is to fall prey to the life-destructive ideal of a pure historical knowledge (see KSA 1:271).

The monumental approach to history is for the active and powerful, those who need idols, teachers, and comforters, but cannot find them in their own times. Such idols and important persons contribute not only to the formation of individual identity, but according to Nietzsche they are also important for developing a common understanding of humanity's cause, and point to what could be possible great historical actions in the future (KSA 1:260). "That the great moments in the fights of the individual establishes a chain, in which . . . the already long gone is still vital, light, and great, that is the basic thought behind the belief in humanity, which expresses itself in the demand for a monumentalistic history" (KSA 1:259). In other words, the monumental relation to history relates to it as inspiration and as a way of evaluating the possibilities as well as the actual achievements of the present. Nietzsche makes clear that this instrumental approach sometimes runs into the danger of blurring the border between fiction and fact. It is a powerful tool in the hands of the powerful, but can also be powerful in the hands of those who are not among the strongest and most excellent.[66]

If the direction of the monumental relation for the subject is from the past to the present, the antiquarian direction is the opposite. Here the relation is marked by a focus on one's own origin; and, as Nietzsche states, this origin has its own dignity and value, so that "the conserving and adoring soul of the antiquarian human moves into these things and makes itself at home there" ("die bewahrende und verehrende Seele des antiquarischen Menschen in diese Dinge übersiedelt und sich darin ein heimisches Nest bereitet," KSA 1:265). It follows that this relation is more passive than the first. It is an approach concerned more with the conservation of life than with developments and production of further life. Hence there is here no real evaluation of the development and the emerging elements in history, such as we can find in the previously described way of relating to history. Hence there is also no real impulse for new elements or novel action (KSA 1:268).

When Nietzsche finally describes the critical approach to history, it is unmistakably a reception of the Enlightenment heritage. Again, his-

---

66. See KSA 1:263-64. Here Nietzsche seems to anticipate one of the basic issues in *Genealogy of Morals*.

tory shall serve life, but in order to do this, one needs sufficient power to dissolve the past and break its chains. The aim of this relation is to gain control over one's own life, and to question the past in order to exhibit all that delimits the present and all that can help us to get more power. The relation toward past history is not concerned with justice or grace, but only with the possibilities of further life. In a statement that anticipates his later idea of power as the driving force, Nietzsche says: "It is not justice that stands trial here, nor is it the grace that proclaims the judgment, but it is life alone, this dark, driving, unsatisfied power that desires itself constantly" (KSA 1:269).

We notice in this quotation another element of interest in the personal and subjective, similar to that which was mentioned earlier in a comparison with Kierkegaard. Nietzsche holds that the enlightened and critical relation to the past is not neutral, but one that exhibits the subject's will to power. Hence he discloses the Enlightenment idea of critique of the past as one that involves an element of power, a power that cannot be viewed as being unrelated to the situation in which the subject exists. This is, I think, one of the elements where Nietzsche turns the modern understanding of reason as a basis for freedom into a more relative and not necessarily freedom-striving, although power-striving, mode of relating to the world. He anticipates here a typical postmodern element, recently best illustrated in the writings of Michel Foucault.

It follows from the above that Nietzsche seems to prefer the critical approach. This approach is also elitist, however, as the critical subject is the one who needs to overcome the past, and to control and evaluate it on her own terms. "Only from the highest powers of the present are you allowed to interpret the past," he writes, thereby indicating how important it is that the past is evaluated from on high. If we are not able to do this, the past will drag us down (KSA 1:293-94).

Nietzsche is thus critical toward any attempt to let the purely historical meaning rule without control. If it does, it cuts off the roots of the future, and destroys our illusions, along with the atmosphere that is necessary if these illusions are to have a place in the present. In other words, if it is not linked to constructive interests in the present, purely historical judgment of the past always involves the annihilation of it. Nietzsche uses the historical investigation of religion as the best example of this. If a religion is transposed into purely historical knowledge and scientifically explored, it will finally be destroyed. The reason for this is that such investigations will always uncover so much falsehood and so many absurdities that the pious illusions, which mark out the present atmosphere for religion, disappear (KSA 1:295-96).

Thus, according to Nietzsche, contemporary theology fulfills Voltaire's aim of destroying religion. Historically oriented theology, when it searches for "the pure historical meaning," destroys its own basis. As long as this is not made transparent by itself, we face an unnatural form of religion, which is unable to understand itself properly (KSA 1:296-97).

Since we are occupied here with the conditions for religion and theology, we note that Nietzsche addresses a position that is overcome by both Lessing and Kierkegaard. They both stress how it is the present appropriation of religion, not the recovering of its ancient, contingent, and historical content as such, that makes it a viable option in the present, postenlightened, and critical period of history. In other words, Nietzsche seems to fall short of the stage of theology that is developed by means of their reflections, as well as by other thinkers in the same period whom we do not consider here (Schleiermacher and Hegel being perhaps the most prominent).

If we reflect on what the approaches to the historical past that Nietzsche describes mean, we first of all note that the monumental and the antiquarian approaches will, when applied to religion, be of interest for the religious subject. The past, from a monumental point of view, offers standards and examples that can guide the present and help one to cope with it. This contributes to active forms of religion and religious practice. From the antiquarian point of view, the past mainly serves as the basis on which one shapes one's identity, and as a possible means of escaping from the past. Here then we find reasons for relating critically to religion, since on those terms it offers the possibility of escaping from reality. Hence these two ways of relating to history, when applied to religion, correlate well with the descriptions of religion found in *The Antichrist* 16 (see above).

The historical-critical approach will dissolve religion. Nietzsche sees clearly, as do Kierkegaard and Lessing, that if religion is to have any meaning, it is necessary to appropriate it in a present context and based on present needs and experiences. But Nietzsche does not find any means to do this in a positive form, as long as he has no vision for the positive content in the contemporary forms of religion he confronts. Hence no appropriation of religious content seems meaningful to him, on the basis of his deconstruction of the religious subject. If such an affirmation had been possible, he would not only have had to emphasize the active and creative elements in the relation to the past (as he actually does), but also to affirm that the historical content of religion could have some positive meaning in the present (which he does not). An independent, historically grounded religion has no value to him.

Also, the critical approach seems to omit the possibility of estimating religion on its own terms, a priori. The constructive and critical relation, indicating active evaluation, criticism, and judgment of the past, is not in accord with a religious self-understanding where the past has something important and new to say to the subject, in addition to that which the subject itself thinks that he or she should know and use from the past. The critical approach leaves no room for history as a genuine other, but invokes it as a means for making the past a function of the same thing that the subject already is. It is no surprise then, that Nietzsche in *Der Antichrist* can elaborate on how Christianity has *constructed* (falsely, of course) its own history and prehistory.[67] This is a natural consequence of the mechanisms that also lie behind the critical understanding of history.

This means that our three authors have different relations to the possible historical basis of faith and religious belief, and its importance for developing the subject:

- Lessing holds that history contains eternal truth that can be illustrated and made accessible by contingent historical events, and that such truth is important for the development of the subject.
- Kierkegaard holds that history only gains value through its personal and existential appropriation. This leaves the merely historical as being relatively uninteresting or secondary. It is only a means for the personal development of the relation toward the divine.
- Nietzsche seems to think that history has given no good reasons for holding a religious position, and is not of interest in terms of defining any position other than the subject's own self-understanding.

Nietzsche is negative to the possibility of using religion to improve or mature humanity. He regards the problem of present humanity to be

---

67. See *Der Antichrist*, §42 (KSA 6:216).

that it understands itself as being incomplete.[68] Religion contributes to the feeling of insufficiency connected to this self-understanding. Hence the only way to overcome this is if the human being alters the relation to herself implied in this: "For one thing is necessary: that the human achieves his peace with himself" ("Denn eins is Noth: daß der Mensch seine Zufriedenheit mit sich *erreiche*").[69] Hence Christianity contributes nothing to the improvement of humanity — quite the opposite.[70] Consequently, it is where humanity lacks the power to affirm reality under the dictum *amor fati* that faith becomes possible: faith in the things that are lacking, faith as compensation for the lack of power and ability to affirm what is. The less a human being is able to command and control her own life, the more she needs someone to do it:

> When a human comes to the basic conviction that he *must* be commanded, then he becomes "a believer." It is possible, however, to imagine the joy and force of self-determination, a freedom of will, by which a spirit departs from every kind of faith, every wish for certainty. . . . Such a spirit would be *the free spirit* par excellence.[71]

It follows from this that the relation to past history is put in negative terms when it comes to religion, because this provides the means for not being content with oneself. Moreover, this also reveals how the will to power must be understood as a creative force. It is as such a force that it becomes apparent how it can make a difference between weaker and stronger subjects. Walter Kaufmann writes: "The one who is powerful is also creative, and when one creates, then one is not hindered by what has been established earlier. A really creative action establishes its own norms, because a creative act is simultaneously a development of new norms."[72]

In sum, the notion of God is thus uncovered and reconstructed as a means for human beings. It is not seen as something that basically constitutes human beings. This is not to be understood as saying that religion cannot serve as a means for constituting human subjectivity. It is obvious also from Nietzsche's reflections that it can. But religion is a human-

---

68. *Die fröhliche Wissenschaft,* §115 (KSA 3:474-75).
69. Ibid., §290 (KSA 3:531).
70. See *Der Antichrist,* §5 (KSA 6:171).
71. *Die fröhliche Wissenschaft,* §347 (KSA 3:583).
72. Kaufmann, *Nietzsche,* 291.

made thing, humanity is not a God-made thing. Hence Nietzsche carries forth the imperative of understanding human subjectivity and experience on immanent terms. He is still willing, however, to admit that religion has had, and can have, some positive functions — but only for those who need to compensate for their lack of will to power.

Concluding Reflections

Nietzsche is not a typical atheist. His self-understanding comes close to the prophetic — and sometimes the pathetic. He thinks that the realization of the death of God has to lead to disaster, and this disaster will in turn end up in a new world order.[73] Therefore he rejects the usual way of dealing with religion in a process of secularization and modernization: it is not enough to confine oneself to the fact that religion and God no longer have any function, because this would create the impression that everything could remain as it is, with no further ado.

Nietzsche seems to think that the usual way of understanding secularization implies an incoherent basic position. As long as morality and religion can continue to live and exist inside their, now restricted, areas of life or their cultural spheres, God continues to cast his shadow on human existence. Culture still seems haunted with nostalgia for God, faith, or meaning.[74]

Consequently, such elements also restrict humanity from climbing new heights and facing the dawn that follows from the death of God. With the metaphors of *dawn* and *high noon* he positions himself as an Enlightenment theorist, but again, we see that the similarities between him and the Enlightenment project of, for example, Lessing are only superficial. Whereas other figures of modernity think that they can rescue the cultural content of Western society by means of a critique of tradition and enlightened rationality, Nietzsche dampens such optimism by showing how this project is itself based on the very elements that it wants to criticize. Modernity is not able to make transparent to itself how the ideas of subjectivity, reason, and moral order are built on suppositions that have become obsolete once religion is made neutral and nonfunc-

73. See Ross, *Der ängstliche Adler*, 585.
74. See Roberts, *Contesting Spirit*, 196-97.

tional in society. I think that this is one of the elements that makes Nietzsche a postmodern more than a modern thinker. It is as a critic of modernity that Nietzsche also appears as a critic of religion.

Accordingly, Nietzsche does not think that humanity can develop itself further by means of a humanized religion; he thinks that humanity in its present state as well as religion must be overcome. These aims are interconnected. As long as religion remains, humanity is unable to rise to new heights. This is the content of the proclamations of *Zarathustra*. No matter how overstated and self-indulgent they may seem, these statements point toward an existential position that differs greatly from Kierkegaard's. Whereas Kierkegaard views religion as a way for developing and deepening the inwardness of the self, the subjectivity of Nietzsche's superman has to cast off religion in order to develop further. Kierkegaard's subjectivity is a subjectivity of morality as well as spirituality, while Nietzsche's is, in contrast, a subjectivity of the amoral, a more bodily oriented individuality.

Another way of describing the differences between Nietzsche and Kierkegaard is to say that whereas Kierkegaard is on the way toward a substantial and sincere self, Nietzsche tries to overcome any notion of a substantial self that builds its existence on a definite idea or content of what the human is meant to be.[75] Even the idea of the superman remains very much defined by the proclamation "away from here, that is my desti-

---

75. I think this understanding of the self is the essential in Nietzsche's scattered writings on this, and to the extent that it has a normative content, it is on this basis. From here on, he can talk about experimenting on oneself (*Zur Genealogie der Moral*, Third Essay, §9 [KSA 5:357]; see also *Morgenröthe*, §501 [KSA 3:294]). Thus, when Nietzsche talks about overcoming oneself, or about self-effort, he seems to talk about a kind of normativity, where there is no talk about pure affirmation of the present position. This is important to see in relation to the fact that the will to power can express itself in different forms: as Kaufmann says, it is a question of how one way of expression can be overcome by another, thus making the subject able to cope with and express new forms of power (Kaufmann, *Nietzsche*, 273). This is different from T. Sadler, *Nietzsche — Truth and Redemption: Critique of the Postmodernist Nietzsche*, who holds that Nietzsche has a stable conception of truth (5-6, 12-13), and counters postmodern readings with this (51, et passim), but without arguing directly from Nietzsche's own texts. Based on this interpretation, he claims that Nietzsche believes in "some kind of essential self which it is possible to 'become' or to return to in a 'homecoming.'" Hence he maintains an idea of "being true to one's own self" (166). Thus he makes Nietzsche more of a modern thinker than he is, also more consequent, less exploring and experimental.

nation." It remains an antithetic notion, applied in order to take care of the basic idea that the human being (for Nietzsche as well as for Kierkegaard and Lessing) has to overcome her present state and develop further in order to realize her potential. I think that all three authors here reflect an experience that is contained in Christian doctrine, as well as in the ethics of Aristotle. A human being is not where she could be; she is directed toward some kind of telos that still lies ahead.[76] This common experience, which expresses itself in Nietzsche's idea of the superman, is, however, contradicted by his demand for the *amor fati* — love thy destiny! The two ideas seem irreconcilable, although they express different concerns, both of which are important for Nietzsche. The only way to reconcile them is to see the ideal of the superman as being not yet realized, still in need of further development of character.[77] Hence the development that Nietzsche pictures in the introduction to *Zarathustra,* where the individual develops from "Thou shall" through "I want to" toward the immediate self-affirmation expressed in "I am!" (KSA 4:29-30), points to a goal that is radically opposed to Kierkegaard's. Nietzsche wants to overcome mediateness and reflectivity, and find a new innocence, a new immediacy,[78] while for Kierkegaard the whole point of development is to overcome immediacy in order to create a subjectivity of depth.

When Nietzsche conflates Christianity with static and never-changing metaphysics, he invites a critical examination of his own position. Even though there is no final definition of what metaphysics really is in his writings, his description of it seems to offer some general traits that make the understanding of it sufficiently clear. I think Stephen Houlgate summarizes this well:

> Perhaps the most obvious characteristic of metaphysical thinking for Nietzsche is its hostility to the transience, contradictoriness and pain

76. This does not, however, imply that Nietzsche has developed any kind of teleological worldview. On the contrary, he holds any kind of teleology to be part of the metaphysical-Christian worldview that he wants to leave behind. But it is not clear that he is able to maintain this position as consistently in his anthropology and understanding of the subject as he does in his more general statements. For this see further (on the basis of the texts of the later Nietzsche) Striet, *Das Ich im Sturz der Realität,* 37ff.

77. For a positive remark on the formation of character, see *Die fröhliche Wissenschaft,* §290 (KSA 3:530).

78. As Schulz comments, this "existential positivism" implies, as a consequence, that all human action becomes indifferent (*Philosophie in der veränderten Welt,* 416).

of human experience. . . . Metaphysical thinking, according to this description, refuses to accept the view, which Nietzsche holds to be self-evident, that everything in human experience — the values, ideas and characteristics of man — has emerged in time and will one day pass away, but it yearns instead for a true world, an unconditioned world, a world free of contradiction, a world of being.[79]

Does this description of metaphysics fit Christianity? Has Christianity no sense of the pain and the transitoriness of human existence? Is it unaware of the contradictory elements in human life and action? By no means. But religion sides with metaphysics in saying that this need not be all there is to say about human existence. We need not take this as all there is to say.

A clear way of exhibiting the difference among the three positions we see in Nietzsche, metaphysics, and Christianity is in how they describe and identify the important elements for human development.

- Nietzsche views religion as repressing human development. Religion offers hope for change, the overcoming of transience, in a way that humanity must do away with if it is to remain faithful to its fate. In his radical affirmation of embodiment and change, religion is not a resource but a hindrance. But this also puts him in a position where he has to seek for alternative forms of subjectivity, and this turns out to be a paradox, as it seems to indicate that something not yet existing serves as a normative point of evaluation for what does exist.
- Christianity can affirm the created world as good, and see the task of human development as being to develop this goodness further in some of its forms, by overcoming that which contradicts it. However, such an overcoming indicates that something is recognized as being necessary to overcome — and thereby submitted to negative evaluation. But is this structurally so different from what I have said is Nietzsche's position? Religion is here a resource since it offers ideals and aims for development, as well as a ground for evaluation. It sets a goal, but this goal is not so strict that it leaves out elements of individuality and personal character.

79. Houlgate, *Hegel, Nietzsche and the Criticism of Metaphysics,* 38-39.

• Metaphysics, as Nietzsche describes it, differs from both the above positions because it focuses on how to overcome all transience and to go beyond the sensual. It is metaphysics and not Christianity that regards the world of experience as inauthentic and as mere appearance. Focusing on eternal concepts, this position contributes only to a personal development that consists in the contemplation of those sides of life that are not marked by transience. Hence it creates the impression that the world of concepts and ideas is the human world, thereby falsely creating a subjectivity that is unable to recognize its own transitory character and its bodily based experiences as being that which constitute humanity.

Having tried to clarify this, I now note that the German theologian Eberhard Jüngel has pointed out that Nietzsche's identification of Christianity and metaphysics leads to problematic conclusions. If we look at how, for example, Paul proclaims his understanding of God, this God is the opposite of a highest, unchangeable being. As Jüngel puts it, "For when Paul proclaims God in the form of the crucified, he fulfills at the same time the negation of a God that is only possible to think of in terms of a supreme being, in infinite contradiction to the finite and transient character of humanity."[80] We can find the resources for developing such an understanding of reality and God, in both the more Christological elements of Christian faith and in the doctrine of creation, where the transience, dependence, emergence, and temporality of the world are expressed.[81] Others have also noted that there seem to be elements and potentials that Nietzsche has missed here:

Nietzsche's criticisms of the suffering and self-denial idealized by Christianity are directed to suffering as the price for or the way to

---

80. Jüngel, "Deus qualem Paulus creavit, dei negatio," 295-96. Jüngel is not the first to make this distinction, which Nietzsche misses. Westphal (*Becoming a Self,* 194) points to how Kierkegaard first distinguishes Platonism from Christianity, and then also separates the positions of Plato and Socrates in his work. By doing this, Kierkegaard establishes insights that Nietzsche seems unable to take into account: "In spite of affinities, there are essential differences between Christianity and both Platonic speculation and Socratic ignorance, based as they are on the universally human."

81. "Without God, there would not be any transience" (E. Jüngel, *Gott als Geheimnis der Welt,* 295).

heavenly bliss; the symbol of the Cross is a symbol for the "hatred of reality" (AC: 161). The question then is whether a theology of the Cross can articulate a Christian life that leads to engagement with reality through a deep love for *this* life. Such a theology would not emphasize the impassable, omnipotent God of metaphysical dualism, one whose apathetic response to pain and suffering becomes an ideal for human response, but a God who suffers with humanity, a God immersed in the this-worldly reality of the human, *out of love.* Here imitating Christ on the Cross would not be a means to another life, but an expression of love for this life — a life in which the deepest suffering is intimately connected with the deepest affirmation.[82]

But to confront Nietzsche with statements like these easily creates the impression that we are arguing with him on the basis of an obsolete, onto-theological basis. That will not serve our case. We have again to insist that the question must be taken up within the framework of subjectivity. To develop an understanding of religion in modernity, it is impossible to ignore how the question of God and the question of subjectivity are inseparably linked. A central point here is the understanding of human freedom, our sovereignty and our ability to transcend and overcome the given and immediate conditions of life. If these elements are not taken seriously, all speech about God becomes arbitrary, and even more so since the modern form of atheism is a consequence of that very same subjectivity.

Another theologian, Wolfhart Pannenberg, formulates this clearly: "The question of the being of God can presently only be posed as a question about the being that the human being has to presuppose in his own subjectivity — that is, as a question about the being to which we are referred as the possibility for our freedom over against the world."[83] Pannenberg here stresses how the other — that which is different from the "subject," is something that must be seen as a condition for subjectivity. In other words, he points to the given elements in human existence, to the factors that humanity cannot control totally, but that serve as conditions for establishing control, creativity, coping, and exhibiting power. The central question that Nietzsche constantly avoids dealing with prop-

82. Roberts, *Contesting Spirit,* 176-77.
83. Pannenberg, "Typen der Atheismus und ihre theologische Bedeutung," in *Grundfragen systematischer Theologie,* 1:356.

erly in his dispute with religion is this: Are we conditioned by something else, in our subjectivity, in our ability to be free, apart from that very subjectivity itself? Nietzsche seems to agree with Christianity that subjectivity is not its own ground or basis (but rather the will to power that it originates from), but then their ways part.

From an outside point of view, it can be argued that Nietzsche's understanding diminishes the variety and complexity in human subjectivity when he describes it as a function of the will to power. This understanding sees freedom only as the experience of how this power can develop and emerge, and nothing else. In Christianity, freedom can be seen as a genuine element in human subjectivity, even when the person does not express him/herself in unrestricted will to power, but rather in devotion or altruism.

From this follows the central question, which I have already presented above: Is religion a product of the will to power, or is religion based on elements that shape human experience, elements that both delimit us *and* make freedom possible, elements that express themselves both in ideas and imaginations of a beyond and of transcendence, as well as in attempts to say what is good and bad for us in exploring the possibilities of human life? If the latter is the case, religion can — at least partly — be understood in Schleiermacher's terms, as an expression of the sense or feeling of absolute dependence on something other than ourselves.[84] This does not exclude our freedom, but is rather the basis for it.

I take this to be an argument for religion as a way of experiencing, and expressing the experience of, how we are referred to "the other" as an instance that delimits and conditions us as humans. This experience is not exclusively expressed in religion, but can be found in science as well. The question this raises is: To what extent can we think of the human being as free on such conditions? The question of freedom raised here is basically a question about what kind of human being we are talking about, and what kind of freedom. On the one hand, if freedom means being capable of acting on no given basis whatsoever, and with no material or cultural elements forming our choices and preferences, such freedom is not possible. It is this kind of freedom that Nietzsche seems to be striving for. On the other hand, if freedom is the ability to live in accord with our

---

84. See *Der christliche Glaube*, §§36ff., where Schleiermacher develops this as the basis for the Christian doctrine on creation.

ideas, and our ability to master and carry out our life according to our given understanding of what it should be, this freedom can be realized while simultaneously accepting our dependence on something else that conditions our existence. It is to the credit of the Enlightenment that it has made clear how these conditions are framed quite differently in a religious and a nonreligious context. For the believer, these conditions constitute the positive substance of his/her life, while for the nonbeliever they must be overcome as much as possible.

Basically, we here face two different understandings of the self: on the one hand, we have a self-creating self that is free because what she makes out of her life is due only to her own actions and efforts, with no given, normative, informing, or externally based content. On the other hand, we have a self that is free due to her ability to act on self-appropriated conditions and affirmed values and ideals. Hence the appropriation of the content of religion on a subjective basis becomes the condition for talking about religion and freedom as being interconnected. One of those who, on this basis, criticizes the way Nietzsche deals with these positions is Falk Wagner:

> Nietzsche is thinking in mutually exclusive terms, so that the human is either dependent on God, or is free by and through himself. On the basis of Nietzsche's critique of religion, every attempt to describe religious consciousness in an affirmative way needs to put itself in front of the question: to what extent is it possible to combine the dependence that is implied in the relation to God with the free subjectivity of the human being? For if the religious consciousness is an implication of the individual subjective being of humanity, then the declared dependence on God from the side of religious consciousness can only be consistently established in so far as it does not contradict the consciousness of freedom.[85]

Hence we see again how the understanding of religion and the understanding of what the human being is, and is to become, are closely interconnected. In the concluding chapter, I deal more with this question on the basis of the resources that Lessing, Kierkegaard, and Nietzsche have offered for further reflection.

85. Wagner, *Was ist Religion?* 106.

Chapter Five

CONCLUSION

In this closing section, I highlight some elements and patterns that I find important in the discussed material, and offer some approaches and perspectives that also seem to be relevant in order to understand the conditions for religion in a postmodern age. I am aware that some readers would probably have liked to see other things highlighted. This, however, is in itself an expression of the unfinished and the perspectival in a postmodern situation. No exposition can be taken to be final. But that does not mean that there is no relevant approach, or that every interpretation is arbitrary. Moreover, the following must be read against the background of the theoretical elements I developed in the introduction.

Formation of the Self

In the introduction, I stated that the principle of subjectivity is a major focus for understanding the importance of religion. This was found to be so for all three of the authors considered. How religion relates to and contributes to the development of subjectivity is an essential element in the way they reconstruct their understanding of religion on modern suppositions. Now, if the self is to be understood in terms of its relations, and these relations can be described in narrative, the role of religious language is clarified. It serves as a tool, or as a means, for the acquisition of a self, by way of telling and shaping the story of the self in the language provided by a religious life stance. One could say that the question the three authors implicitly relate to in their works is to what extent we need such a language, and how we are to use it. The answer to this question is, at the same time, an answer to the question of how we evaluate the appropriation of the religious tradition. As we have seen, they answer this quite differently. They also differ in their assessment of how religion functions in this context: Lessing sees true religion as a common ground for humanity, expressing itself in a morality that can also be used for addressing critical points in traditional, doctrinal religion. Kierkegaard insists on the individual as the starting point and object of religious formation, and has little or no interest in how religion shapes a subject in relation to a common ground. Finally, Nietzsche sees religion as a means for a distorted, nontransparent subjectivity that is unable to see through itself.

Nonetheless, all three writers have in common that they assert that to be a human being also involves a process of becoming, of development and maturation. In the context of this development, based on what was just said, they disagree as to the role of religion.[1] All of them seem, however, to have some kind of normative idea of what it is to be, or to become, human (even Nietzsche, in his conception of the superman). Hence none of the three seems to be fully in favor of postmodern anti-essentialist anthropology.[2]

- Lessing emphasizes the rational and moral, and how it is by using his *ratio* that the human being fulfills his telos. This normative idea of what it means to be human is not very religious in its content. It is more a question of to what extent religion can help to provide means for such development. Lessing's answer to this question is that the content of religious traditions, given specific conditions, does this well.
- Kierkegaard emphasizes the relational, passionate, and religious elements in existence, and his idea of what human development

1. For Kierkegaard on this, see Grøn, *Subjektivitet og Negativitet*, 98; as well as Westphal, *Becoming a Self*.
2. Nietzsche's conception of the superman points to some kind of normative position, which makes at least some people stand under a kind of normatively grounded challenge. But this does not go for all of humanity. Hence the careful use of the word *fully* here.

means is very much shaped by religious resources. As J. Sløk says about Kierkegaard's discussion on how it is possible to live a valid life, Kierkegaard affirms how the given life receives its validity only when it is anchored in the absolute as an existential notion, and how his theological conviction, namely that *Christianity must be interpreted in the light of this problem,* also implies that it is a concrete communication of real existence and not a metaphysical system following a Platonic pattern.[3]

- Nietzsche's idea of the human is deliberately antireligious, often naturalistic in its tone, and his normative concept of the superman exhibits traits that are clearly inspired by a romantic wish for immediacy and a naturalistic affirmation of this world. Nietzsche seems to have no positive understanding of Christianity's contribution to the formation of the self. The same is true of its historical and social function in Western culture. Hence his deconstructive reconstruction is marked by a systematic effort to reveal the most negative sides of subjectivity and to establish clear alternatives, or antipositions, to those developed by the Christian religion in these matters.

It is tempting to say that one of the things this study has clarified is the large range of possibilities for interpretation and theoretical understanding that religion displays in modernity. The frameworks for the reconstructions and reinterpretations of its content, the definitions of its "essence," and so on, can differ greatly. This result itself contributes to the postmodern insight that there is no given and definite interpretation of cultural phenomena. They consequently have to be constantly reinterpreted and reconstructed in order to function as viable frameworks for human self-understanding.

To use the notion of self-understanding here at the same time addresses the common denominator in all three writers. The way religion functions and is theoretically reconstructed as well as practiced in their views says something important about the way a human being under-

3. Sløk, *Anthropologie,* 144. My emphasis, in order to identify how Sløk accords with my results as to how much the struggle for developing an authentic existence serves as the framing question in Kierkegaard's appropriation of the "essence of Christianity."

stands herself. Moreover, Christianity shows itself through the works of Lessing, Kierkegaard, and Nietzsche as having an enormous plasticity, in terms of providing different options of such self-interpretation. This is probably one of the reasons why it has been able to survive for so long as the main religion of Western culture. It is still able to cast light on and provide means or resources for human self-interpretation. It contributes still to the clarification and the construction of the self and the interpretation of its development.

It is interesting to note how both Kierkegaard and Lessing reconstruct their views on religion or Christianity by pointing out how they provide means and frameworks for the interpretation of both development and change, and maintain that this must happen not in order simply to overcome the given, but to improve it (pace Nietzsche). They also side with Nietzsche, however, that it is not what the human being is but what she can become that must be emphasized. Given this background, every construction of religion can be seen as either providing means and conditions for positive development, or as a means for "freezing" and making static the present condition of humankind.

Conservative Protestant theology has usually been critical toward this mode of evaluating religion. Its insistence on the sinfulness of the human being, combined with its emphasis on the external and authoritative basis of religion being found in Scripture, and not in the subject, has to a large extent blocked the way for an affirmative approach to the development of religion on more personal and more modern conditions. But as we saw in the introduction, the analysis of Peter Berger indicates that Kierkegaard and Lessing are more in accord with the contemporary situation than this type of theology.

In a (post)modern society, most people no longer experience the development of this society as a credible personal project. Hence developing the self is the only project that is worthy of commitment. For this purpose, religion offers itself as a means. The "danger" of this is that it easily shapes religion into some kind of sophisticated morality. But religion's potential lies in the possibility of letting the subject recognize her dependence on others, and how the resources in tradition can be personally and positively appropriated in order to develop the human community. Hence religion can compensate for some of the weakened social basis of the subject's life fulfillment.

To interpret modern constructions of religious content as an expression of the anthropological (or even anthropocentric) turn in modernity is a common approach in much of the literature discussing religion and theology in modernity. My emphasis on the anthropological function of religion, as it is displayed in these authors, can be read in the same vein. It is important to see, however, that there is more to it than this, and that there are insights behind their different framings of religion that still need closer consideration and reflection. For example, despite their obvious differences, they can all be said to show how the importance of the adequate framing of the question of identity or self-understanding is related to — and is unavoidable in — a discussion of what religion is. That such identity can be acquired by the means of religious language is illustrated in the following quotation, which emphasizes how the self is situated in traditions and contexts, so that: "Adopting a 'view from nowhere,' the standpoint where any self is replaceable by any other, is both illusory and morally corrupting. What matters is not some kind of disembodied general consciousness, or aggregate of interchangeable selves, but my self — and your self."[4]

Religion is, in a profound way, able to take care of and help to articulate this personal interest. Religion offers at its best not only a framework for the ordering of experience, but also a means for personal development. It contains an idea of the human that affirms and recognizes human existence, as well as challenging its present status (this is true for all of our writers, but in different terms). Religion also articulates how the individual is a relational being, dependent on others, determined by factors he/she cannot control, existing within frameworks that have their origin outside him/herself. Such conditions of "otherness" offer vital means for the development of human existence that all three hold as an important factor in their thinking. However, this otherness also needs to be integrated with each individual's personal life, experience, and challenges. Hence it contributes to the way the individual copes with life:

> *Some* dimensions of importance, or "horizons of significance" (C. Taylor), are necessary to the fabric of a viable self. Individual appropriation or embodiment of social or religious values is central to the project of our becoming selves. And such objects of commitment or appropriation have standing independent of particular wish or de-

---

4. E. Mooney, *Selves in Discord and Resolve*, 8.

sire. Neither they nor the self confronted by them are created *ex nihilo* by a choosing self.[5]

Appropriation of historical content is always personal. As such, it relates the historically given to personal experience. Thus appropriation takes place not for the sake of the historical as such, but in order to relate the historically given to the individual, in order to make self-development possible. Both in Lessing and Kierkegaard we see how appropriation serves as a means for self-development. This presupposes, however, that one has a positive relationship to the historically given and sees it as a fruitful task to relate to it. This is not the case with Nietzsche, although he has developed an understanding of the relation to the past in which religious content also could fit. But we also note that none of the three has a positive emphasis on the institutional side of religion. Positive affirmation of religion is — if at all — something that takes place on the individual level. Hence Berger's point on the subjectivization of religion in modernity finds clear support in my analysis of these three reconstructions of religion.

By relating self-development to the appropriation of the given resources in history, Lessing and Kierkegaard reconstruct a typically modern understanding of religion. As autonomous, overcoming the authority of tradition, the subject they describe anticipates postmodernism in terms of self-development and the insistence on a personal and double-reflexive relation to the past (both affirming and critical, both on the inside and outside, both ironical and committed). We note, however, that they also try not to be bound to the historically given in a way that makes them subject to the mere historically given past. They attempt the opposite: to subject the historically given to their own concerns.

Religion's Contribution to Humanity

We have seen how the idea of a common humanity in Lessing (a typically modern idea), which provides the basis for tolerance, also serves as a basis for understanding religion and ethics. Kierkegaard and Nietzsche develop and criticize this approach in different directions. Kierkegaard em-

5. Ibid., 9.

phasizes how the individual needs to develop and deepen her faith outside any kind of tradition or religious *Sittlichkeit.* Hence he also is critical toward understanding religiosity in general terms. What counts for him is the individual task of becoming a self. This "religious individualism" is not totally counter to Lessing, but Lessing is clearly more positive toward the idea of religion — at its best — as expressing a common human core. This partly also lies with the emphasis that Lessing puts on the idea of a natural religion, an idea that Kierkegaard does not use at all.

Nietzsche's criticism of religion and religious communities goes in a different direction. He sees, or recognizes, none of that which is important to both Lessing and Kierkegaard, namely, how religion and history can prove to be the occasion for the individual's personal development. For him, religion only serves as a means for the repressing socialization of individuals into one uncritical herd, which is incapable of making its own subjectivity transparent. When Nietzsche speaks of the herd animal, he denounces the option of gaining subjective transparency through religion. He also rejects a positive understanding of the human community or of something that is common to all in religion.

Thus the three agree on the individual's need to be involved in a development of her own. They disagree, however, on the function religion has in this (here Kierkegaard sides with Lessing on how religion contributes positively to the development of the subject). They agree on the individualism that grows out of a modern way of understanding the individual's relation to religion, which is emphasized even more in the postmodern configurations of religious subjectivity.[6] Hence they confirm Berger's understanding of religion as something that becomes increasingly privatized, and show how this is the case also in terms of how religion is reconstructed theoretically in its relation to the subject. In the modern reconstruction of religion, the individual is the constructor, not the religious or the social community. We see how this is the case in both Kierkegaard's affirmation of the individual *(den Enkelte)* as the Christian (an affirmation in which he also exemplifies modern attitudes toward religion in emphasizing the heretical imperative, i.e., the challenge to choose for oneself). The paradox is that Kierkegaard's and Nietzsche's

---

6. It is, however, important to be aware that Kierkegaard's individual is not easy to accommodate to the common theoretical frameworks for the description of modern individualism. See Matuštík, "Kierkegaard's Radical Existential Praxis."

understandings of the Christian here are in sharp conflict. Nietzsche sees the Christian as the typical herd animal, and on this basis he develops the same ideal of the human as Kierkegaard. This is the individual that takes on the personal challenge of developing herself, knowing that it involves suffering and loneliness, with no shelter or escape into the ideal of the so-cial commonality.

With this background, however, we can also read one of the most important differences between Nietzsche and Kierkegaard in the way they understand the "direction" of subjectivity. Kierkegaard directs his atten-tion inward, but via the way outward toward the loving, relating, commu-nicating relationship to the other (the God in time, or the fellow neigh-bor).[7] The self matures by trusting in and relating toward something out-side itself, and this relationship is the occasion for the development of the inner self. By contrast, Nietzsche is far more one-dimensional, and goes only inward, into the self, without any positive and trusting relation to the world of others. Hence he sees only the interests of the ego, its desires and drives, its anxiety and its passion. Consequently, he rejects the social and historical world as an occasion for the positive development of humanity. In other words, Kierkegaard and Nietzsche exhibit a different relation to the other, a relation that is also mirrored in their understanding of religion and religious life.[8]

The Relation to History: Criticism and Suppositions

In Kierkegaard's work, there is an insistence on the commitment and the devotion *(inderlighed)* of the subject in her relation to the objectively inse-cure. Kierkegaard leaves little room for what we can call explicit struc-tural criticism of Christianity, apart from the shape he finds that it has taken in some deviant forms in his own local circumstances. This does not mean that Kierkegaard is uncritical. He is critical all the time, both toward the contemporary Hegelian theology and the attempts to base faith on research into and reconstructions of the historical Jesus.[9] How-

---

7. In Kierkegaard God is the other that has established the self — in its relation to itself. Cf. Grøn, *Begrebet Angest hos Søren Kierkegaard*, 140.

8. For more on the function of the other, see the next section.

9. For this see also Hannay, *Kierkegaard*, 97.

ever, his critique is always based on his own positive and normative idea of what Christianity essentially is, so that the critique is carried out in order to clarify the positive content of religious faith and what it can mean for the positive development of personal existence. Thus Kierkegaard is perhaps the one among our writers that has the most clearly developed idea of religious faith's contributions to anthropology. Lessing seems to be much vaguer about this, and Nietzsche has little or no positive understanding of this at all. Apart from *EdM* and *Nathan,* Lessing is not very clear on what his personal opinions are in these matters, and Nietzsche uses all his space to criticize any given position.

Now, none of the three seems to hold that a positivistic approach to history is a fruitful way to access what religion is all about. They all provide anthropological and theoretically founded elements as the basis for an approach to history. This means that their attitude toward past history is marked by both criticism and a struggle for an adequate appropriation on the anthropological basis I have described above. There are two "postmodern" concepts that can clarify this relation to history, namely, perspectivism and constructivism. The perspectivistic element shows itself in how the subject takes no neutral stand, but always relates to the historically given from his or her own personal stance. He or she is situated in a historical and existential situation that prescribes how the relation to the past is configured. This configuration is then also the result of a reconstruction based on anthropological principles, and not only the principles offered by a given historical situation or a specific religious configuration that expresses itself in a specific community.

From this perspective, the basis of faith is given in the experience that the past offers resources that are possible and meaningful for the subject to appropriate. Without this experience, summarized in the experience of the development and sustaining of personal identity, the past is without meaning. This goes for all our authors. Again, however, this statement needs to be qualified as to how they then mean that the past is best appropriated. We have seen that in this respect they differ considerably. Hence they exhibit how tradition, as a "given" element, cannot be taken for granted, but has to be scrutinized in order to function as it was meant to (Lessing, Kierkegaard), or in order to be revealed in its repressive form (Lessing, Kierkegaard, and Nietzsche).

Reflections on the Role of the Other and of Otherness

The figure of "the other" is used in a wide sense here, in order to depict how, in their reconstructed framework for religion, the three authors understand the contribution of the social world or frame that which is alien or new to the subject. Hence it has a rather broad scope, and the intention in using it is to provide a means for the following reflections.

In Lessing the true religious content of history is not basically different from that which can be disclosed by reason. Hence it would be wrong to say that history, in a religious sense, presents the subject with new conditions for its formation, other than those already in principle accessible to the subject by reason.[10] This is quite contrary to Kierkegaard, for whom the God-in-time provides quite new conditions for the subject, different from those developed and utilized by religiosity A (or a Socratic approach). In this sense Kierkegaard also maintains the necessity of a revelation that transcends or surpasses the given content of a "natural religion." He thereby makes it possible to distinguish between theology and religious reflection based on this revelation, on the one hand, and philosophical theology or natural theology, based on "natural religion," on the other hand. In this he also takes care of a concern that Lessing expresses over against neology's unsound blend of reason and faith, where the distinction between the two tends to collapse. Although reason, according to Lessing, must discern when the individual is confronted with a revelation, this does not mean that the revelation only says what is already inside the framework of reason: "Denn was ist eine Offenbarung, die nichts offenbaret?" ("For what's a revelation that reveals nothing?").[11] The content of this revelation, however, is for Lessing confirmed in and by reason.

The differences between Lessing and Kierkegaard can be summarized as follows. For Kierkegaard, the subject's other is primarily a *religious* category, which constitutes its personal mode of religious existence. For Lessing, the subject's other is primarily a *moral* category, which challenges the subject to develop his reason and tolerance so that the integrity of the other is conserved with no attempt at assimilation. In addition to this, both of them have a profound sense of the social dimension in

---

10. This point is the background for why I discussed the different possibilities of the interpretation of revelation and reason in *EdM* somewhat extensively.

11. Lessing, *Werke*, VII, 461-62, quotation 462.

the constitution of subjectivity. Kierkegaard's understanding of the self as a relational entity is the most developed in this connection. Among the authors in our material, Kierkegaard seems to stand alone in his understanding of religious subjectivity as being constituted by something unique, which is to be identified neither by the historical as such nor by some subjective dispositions and conditions alone (as in Nietzsche).

I would like to emphasize that, both as a moral and as a religious category, this understanding of otherness is important in a positive sense, as it makes the individual's relation to history more concrete, and helps in understanding its importance for Lessing and Kierkegaard. Even more so, as in Nietzsche the relation to otherness is constantly viewed in negative terms and understood as a figure of thought that threatens to make the subject subjected to new types of repression and false or opaque modes of self-understanding. Nietzsche's philosophy can be seen as a permanent attempt to overcome any kind of externally based otherness that works as being constitutive in the subject's self-development.[12] While Lessing and Kierkegaard see otherness as something that also provides important occasions for development, Nietzsche tends to isolate the subject from otherness and the social world when he develops his ideas of how a human being should fulfill her life. Both as a moral and as a religious category, otherness is thus a severe threat to Nietzsche's position. I think that in this he is not only too negative in his basic construction of what it means to fulfill one's destiny; he also seems to have no positive view of the possibilities provided by religion in terms of developing a broader and richer narrative for the constitution of the subject and her resources. In other words, Nietzsche's subject is far narrower than a social subject and has fewer resources. The contribution of both Lessing's and Kierkegaard's reconstructions of religion is that they provide a fresh understanding of otherness and of the subject's self-relation as it is mediated by participation in the social world. This they do at the same time as they also — along with Nietzsche — stress how it is the *individual's* life, religious understanding, and responsibility that are in focus, and not the social world as such. Hence the subject, in Lessing and

12. It is necessary to distinguish between internal and external otherness in relation to the subject in Nietzsche, because he grounds subjectivity itself in the otherness of the instincts or the will to power (internally). This gives rise to how some persons try to establish a kind of otherness (externally) that shapes or attempts to shape the lives of others.

Kierkegaard, does not seem to suffer the type of subjection by religion that Nietzsche seems to fear so much.

One more element in relation to the framing of "otherness" is of relevance here. There is a trend in modern forms of thinking that runs counter to the recognition of plurality and the invitation to "heresy." This is the struggle to integrate, rationalize, and handle the existing cultural (and religious) differences in one comprehensive whole. We find the best example of this position in Lessing's combination of tolerance of plurality and the idea of a common rational and moral core in true religion. Here we also face one of the differences between modernity and postmodernity. For example, it is by using concepts or ideas like "natural religion," partly also "humanity" (in itself necessarily a comprehensive concept) and "morality," that differences are softened and ironed out in order to be less threatening for the establishment of a (religiously founded) identity.

Now, one can ask to what extent this presupposes an understanding that only takes into account what I would call soft pluralism, that is, a pluralism that is considered possible to overcome. This would imply that within this frame of thought there could be no talk of basic differences. The recognition of otherness is based on its relation to the common, and can thus easily lead to the struggle to make everything an expression of the same. I think this problematic is vividly illustrated in Lessing's play *Nathan,* and this reveals Lessing to be a typically modern thinker. Heresy and difference need not in his eyes turn into irreconcilable separation and divergence; they are simply different witnesses to the same human struggle and the same human needs. This is a position that is countered very clearly by Nietzsche, who recognizes how this might be another way of subjecting everyone to the same standards — the standards set by the mediocre flock.

Moreover, I have noted how all three authors make communication an issue, and are critical of any kind of direct communication. I think this issue also can be seen as an attempt to maintain the other's otherness. It is by making the other into herself that the communication they attempt attains its goal. Any direct communication suffers under the danger of subjecting the other to something that is alien, and to conform her to the one who communicates. The thought of all three authors does not have the aim of making disciples, but of communicating something that makes the subject realize his or her own specific tasks. This takes care of the other as other, as an individual. At the same time, this opens one up to a kind of communication that is humanly far more fulfilling than the mere preaching of some message. It develops a basis for human interaction in which social life probably has better and more symmetrical conditions than in some kind of asymmetrical communication, as this is expressed in more traditional (!) forms of religion. In this, their different reconstructions of religion also imply a critique of previous and contemporary forms for communicating religious content.[13]

Finally, I want to discuss briefly a related question that is of importance for understanding the relationship between (religious) self-development and the realization of otherness (including some idea of what external reality is like). The question is: What is the point of self-development if reality has no sense? In Lessing and Kierkegaard reality is presupposed to have some kind of meaning that can be acquired by the subject. This acquisition is also important in the development of the subject's relation to world and self. But can we affirm that reality has no meaning, as Nietzsche does, and still maintain the process of self-development as a meaningful task, or a task worth fulfilling? I think that, in every kind of quest for self-development, there is a tacit recognition or affirmation that our own interaction with reality reveals its potential for meaning — no matter how much we must revise, alter, and criticize our conceptions of what this meaning is. To become something else is hard to hold up as a goal unless one has a clear idea of something meaningful that is not yet realized, something beyond and transcending the present situation. In these matters Nietzsche is not clear.

Such self-development demands some kind of stability, as it is a *self that will develop*.[14] The cultural framework that establishes a specific world, including morality and religion, seems to provide the means for this. On this background, religion can also be understood as pointing to

---

13. It is interesting to note an element that Grøn has pointed out in relation to Kierkegaard: What saves the subject for closure is communication, community, and language. As a specific configuration of this communication, faith is an anthropological constituent in Kierkegaard's way of describing the subject's way of overcoming oneself (in quite another way than the Nietzschean superman). Cf. Grøn, *Begrebet Angest,* 106; and *Subjektivitet,* 38, with reference to *Concept of Dread* (6:207, 220).

14. In his critique of subjectivity Nietzsche seems to dissolve the basis for this *ipseity of the self,* to use Ricoeur's notion (*Oneself as Another,* passim), while it still remains an important presupposition in Lessing and Kierkegaard.

resources and ideals for development — not only as a hindrance, or as maintaining a stiff stability. Nietzsche seems to have dispensed with such a framework for his understanding of self-development, and hence it is hard to see how he can affirm such development as a meaningful task at all.

By contrast, Lessing and Kierkegaard reconstruct religion so that it contributes to both the personal and social challenges of their context. Lessing discusses and develops a theoretical understanding of religious pluralism and tolerance, while Kierkegaard, more than any of the others, shows how religion can develop the transparency of the subject, thereby also securing (in an anticipation of postmodernity) the insight into the unfinished, not yet fully transparent and rational subject, as well as the constitutive contribution of otherness, which is more and more realized in a pluralist society.

Irony and Double Reflexivity

I have noted how the historical past achieves its function in relation to the self-development of the subject. This "occasionalism"[15] in relation to the historical (seen most clearly in Kierkegaard's description of romantic irony) seems at the same time to solve the problem of historical insecurity. This insecurity is not so threatening as long as history still provides the basic presupposition for the self-development that the subject thinks she needs. But the emphasis on the individual and the subjective in all three authors seems to compensate for historical insecurity in a way that makes this insecurity less of a challenge in a Christian framework. It is in the light of this that we can also see the emphasis of Lessing and Kierkegaard on self-relation and self-formation more than on doctrine. This is a natural consequence of making the present the actual starting point for the religious position. Here they also anticipate what sociologists can tell us about the development of religious preferences in a postmodern situation.[16]

15. For the relation between occasionalism and irony in the romantic period, see O. Krogseth, Den tyske historismen, 160ff. Here he develops the relation in a way that makes it interesting to view it as a background for all our authors (although none of them is distinctively romantic), as well as for postmodernity.

16. See, e.g., W. C. Roof et al., Generation of Seekers, passim.

Historical insecurity also provides the background for another element in religious subjectivity: irony. In all three authors, irony is related to the way they communicate.[17] However, I think there is one more important element behind this, namely, the insight that every position has its limitations, so that there is a built-in reservation in the theoretical articulation of any religious or philosophical position. This reservation makes it even more important to stress how necessary it is to personally appropriate a position.

Irony is marked by a double relation: it indicates a both-and position, a fluid and provisional position, a position that still is open to revision and change. Hence I suggest calling irony an expression of double reflexivity. I think that in terms of modernity, the very fact that the religious subject lives under the "heretical imperative" and is challenged to decide his or her position presupposes a given position as the background of the choice, and this background is not taken for granted. Religious faith is thus both something that can be deliberately chosen and something that presupposes a kind of critical attitude toward this background. A believing subject, expressing the double reflexivity I speak of here, is then both committed (in faith) to and critical (by reason) of the tradition of faith.[18]

In our material we see this approach clearly in both Lessing and Kierkegaard. The tension between commitment and criticism is perhaps strongest in Kierkegaard, who emphasizes the passion of faith, and at the

17. The irony in the *Postscript* is distinguished most in the fact that Kierkegaard in the closing section of the book retracts the whole text (10:280, 286).

18. What I here describe as double reflexivity, in earlier versions of this study I named "double consciousness." This is partly inspired by, but should not be confused with, Kierkegaard's notion of "Dobbeltreflexiviteten." I discovered that this is a notion that, although it captures what I am driving at, is used in different ways in recent psychology. In order to indicate the similarity and also to give a further idea of what I understand by this notion, I quote Rom Harré, *The Singular Self: An Introduction to the Psychology of Personhood* — a distinctively postmodern book: "'Double consciousness' refers to two sets of beliefs about oneself that are distinct but held together, clusters of belief that may in extreme cases be logically incompatible. In most cases of 'double consciousness' of this sort the incompatibility is pragmatic, in that in implementing the one, implementation of the other is blocked" (113). I think Harré here captures both the pragmatic character in the reflexivity, as the perspectives are there in order to take care of specific interests, as well as the mutual exclusiveness where the two perspectives can neither replace each other nor be merged into one coherent perspective.

195

same time points out very well how the disinterested, not-fully-committed attitude of an aesthetical position leaves the subject devoid of any lasting content. The aesthetical position also excludes the decision for a definitive option in terms of modes of existence.[19] In many ways this is also a position expressed in Dietrich Bonhoeffer's famous statement about the Christian who has to live in this world as if God does not exist *(etsi Deus non daretur).*[20]

In a modern context, the subject is challenged to develop a kind of double competence, where the immediate and the mediate relation to the given historical and religious position are combined, and where critical reflection and trusting devotion exist together in an unreconciled contemporaneous existence. The lack of reconciliation is important to maintain in order to make sure that theological reflection does not turn into mere subjective expressions of faith, but also in order to secure that faith does not drown in the tempest of unlimited criticism.

I use here the notion of an unreconciled contemporaneous existence because I do not think it is possible to synthesize these two approaches to the content of faith. Moreover, it is necessary to maintain that these different approaches cannot be replaced by each other. Faith cannot replace criticism, and criticism cannot replace faith, without loss.

If we relate the double position I am trying to spell out here also to what I have already written on otherness, one reflection presents itself that expresses a more postmodern concern as well: I think this double reflexivity serves as a condition for facing the other as an other, without having to integrate it, make it known, turn it into the sameness of what is already known. Otherness implies a position where something transcends the subject, or is a stance that is not fully integrated in the person that relates to it. The conscious awareness of otherness then implies some kind of recognition of a position that is not my own — but this position is still a position that I am able to recognize, and notice the importance of, despite it not being my own.

This can also be seen in relation to another element that is common to all three authors. Rationality is not everything to any of them. Even Lessing, most inspired by the Enlightenment ideas, sees that "the

---

19. This can also be viewed in the light of Kierkegaard's statement that to choose is to choose a history, by which you are given an identity and a belonging (3:200).

20. Cf. Bonhoeffer's *Letters and Papers from Prison.*

feelings of the heart" have an important part to play in the question of religion. Furthermore, both Kierkegaard and Nietzsche express their condemnation of a rational approach to the important questions of existence. This should not, however, be seen as a leap into mere irrationalism, but as a means for pointing out that there are elements that are not fully disclosed in a rational approach to reality. As long as one recognizes this, one also needs to keep a distance from one's own religious constructions, as they are expressed in a rational framework.

In many ways this double approach toward religion and reconstructions of religion as well can be seen as being conditioned by the secularization process, which ascribes to the religious sphere a certain extension, and allows for its perspective only in particular settings of cultural and social life. In terms of understanding what is taking place, however, I think we have to note that the double reflexivity that is conditioned by secularization (and pluralism) leads to a philosophy of religion that runs parallel to the dogmatic or the internal ecclesiastical theology. It is precisely this double approach to religious life that is demanded if one is to understand what the reconstructions of religion offered by Lessing, Kierkegaard, and Nietzsche mean, both in historical and in philosophical terms. Their positions are not understood fully if they are only viewed from a position inside the church, nor if they are viewed only from the outside. They demand that we establish a first-person perspective and a third-person perspective to what they say and what they criticize.

It is worth reflecting on to what extent this challenge of combining a first- and a third-person perspective is fulfilled in our three authors. This is most clearly the case with Kierkegaard, where religiosity has become a problem — perhaps the main problem — for itself; hence the need for distance, irony, questioning. In his work Kierkegaard then integrates the first- and third-person perspectives, and this integration is itself part of his whole enterprise of communicating religious truth in a specific manner. Lessing also seems to combine the two perspectives, but not in such a theoretically thought-through way as Kierkegaard. With Nietzsche this is not the case at all, since he both lacks the first-person perspective on religion and ignores what Kierkegaard makes clear, namely, that the reflexive dimension of religiosity can make it transparent to itself. All together, however, the three contribute by their work to a relation to religion that heightens its level of reflection and recognizes the modern insight into the construction of religion under the conditions of heresy and pluralism.[21]

*   *   *

After modernity, in the positions anticipated by Kierkegaard and Nietzsche, human beings must recognize their fragility, the fragility of the project of self-development, and religion's ambiguous place in this project. Human beings are finite, and the recognition of finiteness is the condition on which the reconstruction of religion has to take place (hence also the insistence on the necessity of a plurality of perspectives, and of different reconstructions in different historical circumstances, as advocated by Lessing). On this, W. Schulz, writing in the vein of existential philosophy, has made an apt remark:

> All characteristics of existence that follow from this finitude, the links to the situation, the necessity of a decision without recurrence on given orders, the knowledge of a threatening death; all these are seen as something negative in the perspective of tradition. However, not only to endure this negation but also to appropriate it in the innermost of oneself is now the real task. This essential core of existence is not given. It is something to be acquired through the personal effort of integration *(Verinnerlichung)*, in which and through which I constitute myself as the finite subjectivity that I have to exist as.[22]

This is, in different ways, the insight of our three authors as well. But there is something Humean about the conclusion. We have to live with uncertainty, and with the insight that what we construct may be fragile and subject to criticism. That Lessing, Kierkegaard, and Nietzsche use various positions as points of departure for their thinking shows not only how they are familiar with these effects of historicity and fini-

---

21. We find a related but partly different approach to the same problem in Mooney, who talks about how we are challenged to have a double vision of the world. We relate to the world as external and objective, but also as subjective and personal. The challenge lies in the reconciliation of the two approaches. See Mooney, *Selves in Discord*, 77ff., where he develops this with an interesting reference to Thomas Nagel's *View from Nowhere*.

22. W. Schulz, *Philosophie in der veränderten Welt*, 326.

tude,[23] but also that their understanding of the issues that are central to the understanding of what it means to be human are based on the insight that *closure* and *system* are not viable options if we want to safeguard a true development of humanity, human existence, and human freedom (most profoundly so in Kierkegaard, but also in different other ways in the others). This is a lesson here to be learned as well for those who think that religion is linked to existing as truly human.

At the same time, religion is always a reconstruction of a cultural form in which we interpret our own experience and cultural framework with the resources available to us. Thus religion is in constant need of reappropriation, and it offers no secure and lasting stability. To accept this, however, need not imply subscription to a nonreligious position. But this acceptance is offering the faith, trust, and identity that religion establishes, a framework that should be recognized in the double reflexivity that a mature believer needs in our times. As "all that is solid melts into air" also goes for our religious constructions, reconstructions of religion in theory, philosophy, theology, and thinking exist under that heading. To make a twist on Lessing, however, that constructions fall apart does not need to imply that the material on which basis they were constructed (i.e., the religious experience, the Scriptures, and the historical events they are related to) are destroyed. Such materials are "the given," to which any philosophical or theological approach to religion has to relate, be it affirmatively, critically, or deconstructively. Hence reflection on religion goes on, as a Sisyphean work. There are enough mountains to climb and stones to carry.

---

23. Cf. Westphal's apt remark on Kierkegaard's pseudonym Johannes Climacus, a remark that can fit Lessing and Nietzsche as well: "As with Kant before him and Derrida after him, Climacus finds the radical temporality of human existence to be the barrier to absolute knowledge" (*Becoming a Self,* 115).

Literature

The text editions that have been used as a basis for the study are:

Kierkegaard, Søren. *Samlede Værker.* 3d ed. Copenhagen: Gyldendal, 1963.

Lessing, Gotthold Ephraim. *Werke.* Darmstadt: Wissenschaftliche Buchgesellschaft, 1996.

Nietzsche, Friedrich. *Kritische Studienausgabe.* Ed. G. Colli and M. Montinari. Berlin and New York: de Gruyter, 1988.

Adorno, T. W. *Kierkegaard: Konstruktion des Äesthetischen.* Frankfurt: Suhrkamp, 1974.

Allison, H. *Lessing and the Enlightenment.* Ann Arbor: University of Michigan Press, 1966.

Arendt, H. *Von der Menschlichkeit in Finsteren Zeiten.* Munich: Piper, 1960.

Augsburg Confession, I. *Die Bekenntnisschriften der VELKD.* Göttingen: Vandenhoeck & Ruprecht, 1979.

Berger, P. L. *The Heretical Imperative.* Garden City, N.Y.: Anchor, 1979.

Berman, M. *All That Is Solid Melts into Air: The Experience of Modernity.* New York: Penguin, 1988.

Beyschlag, K. "Kommentar zu *Erziehung des Menschengeschlechts.*" *Lessings Werke* 3. Hereafter Lessing: Werke VIII, 71.

Boethe, B. *Glauben und Erkennen: Studien zur Religionsphilosophie Lessings.* Meisenheim am Glan: Anton Hain, 1972.

Bohlin, T. *Kierkegaards Dogmatiska Åskådning i dess historiska sammanhang.* Uppsala: Almquist & Wiksell, 1925.

Bohnen, K. *Geist und Buchstabe: Zum Prinzip des kritischen Verfahrens in Lessings litteraturästetischen und theologischen Schriften.* Cologne: Böhlau, 1974.

Bollacher, M. *Lessing: Vernunft und Geschichte: Untersuchungen zum Problem religiöser Aufklärung in den Spätschriften.* Tübingen: Niemeyer, 1978.

Bonhoeffer, D. *Letters and Papers from Prison.* London: SCM, 1971.

Bucher, R. *Nietzsches Mensch und Nietzsches Gott.* Frankfurt: Peter Lang, 1993.

Bultmann, R. *Glauben und Verstehen.* Vol. 1. Tübingen: Mohr, 1933.

Cassirer, E. *Die Philosophie der Aufklärung.* Tübingen: Mohr, 1974.

Deuser, H. *Kierkegaard: Die Philosophie des religiösen Schriftstellers.* Darmstadt: Wissenschaftliche Buchgesellschaft, 1985.

Evans, C. S. *Faith beyond Reason: A Kierkegaardian Account.* Grand Rapids: Eerdmans, 1998.

Farley, W. *Eros for the Other: Retaining Truth in a Pluralistic World.* University Park, Pa.: Pennsylvania State University Press, 1996.

Figl, J. *Dialektik der Gewalt: Nietzsches hermeneutische Religionsphilosophie mit Berücksichtigung unveröffentlichter Manuskripte.* Düsseldorf: Patmos, 1984.

Fittbogen, G. *Die Religion Lessings.* Leipzig: Mayer und Müller, 1923.

Fleischer, M. *Der Sinn der Erde und der Entzäuberung des Übermenschen. Eine Auseinandersetzung mit Nietzsche.* Darmstadt: Wissenschaftliche Buchgesellschaft, 1993.

Foucault, M. "What Is an Author?" In *The Foucault Reader.* Ed. P. Rabinow. London: Penguin, 1991.

Gadamer, H. G. *Wahrheit und Methode.* Tübingen: Mohr, 1975.

Gay, P. *The Enlightenment: An Interpretation,* vol. 1: *The Rise of Modern Paganism.* New York: Norton, 1977.

Göpfert, H., ed. *Das Bild Lessings in der Geschichte.* Wolfenbütteler Studien zur Aufklärung. Heidelberg: Lambert Schneider, 1981.

Gregersen, N. H. *Teologi og Kultur: Protestantismen mellem assimilation og isolation.* Århus: Aarhus Universitetsforlag, 1988.

Grøn, A. *Begrebet Angest hos Søren Kierkegaard.* Copenhagen: Gyldendal, 1994.

―――. *Subjektivitet og Negativitet: Kierkegaard.* Copenhagen: Gyldendal, 1997.

―――. "Kierkegaards 'zweite' Ethik." *Kierkegaard Studies Yearbook* 1998, 358-68. Berlin: de Gruyter, 1998.

Hannay, A. *Kierkegaard.* London: Routledge & Kegan Paul, 1982.

Harré, R. *The Singular Self: An Introduction to the Psychology of Personhood.* London: Sage, 1998.

Harth, D. *Gotthold Ephraim Lessing: Oder die Paradoxien der Selbsterkenntnis.* Munich: Beck, 1993.

Hegel, G. W. F. *Vorlesungen über die Philosophie der Religion.* Vol. 2. Werke 17. Frankfurt: Suhrkamp, 1986.

Henriksen, J.-O. *På Grensen til Den andre: Om teologi og postmodernitet.* Oslo: Ad Notam Gyldendal, 1999.

————. *Religion og vilje til makt.* Volda: Volda College Publications, 1993.

Hornig, G. *Die Anfänge des historisch-kritischen Theologie.* Göttingen: Vandenhoeck & Ruprecht, 1961.

Houlgate, S. *Hegel, Nietzsche and the Criticism of Metaphysics.* Cambridge: Cambridge University Press, 1986.

Houmann, I. *Nihilismen: en sprogfilosofisk analyse af Friedrich Nietzsches syn på den nihilistiske problematik med særligt henblik på dennes konsekvenser for en mulig religionsfilosofisk tydning.* Copenhagen: Borgen, 1983.

Jaspers, K. *Nietzsche og kristendommen.* Oslo: Solum, 1977.

Jüngel, E. "Deus qualem Paulus creavit, dei negatio." *Nietzsche-Studien* 1 (1972): 286-96.

————. *Gott als Geheimnis der Welt.* 5th ed. Tübingen: Mohr, 1986.

Kaufmann, W. *Nietzsche: Philosoph, Psychologe, Antichrist.* Darmstadt: Wissenschaftliche Buchgesellschaft, 1988.

Kellenberger, J. *Kierkegaard and Nietzsche: Faith and Eternal Acceptance.* Basingstoke: Macmillan, 1997.

Krogseth, O. *Den tyske historismen: En idéhistorisk undersøkelse av en tyske historismens utvikingshistorie.* Oslo: Solum, 1984.

Küng, H. "Religion im Prozeß der Aufklärung." In *Dichtung und Religion.* Ed. W. Jens and H. Küng, 82-101. Munich: Piper, 1989.

Law, D. R. *Kierkegaard as Negative Theologian.* Oxford: Clarendon, 1993.

Lindstrøm, V. *Stadiernas Teologi: En Kierkegaard-studie.* Lund: Gleerup, 1943.

Luther, M. *The Large Catechism* (Philadelphia: Fortress Press, 1959).

Lyotard, J. F. *The Postmodern Condition.* Minneapolis: University of Minnesota Press, 1984.

Lønning, P. *Samtidighedens Situation: En studie i Søren Kierkegaards Kristendomsforståelse.* Oslo: Land og Kirke, 1954.

Malantschuk, G. *Frihedens problem i Kierkegaards Begrebet Angest.* Copenhagen: Rosenkilde & Bagger, 1971.

Matuštík, M. J. "Kierkegaard's Radical Existential Praxis, or: Why the Individual Defies Liberal, Communitarian, and Postmodern Categories." In *Kierkegaard in Post/Modernity*. Ed. M. J. Matuštík and M. Westphal, 239-64. Bloomington: Indiana University Press, 1995.

Matuštík, M. J., and M. Westphal, eds. *Kierkegaard in Post/Modernity*. Bloomington: Indiana University Press, 1995.

Moles, A. *Nietzsche's Philosophy of Nature and Cosmology*. New York: Lang, 1990.

Mooney, E. *Selves in Discord and Resolve: Kierkegaard's Moral-Religious Psychology from Either/Or to Sickness unto Death*. New York: Routledge, 1996.

Morris, P. "Communities Beyond Tradition." In *Detraditionalization: Critical Reflections on Authority and Identity at a Time of Uncertainty*. Ed. P. Heelas et al. (Oxford: Blackwell, 1996) 223-49.

Nagel, T. *The View from Nowhere*. New York: Oxford University Press, 1996.

Oelmüller, W. *Die unbefriedigte Aufklärung*. Frankfurt: Suhrkamp, 1979.

Pannenberg, W. "Typen der Atheismus und ihre theologische Bedeutung." In *Grundfragen systematischer Theologie: Gesammelte Aufsätze*, vol. 1:347-60. Göttingen: Vandenhoeck & Ruprecht, 1967.

————. *Gottesebenbildlichkeit als die Bestimmung des Menschen in der neueren Theologiegeschichte*. Munich: Bayerischen Akademie der Wissenschaften, 1979.

————. *Anthropologie in theologischer Perspektive*. Göttingen: Vandenhoeck & Ruprecht, 1983.

————. *Metaphysik und Gottesgedanke*. Göttingen: Vandenhoeck & Ruprecht, 1988.

Peter, K. *Stadien der Aufklärung: Moral und Politik bei Lessing, Novalis und Friedrich Schlegel*. Wiesbaden: Athenaion, 1980.

Ricoeur, P. *Oneself as Another*. Chicago: University of Chicago Press, 1993.

Rilla, P. *Lessing und sein Zeitalter*. Munich: Beck, 1973.

Ringleben, J. *Aneignung: Die spekulative Theologie Søren Kierkegaards*. Berlin: de Gruyter, 1983.

Roberts, T. T. *Contesting Spirit: Nietzsche, Affirmation, Religion*. Princeton: Princeton University Press, 1998.

Rohrmoser, G. "Lessing und die religionsphilosophische Fragestellung der Aufklärung." In *Lessing und die Zeit der Aufklärung*, 116-29. Göttingen: Vandenhoeck & Ruprecht, 1968.

Roof, W. C., et al. *A Generation of Seekers: The Spiritual Journeys of the Baby Boom Generation*. New York: HarperCollins, 1994.

Rorty, R. *Contingency, Irony, and Solidarity.* Cambridge: Cambridge University Press, 1989.

Ross, W. *Der ängstliche Adler: Friedrich Nietzsches Leben.* Stuttgart: Deutsche Verlagsanstalt, 1980.

Sadler, T. *Nietzsche — Truth and Redemption: Critique of the Postmodernist Nietzsche.* London and Atlantic Highlands, N.J.: Athlone, 1995.

Saine, T. P. *The Problem of Being Modern: Or the German Pursuit of Enlightenment from Leibniz to the French Revolution.* Detroit: Wayne State University Press, 1997.

Schilson, A. "Lessing und die Aufklärung: Notizen zur Forschung." *Theologie und Philosophie* 54 (1979): 379-405.

————. "Zur Wirkungsgeschichte Lessings in der katholischen Theologie." In Göpfert, *Das Bild Lessings in der Geschichte,* 69-91. Heidelberg: 1981.

Schleiermacher, F. *Reden über die Religion.* Stuttgart: Reclam, 1799.

————. *Der christliche Glaube.* Berlin: de Gruyter, 1821.

Schrag, C. O. "The Kierkegaard-Effect in the Shaping of the Contours of Modernity." In *Kierkegaard in Post/Modernity.* Ed. M. J. Matuštík and M. Westphal, 1-17. Bloomington: Indiana University Press, 1995.

Schrift, A. D. *Nietzsche and the Question of Interpretation between Hermeneutics and Deconstruction.* New York: Routledge, 1990.

Schultz, H. *Eschatologische Identität: Eine Untersuchung über das Verhältnis von Vorsehung, Schicksal und Zufall bei Søren Kierkegaard.* Berlin: de Gruyter, 1994.

Schultze, H. *Lessings Toleranzbegriff: Eine theologische Studie.* Forschungen zur systematischen und ökumenischen Theologie 20. Göttingen: Vandenhoeck & Ruprecht, 1969.

Schulz, W. *Philosophie in der veränderten Welt.* Pfüllingen: Neske, 1972.

Sløk, J. *Die Anthropologie Kierkegaards.* Copenhagen: Rosenkilde and Bagger, 1954.

Striet, M. *Das Ich im Sturz der Realität: Philosophisch-theologische Studien zu einer Theorie des Subjekts in Auseinandersetzung mit der Spätphilosophie Friedrich Nietzsches.* Regensburg: Pustet, 1998.

Thielicke, H. *Vernunft und Offenbarung: Eine Studie über die Religionsphilosophie Lessings.* Gütersloh: Gerd Mohn, 1959.

————. *Vernunft und Existenz bei Lessing: Das Unbedingte in der Geschichte.* Göttingen: Vandenhoeck & Ruprecht, 1981.

————. *Glauben und Denken in der Neuzeit: Die Großen Systeme der Theologie und Religionsphilosophie.* Tübingen: Mohr, 1983.

Timm, H. *Gott und die Freiheit: Studien zu Religionsphilosophie der Goethezeit.* Vol. 1. Frankfurt: Klostermann, 1974.

Trillhaas, W. "Zur Wirkunfsgeschichte Lessings in der evangelischen Theologie." In *Das Bild Lessings in der Geschichte* H. Göpfert, 57-67. Heidelberg: 1981.

von Lüpke, J. *Wege der Weisheit: Studien zur Lessings Theologiekritik.* Göttingen: Vandenhoeck & Ruprecht, 1989.

Wagner, F. *Was ist Religion? Studien zu ihrem Begriff und Thema in Geschichte und Gegenwart.* Gütersloh: Gerd Mohn, 1986.

Wessel, L. P. *G. E. Lessing's Theology — A Reinterpretation: A Study in the Problematic Nature of the Enlightenment.* The Hague: Mouton, 1977.

Westphal, M. *Suspicion and Faith: The Religious Uses of Modern Atheism.* Grand Rapids: Eerdmans, 1993.

————. *Becoming a Self: A Reading of Kierkegaard's Concluding Unscientific Postscript.* West Lafayette, Ind.: Purdue University Press, 1996.

Index